# Relocating to Seattle and Surrounding Areas

# Relocating to SEATTLE and Surrounding Areas

Everything You Need to Know Before You Move

and After You Get There!

GUY STEELE

PRIMA PUBLISHING
3000 Lava Ridge Court • Roseville, California 95661
(800) 632-8676 • www.primalifestyles.com

Every effort has been made to make this book complete and accurate as of the date of publication. In a time of rapid change, however, it is difficult to ensure that all information is entirely up-to-date. Although the publisher and author cannot be liable for any inaccuracies or omissions in this book, they are always grateful for corrections and suggestions for improvement.

**Library of Congress Cataloging-in-Publication Data**

Steele, Guy.

Relocating to Seattle and surrounding areas : everything you need to know before you move and after you get there! / Guy Steele.

p. cm.

Includes index.

ISBN 0-7615-2568-8

1. Seattle Region (Wash.)—Guidebooks. 2. Moving, Household—Washington (State)—Seattle Region—Handbooks, manuals, etc. I. Title.

F899.S43 S73 2000
979.7'77044--dc21

00-042100

00 01 02 03 04 05 HH 10 9 8 7 6 5 4 3 2 1

Printed in the United States of America

**HOW TO ORDER:**

Single copies may be ordered from Prima Publishing, 3000 Lava Ridge Court, Roseville, CA 95661; telephone (800) 632-8676, ext. 4444. Quantity discounts are also available. On your letterhead, include information concerning the intended use of the books and the number of books you wish to purchase.

**Visit us online at www.primalifestyles.com**

To Ashley and Alexa, for your love, patience, and understanding.

# CONTENTS

# ACKNOWLEDGMENTS

I wish to acknowledge several people for the moral and technical assistance they gave me throughout the writing of this book.

To Mom and Dad, for your unflappable support and insistence that I use all twenty-six letters of the alphabet.

To Pat and Mike, for your native insights and adding a combined 107 years of residency to my ten.

To Alice and David, for taking a chance on a guy with only a travel bag full of adjectives and adverbs.

And to Andrew, for helping me find—and cross—the finish line.

# INTRODUCTION

This is my favorite part of the book, where I get to gush about my city: Seattle, the Emerald City.

All the great metropolises have nicknames. Los Angeles is the City of Angels. Chicago is the Windy City. And when Sinatra crooned about New York, it was indeed the City That Never Sleeps. Although considering the Greater Puget Sound area has the highest per capita consumption of coffee products in the United States, we are surely more . . . ahem . . . sleepless in Seattle. Come to think of it, Washington State is also the world's leading apple producer. Perhaps we should lay claim to the Big Apple. Nah.

So how did Seattle become known as the Emerald City? It boasts no precious gemstone mines and has never been home to the Wizard of Oz. The moniker refers to Seattle's brilliant green palette and how the trademark raindrops polish the city to a lustrous sparkle.

Oops! I mentioned rain. Let's talk about that for a moment.

"Seattle" is not an Indian word for "rain." Your feet will not become webbed from living here, nor will you be scraping moss off your windshield. And no, umbrellas are not dispensed by street corner vending machines. Contrary to popular myth, Seattle rainfall does not approach Biblical proportions. Factually, our annual precipitation ranks 46th among the 100 most populated cities in America, well below Houston and Miami.[1]

But I won't kid you. It rains here. Occasionally for days at a time during the winter. However, it's more of a gentle drizzle than a torrential downpour. How else could the local landscapes remain so lush and alluring? It is this seasonal rain that keeps our rivers teeming with prize steelhead and trophy chinook salmon. It keeps our ski areas dusted with fresh powder and our air crisp and pure. Water is, after all, the source of life. You'd be hard-pressed to find a quality of life higher than that found here. Seattle has sunny days, too. Lots of them. According to the National Oceanographic and Atmospheric Administration, the sun generously shines upon this city an average of 191 days per year.[2] Still not convinced? Seattle is our nation's third most popular city for recreational boating and is second only to Albuquerque, New Mexico, for hot air ballooning: definitely fair weather hobbies! The third line of "Washington, My Home"—the official State song—boasts, "Small towns and cities rest here in the sun, filled with our laughter, thy will be done."

But enough about rain. Let me tell you why this book is important.

When I relocated to Seattle, windows upgraded a kitchen, not a computer. The area's richest man, Bill Gates, was worth a paltry $900 million. That was about $89 billion ago.[3] In less abstract terms, ten years—that's not a long time.

Why, then, was I entrusted with writing a book about Seattle? Because it's not just about Seattle. It's about relocating to Seattle: an odyssey that's still fresh on my mind. Living here a decade has allowed me to grasp the sweet, enchanting spirit that is the very signature of this great city. Yet I haven't lived here so long that I've forgotten the myriad emotions that churned inside me during the fall of 1989. My anxieties, fears, hopes, and dreams were at the same time daunting and exhilarating. So I know how you feel.

I can't say I struggled much with the prospect of relocating to Seattle. Huge cutbacks in defense contracting and plummeting real estate prices had crippled the southern California economy. At the time, there was an exodus taking place. En masse, Angelinos were abandoning the snarled traffic jams that paralyzed L.A. freeways, and bidding farewell to their beloved Dodgers and Lakers. Left behind in a rust-hued veil of smog was the once-booming county of Orange and the renowned San Fernando Valley. Notions of Seattle as a sleepy port town yielded to the promises of a second Silicon Valley and the clean-burning engines of a mighty software-driven economy.

Unabashedly, I joined the northern migration. It was like a high-tech Grapes of Wrath. Several hours into my trek up Interstate 5, I witnessed the horrifying aftermath of the San Francisco earthquake. Somebody labeled it the "World Series Earthquake" and the name stuck. The devastation was surreal. Entire expanses of double-decker freeways were pressed together like thin slices of bread on a poor man's sandwich. It was a consciousness-raising experience. At that moment I was determined not only to make my new life in Seattle purposeful, but I was going to make the balance of my trip an adventure, not just a chore.

So many Californians had targeted Seattle that it wasn't hard to "piggyback a rig." That is, share the expense of a northbound eighteen-wheeler. My furniture stayed the course, but I deviated from the red line scrawled up the left side of my map. I took the scenic route. Northern California's coast is something everyone should experience. Its jagged shoreline and rugged, windswept cliffs are rich in color and texture. The untamable seascapes are the challenge of countless artists.

As California license plates gave way to Oregon license plates, I found myself veering inland and splicing through an endless constellation of evergreens. Timbers blanketed the mountains like a dense velvet, interrupted occasionally by opalescent lakes. The water was inviting and I stumbled upon a lodge that rented modest houseboats. Inspired to match wits with native cutthroat, I prepared tackle and fished until nightfall.

Oregon was soothing and unpretentious. But I'll never forget the sensations that enveloped me as I crossed the timeless Columbia River into Washington. Almost instantly the unwavering forest-green tint of Oregon was shattered by an explosion of color. It was a spectacular welcoming. Bursts of crimson, orange, and ochre seemed to ignite the landscape.

I felt toe-curling anticipation. My eyes registered everything. Sprawling countryside. Quaint roadside cafés. Noble mountain peaks. Even an eagle in flight! As I crested the highest point of the freeway, the corridor broadened dramatically, unfurling a panoramic view of Puget Sound. Revealed was the Seattle skyline shimmering in the final rays of an October sun, creating the unmistakable silhouette of the world-famous Space Needle. I considered it my personal Hallmark greeting, and confirmation that what I had found was home.

Although constructed as a showpiece for the 1962 World's Fair, the Space Needle has endured as a visual synonym for the city. For me it was a beacon. My Magnetic North. As I would soon discover, the structure—from *The Jetson's* school of architecture—is just one of many unique offerings of Seattle.

## History of Seattle

To fully appreciate the Emerald City, let's make a quick visit to a few facets of the history of the Evergreen State's crown jewel.

In 1851, an expedition party of prominent families led by Arthur Denny anchored the schooner *Exact* off the shores of Alki Point, now West Seattle. A permanent moorage was later established in nearby Elliot Bay. Along with Denny, industrialists Henry Yesler and William Bell infused the fledgling "Belltown" with crucial investment capital. By 1859, Yesler had built Puget Sound's first steam-powered mill. His operation nourished the township and attracted laborers, eventually supporting a village that is now Pioneer Square.

Meanwhile, a charismatic member of the Denny party, Carson Dobbins Boren, was developing a bond with the local Suquamish Indians. In 1860, the settlers dedicated their village to Chief Seattle of that tribe. A city was born. Boren was appointed sheriff, a position that enabled him to continue nurturing good relations with the Suquamish.

A year later, the University of Washington was established, with Asa Mercer as its first president. To better balance the largely male mill worker population and spark the creation of second-generation Seattleites, Mercer "imported" women from New York. His strategy worked. By 1880 Seattle boasted 3,000 citizens and was the second-largest city in Washington Territory. That population would rise to 230,000 over the next three decades.[4]

This boom was the product of two windfalls.

The first was when miners discovered Klondike gold in 1896. This positioned Seattle as the "Gateway to Alaska." Savvy merchants established themselves as outfitters for the legions of northbound prospectors. Upon returning, the luckier prospectors spent their newfound wealth lavishly. "Bobtail trolleys" and their electric successors shuttled thousands of shoppers through the burgeoning retail district.

During those same decades, Puget Sound acquired homeport status to the famed "Mosquito Fleet" of steamships. Ferries zigzagged across the Sound at the same time that Seattle's roads expanded to accommodate a proliferation of automobiles. The *Kalakala*, touted as the world's first streamlined ferry, would become an international symbol of the Sound. Increased waterway and road traffic gave rise to growth and development, stoking the fires of the building industry.

With the arrival of the Great Northern Railroad and the monumental efforts to regrade much of Seattle's hilly terrain, the city was poised to continue its phenomenal expansion into the twentieth century. From 1895 to 1925, sixty city blocks were developed and a formidable financial center emerged. First Hill sprouted stately homes of the Seattle elite, and in 1907, the landmark Pike Place Public Market was founded as the epicenter of fish and produce trade. The Alaska, Yukon, and Pacific Exposition of 1909 inspired magnificent creations in architecture and landscape design.

Bill Boeing's 1916 maiden voyage of the B & W, his company's first airplane, ushered in an unending era of technology that continues to this day. Paralleling the meteoric growth of The Boeing Company and other corporate giants was the city's development of additional infrastructure. Thirty-five years spanned the creation of Lake Washington Ship Canal, Fremont Bridge, Pacific Highway, and the 1940 dedication of the Lake Washington Floating Bridge. These engineering marvels linked Puget Sound with vast freshwater harbors and the sprawling suburbs of the Eastside.

Seattle grew exponentially during the next twenty years. In 1962, Interstate 5 was extended nearly two hundred miles, connecting Portland to Seattle. Then, in 1970, Seattleites decided to curtail that growth. In an effort to thwart national trends of "urban renewal," they voted to restrict unbridled expansion and preserve their great historic landmarks.

Nevertheless, since that time, the Puget Sound area has become an international hub of commercial trade and advanced technology. Its three million residents live amidst rich cultural diversity.[5] Anchoring the state's thriving tourism industry, Seattle offers visitors limitless arts and entertainment possibilities. The Fifth Avenue Theater and historic Paramount Theater host world-class performing arts companies. Our treasured Seattle Symphony receives international recognition, and dozens of indoor and outdoor concert venues feature superstar headliners. Casual arts and leisure venues include village galleries and boutiques, underground comedy clubs, and jazz coffeehouses. Landmarks Pioneer Square, Pike Place Public Market, and the First Avenue Boardwalk gently link past with present, captivating locals and visitors alike.

Dining runs the gamut from cozy neighborhood eateries to exquisite five-star restaurants. Eclectic Pacific Rim cuisine and traditional Northwest fare will satisfy a broad spectrum of culinary tastes. Wineries, microbreweries, espresso parlors, and juice bars abound. Visitors and residents alike may quench their intellectual thirsts at the acclaimed Seattle Science Center and Woodland Park Zoological Gardens.

With a Triple Crown of NFL, NBA, and MLB franchises, Seattle is a sports fan's Utopia. You'll never be far from a spirited conversation about the Seahawks, Sonics, Mariners, or Huskies!

In short, Seattle has enjoyed an astounding ascent over the last century and a half. In its journey from a single trading post to a cosmopolitan gem of the Pacific Rim, The Emerald City united a colorful past with a vibrant future. Today, Seattle is known as the birthplace of the Starbucks latté, nesting ground for Boeing's proud airliners, and home of Wall Street juggernaut Microsoft. You will soon find yourself in one of the most dynamic and yet livable cities on the planet. Welcome to Seattle!

Putting it simply, you're going to love this town.

## Seattle Statistics

### CLIMATE

#### Location

*Latitude: 47° 39′North*
*Longitude: 122° 17′ West*

### Temperature

| | Winter | Spring | Summer | Fall |
|---|---|---|---|---|
| High | 46°F | 56°F | 77°F | 67°F |
| Average | 40°F | 51°F | 68°F | 59°F |
| Low | 35°F | 45°F | 58°F | 50°F |

### Precipitation

*Rainfall:* *36.20 inches per year (average)*
*Snowfall:* *09.00 inches per year (average)*

### Population

| | |
|---|---|
| *Washington State:* | *5,606,800* |
| *Greater Puget Sound Area:* | *3,149,700* |
| *King County:* | *1,712,200* |
| *Seattle:* | *539,700* |

### Density

| | |
|---|---|
| *Seattle Density per Square Mile:* | *6,425* |
| *Seattle College/University Students:* | *75,413* |

### Population by Ethnicity

| | |
|---|---|
| *Caucasian:* | *75.30%* |
| *Asian:* | *11.20%* |
| *African American:* | *10.10%* |
| *Hispanic:* | *3.60%* |

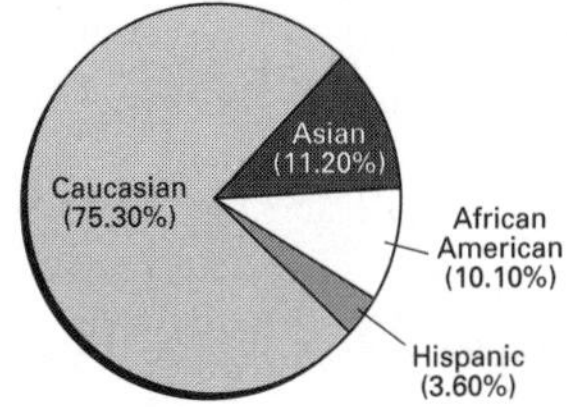

### Population by Age

| | |
|---|---|
| *<1:* | *01.40%* |
| *01–04:* | *5.8%* |
| *05–14:* | *14.4%* |
| *15–19:* | *5.93%* |
| *20–24:* | *6.07%* |
| *25–34:* | *14.66%* |
| *35–44:* | *16.31%* |
| *45–54:* | *12.25%* |
| *55–64:* | *7.38%* |
| *65–74:* | *10.5%* |
| *75–84:* | *3.97%* |
| *>85:* | *1.33%* |

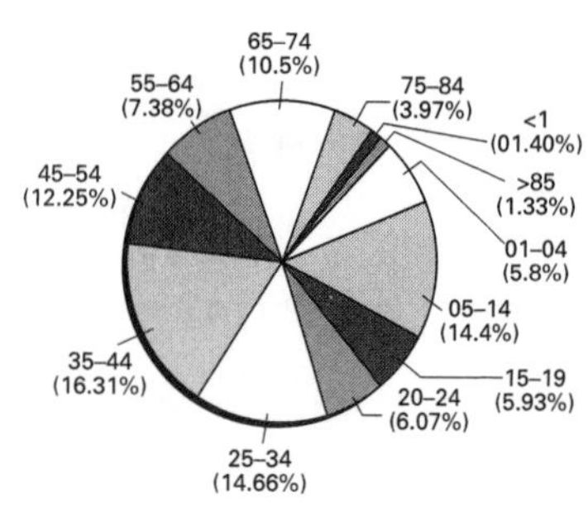


### Education

| | |
|---|---|
| *High school graduate:* | *86.4%* |
| *BA/BS or higher:* | *37.9%* |

## FINANCE

### Income

| | |
|---|---|
| *Median annual family:* | *$62,600* |
| *Median annual individual:* | *$26,707* |

### Housing

*Average cost per single-family residence:* *$175,000*

### Average Rent

| | |
|---|---|
| *Studio:* | *$563* |
| *1-Bedroom:* | *$654* |
| *2-Bedroom:* | *$890* |
| *3-Bedroom:* | *$1,210* |

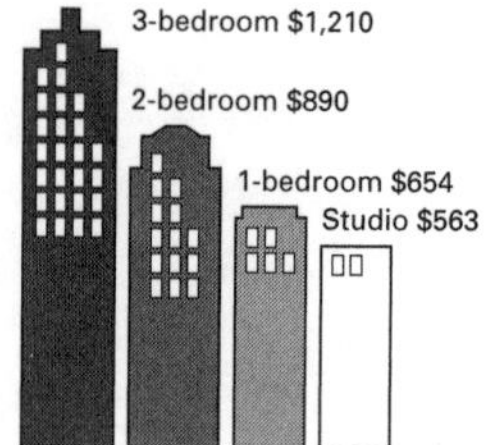


### Cost of Living: High

| | |
|---|---|
| *Seattle:* | *105* |
| *Average:* | *100* |

## Resources

### About.com

www.ci.seattle.wa.us/oir/facts

### Digital City-Seattle-Visitor's Guide

www.home.digitalcity.com/seattle

### MenuHunter.com

www.menuhunter.com/seattle

### Seattle, Washington, Live WebCams

www.leonardsworld.com/info/seattle

### Seattle/Tacoma, Washington-Home Page

www.seattle.about.com/local/pacnwus/seattle

## Notes

1. Ruffner, James A., and Blair, Frank E., *Weather of U.S. Cities*, 3rd Edition, Volume 2, 1998, Gale Research Co.

2. Ibid.

3. "Four Hundred Wealthiest Americans," *Forbes*, September 1989, and "The World's Richest Man," *Fortune*, March 1999.

4. Welcome to HistoryLink, *www.HistoryLink.org/welcome*

5. "Greater Seattle Datasheet," Office of Intergovernmental Relations, Seattle, Washington, October 1999.

## SEATTLE AREA

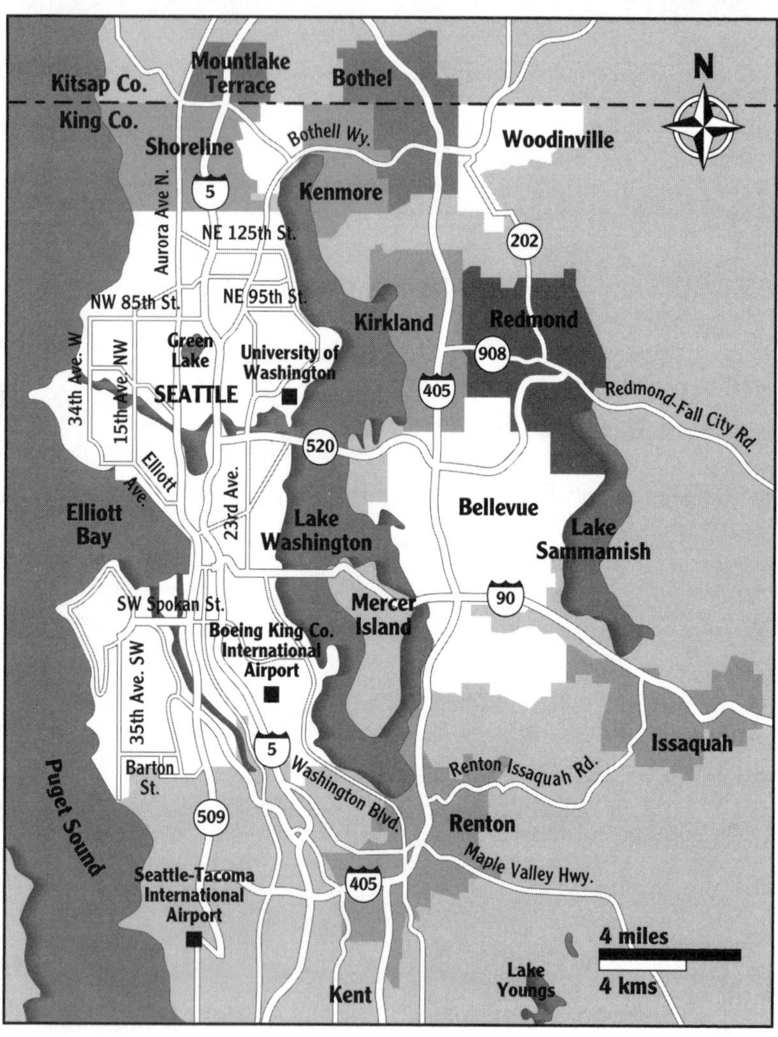

SECTION ONE

# Places to Live

CHAPTER 1

# Neighborhood Descriptions

The Emerald City is a colorful quilt, and the neighborhoods are its patchwork. Holding these neighborhoods together, like fine stitching, are Seattle's citizens. They give our communities a rich diversity and strength of unity. You won't need a map to show where one neighborhood ends and another begins. "Borders" can be as obvious as architectural styles. They can also be subtle, like storefront window dressings, friendly street corner newsstands, or kitschy sidewalk cafés. If you toured Seattle's neighborhoods in chronological order each would reveal a remarkable history. The cultural enrichment and economic growth of the 1990s, however, was perhaps the most remarkable of all . . . and a harbinger of things to come.

Most of Washington is static. It's timeless and unchanging, and I like that. Central and eastern Washington provide perfect counterbalance to the breakneck clip at which Seattle effects change. Technology never sleeps, and evidence of Seattle's insomnia is the proliferation of native dot-com companies. Tech start-ups have given rise to sexy glass skyscrapers and ultra-contemporary "smart parks" that didn't exist on the pre-Internet landscape.

Entertainment and leisure have reshaped the skyline, too. The city channeled more than a billion dollars into new playgrounds for the Sonics, Mariners, and Seahawks. Historical venues have undergone dramatic facelifts, too. New theaters, restaurants, and shopping districts sprout like mushrooms after a rain. Paralleling commercial growth is residential development. More than 50,000 single-family houses were built in King County between 1990 and 2000.

Growth is often accompanied by pain, and Seattle is hardly immune to the ills of rapid expansion. Peak-hour traffic can be nightmarish. Downtown parking spaces are all but extinct. Road crews are becoming a more common curbside sight than fire hydrants. So why do we put up with the irks of commuting?

Because getting home is worth it.

Wherever your welcome mat lies—at the door to a modest apartment, stately lakefront estate, or woodsy suburban ranchette—home is, indeed, sweet. Home is both refuge and reward, the place that restores peace and order at the end of a chaotic day. Where you choose to create your new home is critical. It could be the most important decision you make.

What follows is a brief description of neighborhoods in and around Seattle. The list is incomplete. To include every neighborhood would have been impossible, so I strove for balance—of geography, culture, and economics. A note of caution: The descriptions are candid. Some contain superlatives associated with glossy travel advertisements. Others cut with a sawtooth edge. I've tried to temper frankness with fairness. As you will discover, most neighborhoods receive high marks. That's why I live here. And though I haven't lived here long enough to become jaded, with a few neighborhoods, the honeymoon's over.

The areas discussed in this chapter are:

### City Neighborhoods

- Beacon Hill
- Capitol Hill
- Fremont/Wallingford
- Green Lake
- International District

- Lake Forest Park/Lake City
- Laurelhurst
- Madrona
- Magnolia
- Montlake
- Queen Anne
- University District/University Village
- West Seattle

**Suburbs**

- Bellevue
- Bothell/Kenmore
- Hollywood Hill
- Hunt's Point/Yarrow Point
- Issaquah
- Kirkland/Juanita
- Medina/Clyde Hill/Beaux Arts
- Mercer Island
- Redmond
- Renton
- Shoreline
- Woodinville

## City Neighborhoods

### BEACON HILL

Beacon Hill has a history of social turmoil. Early Dutch settlements were burned down during the Indian Wars of the 1850s. Following the turn of the nineteenth century, the city used the neighborhood to house the unfit and unruly. The "Pesthouse" was a sanitarium and quarantine station. The "Lazy Husbands Ranch" was where neglectful fathers were sentenced to labor. Asian immigration surged after World War II, and conflict erupted within the predominately white population. Today, the multicultural neighborhood exists in relative

## BEACON HILL

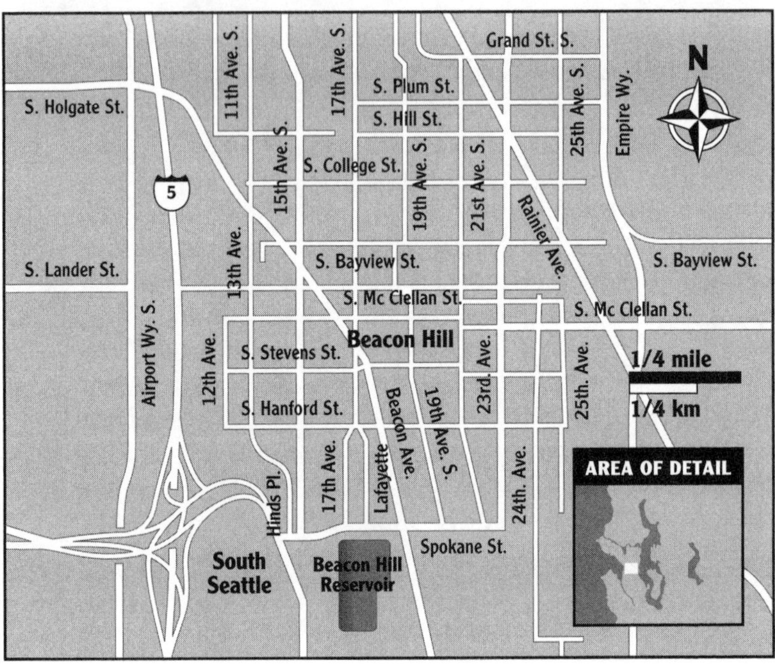


harmony. In fact, the average home owner has lived in the community for an astounding twenty-five years. The greatest challenges facing Beacon Hill's proud and tenacious residents are crime prevention and air traffic patterns. The former is being dutifully addressed by the South Seattle Crime Prevention Council, and the latter by homeowner associations and community coalitions. With the influx of Chinese, Japanese, African, and Filipino nationals, however, language barriers make it difficult to create united support.

Still, cultural diversity is Beacon Hill's greatest asset, and it's reflected in the ethnic shops and eateries. Outdoor markets showcase an impressive variety of exotic produce. The annual International Food Fair is magnificent. Along with culinary arts, another passion seems to unite families from all walks of life: Golf. The Chamber of Commerce and City Council might just as well set up shop by the

Jefferson Park Golf Course. This place is a magnet for Beacon Hill's citizens. The outrageously popular facility also offers lawn bowling and a playground.

## Neighborhood Statistical Profile

**Population:** 34,867

**Median family income:** $27,392

### Population by Ethnicity

*14%* *Anglo*
*29%* *Black*
*39%* *Asian*
*18%* *Hispanic*

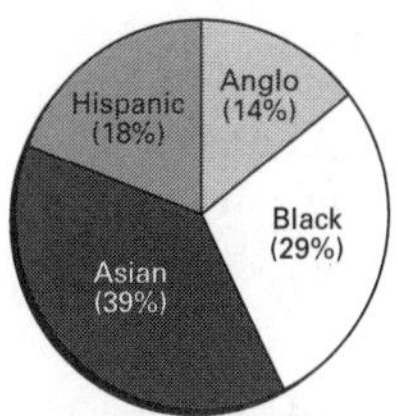


### Population by Gender

*54%* *Male*
*46%* *Female*

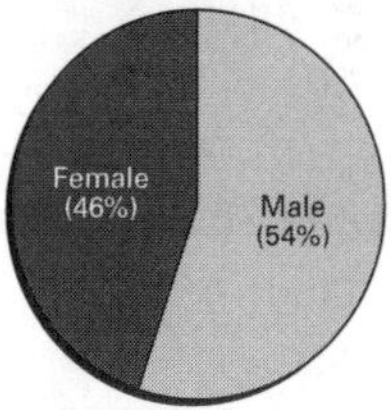


### Population by Age

*Median age:* 33
*19%* *under 18*
*32%* *18–39*
*31%* *40–59*
*18%* *over 59*

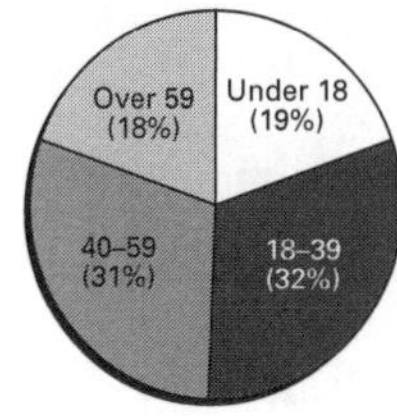

**Average Housing Costs**

| | |
|---|---|
| *Low:* | *$95,830* |
| *High:* | *$157,246* |

**Average Rental Costs**

| | |
|---|---|
| *Apartment:* | *$440* |
| *2–3-bedroom house:* | *$695* |

## Important Places Nearby

### Grocery Stores

**Beacon Hill Foods**
*4347 15th Street S*
*(206) 763-9217*

**Beacon Market**
*2500 Beacon Avenue S*
*(206) 323-2050*

**La Bodeguita Specialty Foods**
*2528-A Beacon Street S*
*(206) 329-9001*

### Pharmacies

**Eastern's Pharmacy**
*515 Minor Avenue*
*Seattle*
*(206) 622-3667*
www.easternsrx.com

### Banks

**United Savings & Loan Bank**
*2800 Beacon Street*
*Seattle*
*(206) 324-1884*

### Hardware Stores

**Home Depot**
*2759 Utah Street S*
*Seattle*
*(206) 467-9200*

### Hospitals/Emergency Rooms

**Group Health Central Hospital**
*201 16th Avenue E*
*Seattle*
*(206) 326-3000*

**Harborview Medical Center**
*325 9th Avenue*
*Seattle*
*(206) 731-3000*

**Providence Seattle Medical Center**
*500 17th Avenue*
*Seattle*
*(206) 320-2000*

**Swedish Medical Center**
*747 Broadway*
*Seattle*
*(206) 386-6000*

**Virginia Mason Hospital**
*925 Seneca Street*
*Seattle*
*(206) 223-6600*

## CAPITOL HILL

Often called "Pill Hill" for its preponderance of hospitals, this urban neighborhood—one of Seattle's oldest—has endured iterations of changes. Thankfully, a few vestiges of its original form are still evident. City Park was the pride of The Hill's original residents and was renamed Volunteer Park to pay homage to supporters of the Spanish-American War. Capitol Hill was once Seattle's majestic mantle adorned with large, prestigious homes of early Catholic settlers. Over the years these giant, boxy houses were converted to apartments and, later, back to houses. For Capitol Hill, the adage is "the more things change, the more they stay the same."

Vintage buildings, worth less than the land they sit upon, are being razed and replaced with urban villages and boutiques. Culturally, the avant-garde neighborhood scene is a melange. Yuppies, generation-Xers, bohemians, and pseudobohemians roam the urban jungle along Broadway, Pike, and Pine.

Funky cafés and intimate venues serve food and music from the fringe. Classic hangouts include legendary Dick's Drive-In, Dilettante Chocolates, Ileen's Sports Bar, and Gravity Bar.

In spite of easy access to the I-5 freeway, The Hill crowd prefers walking and public transportation. Parking is scarce and expensive. The majority of locals are single renters. Students and musicians seem to predominate. East of 15th Avenue, however, residents are older, and owners outnumber renters three-to-one.

But don't hold my feet to the fire. On Capitol Hill, everything changes.

## CAPITOL HILL

### Neighborhood Statistical Profile

**Population:** 36,120

**Median family income:** $27,875

## Population by Ethnicity

*58%* *Anglo*
*14%* *Black*
*19%* *Asian*
*9%* *Hispanic*

## Population by Gender

*49%* *Male*
*51%* *Female*

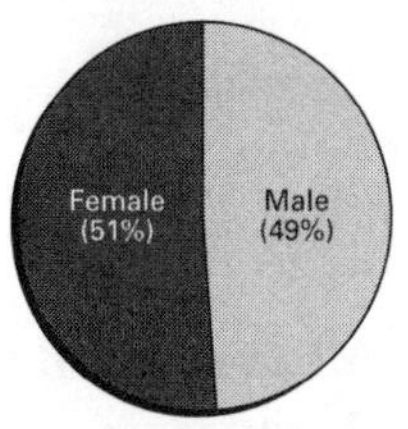


## Population by Age

*Median age:* *33*
*4%* *under 18*
*43%* *18–39*
*31%* *40–59*
*22%* *over 59*

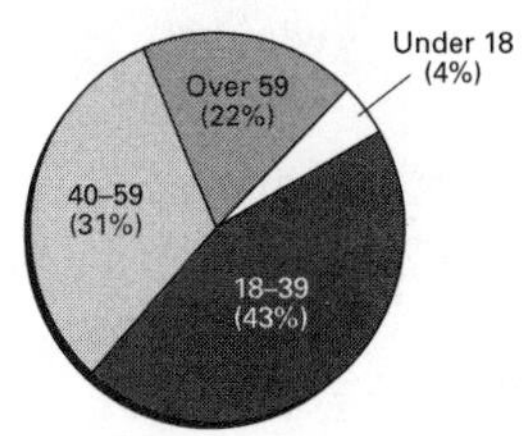


## Average Housing Costs

*Low:* *$211,455*
*High:* *$379,400*

## Average Rental Costs

*Apartment:* *$520*
*2–3-bedroom house:* *$1,776*

## Important Places Nearby

### Grocery Stores

**Capitol Hill Market**
*1728 12th Street*
*(206) 329-4425*

**European Common Market**
*2351 10th Avenue E*
*(206) 322-6632*

**Madison Market Natural & Organic Grocery**
*1600 E Madison Street*
*(206) 329-1545*
www.madisonmarket.com

### Pharmacy

**Cabrini Medical Tower Pharmacy**
*901 Boren Avenue, Suite 100*
*Seattle*
*(206) 682-1011*

### Banks

**Key Bank**
*321 15th Avenue*
*Seattle*
*(206) 585-9315*
www.key.com

### Hardware Store

**City People's Mercantile**
*500 15th Street E*
*Seattle*
*(206) 324-9510*

### Hospitals/Emergency Rooms

**Group Health Central Hospital**
*201 16th Avenue E*
*Seattle*
*(206) 326-3000*

**Harborview Medical Center**
*325 9th Avenue*
*Seattle*
*(206) 731-3000*

**Providence Seattle Medical Center**
*500 17th Avenue*
*Seattle*
*(206) 320-2000*

**Swedish Medical Center**
*747 Broadway*
*Seattle*
*(206) 386-6000*

**Virginia Mason Hospital**
*925 Seneca Street*
*Seattle*
*(206) 223-6600*

## FREMONT/WALLINGFORD

*"Won't you take me to . . . Funkytown?"* The lyricist who penned these words to a 1970s disco beat would've been happy to find Fremont.

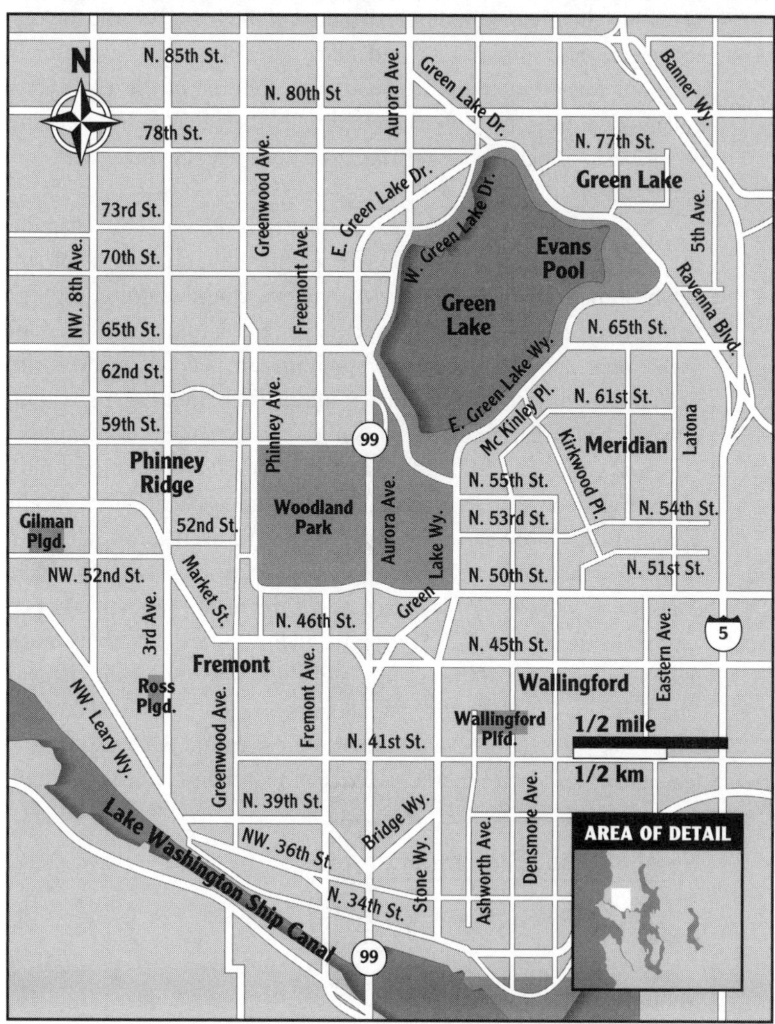

"bohemian," "funky," "artistic," "hippy-ish," and "political" are words Fremont locals use to describe their town. And believe me, it's *their* town. This eclectic urban neighborhood is so protective of its turf that a town square statue was dedicated to social activism. Richard Beyer's *People Waiting for the Interurban* is a centerpiece for weekly activism and soapbox ranting.

It all started during the 1920s and 1930s, when the Great Depression ravaged Seattle mills and threw many people out of work. Hard-luck laborers settled in Fremont, and the town became the center of socioeconomic angst and fierce liberalism. Not surprisingly, Fremont was adopted by Seattle's flower children of the 1960s. Blue collars gave way to tie-dyed tee-shirts as the rank-and-file became shopkeepers. Social rebels on Harleys cruised avenues lined with craft and granola shops.

Today, things are remarkably similar in some ways, but changing in others. Fremont is still where tireless watchdogs of the Establishment plant their flags. Alternative clothing stores, espresso parlors, and bungalows are abundant, as are natural food cafés and herbal pharmacies. Initiatives and petitions are peddled on street corners, often with positive results. Fremont is credited with spawning down-zone legislation that curbed high-rise apartment dwellings.

Sadly, though, this offbeat and free spirited town is becoming more transient and less artsy. The average resident now lives in Fremont only two years: one-third the Seattle average for neighborhood residency. Although its local reputation as such lingers, Fremont is no longer a hotbed of local artists. Of the town's residents, 11 percent make their living in performing and literary arts. Seattle's average is 20 percent. Much of the essential spirit remains, despite the changes. The Fremont Fair & Solstice Parade attracts more than 100,000 spectators and participants every June, and the Fremont Bridge still has its legendary Sunday flea markets, a beacon that draws crowds.

## Neighborhood Statistical Profile

**Population:** 13,712

**Median family income:** $29,800

## Population by Ethnicity

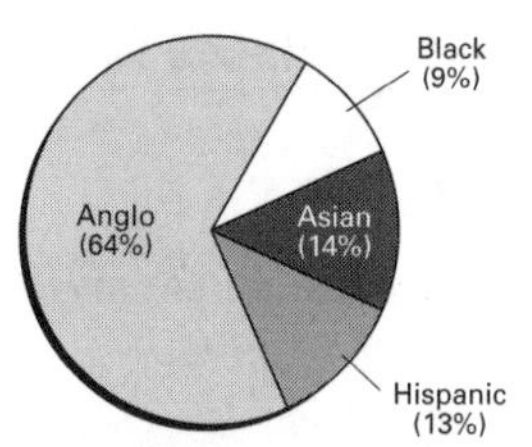


| | |
|---|---|
| *64%* | *Anglo* |
| *9%* | *Black* |
| *14%* | *Asian* |
| *13%* | *Hispanic* |

## Population by Gender

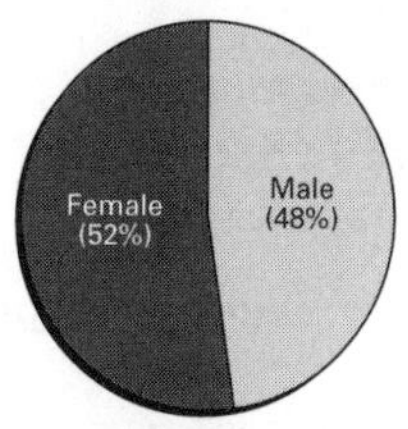


| | |
|---|---|
| *48%* | *Male* |
| *52%* | *Female* |

## Population by Age

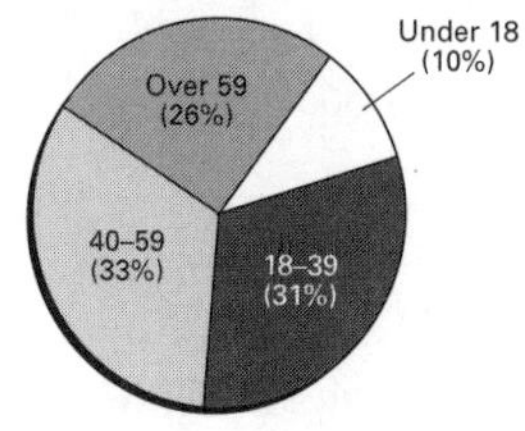


*Median age:* *31*

| | |
|---|---|
| *10%* | *under 18* |
| *31%* | *18–39* |
| *33%* | *40–59* |
| *26%* | *over 59* |

## Average Housing Costs

| | |
|---|---|
| *Low:* | *$163,115* |
| *High:* | *$226,112* |

## Average Rental Costs

| | |
|---|---|
| *Apartment:* | *$571* |
| *2–3-bedroom house:* | *$1,632* |

## Important Places Nearby

Grocery Stores

**The Durn Good Grocery**
*4002 Wallingford N*
*(206) 633-0500*

**PCC Natural Markets**
*716 North 34th Street*
*(206) 632-6811*
www.pccnaturalmarkets.com

**Fremont Fresh Market**
*3601 Fremont Street N*
*(206) 633-3663*

Pharmacies

**Bartell Drugs at Wallingford**
*1820 North 45th Street*
*Seattle*
*(206) 632-3314*

Banks

**Fremont First National Bank**
*600 North 36th Street*
*Seattle*
*(206) 632-0200*

**Washington Mutual**
*1919 North 45th Street*
*Seattle*
*(206) 461-3125*
www.wamu.com

Hardware Stores

**Hardwick's "Seattle's Oldest" Hardware Store**
*4214 Roosevelt Way NE*
*Seattle*
*(206) 632-1203*

Hospitals/Emergency Rooms

**Northwest Hospital**
*1550 North 115th Street*
*Seattle*
*(206) 364-0500*

**University of Washington Medical Center**
*1959 Northeast Pacific Street*
*Seattle*
*(206) 598-3300*

## GREEN LAKE

The centerpiece of Green Lake (the town) is Green Lake (the lake). In the 1970s, the town was a haven of singles hedonism. In the 1980s, opportunistic developers tried to jam cheap "skinny houses" between regal homes, many of which were registered with historical societies. And then there was the cayman (read "pet alligator") that escaped and found refuge in the lake.

For decades, fitness freaks have circumnavigated a three-mile asphalt oval surrounding the "lake." In the 1990s, in-line skaters weaved between sinewy joggers and not-so-sinewy walkers. Frisbees and hackysacks remained the toys of choice for unemployed sun worshippers.

Today Green Lake is undergoing a renaissance, and it's really cleaning up its act. The town has become a delightful place for singles and seniors who want to live within a short walk of life's pleasures. A pedestrian village now has bistros that rival Seattle's famed First Avenue. The town awakens to the aroma of lattes and fresh-baked scones, and microbrews flow until the late hours. New architecture blends with old, and village shops are always engaging.

### Neighborhood Statistical Profile

**Population:** 15,322

**Median family income:** $34,816

**Population by Ethnicity**

*73%* *Anglo*
*9%* *Black*
*12%* *Asian*
*6%* *Hispanic*

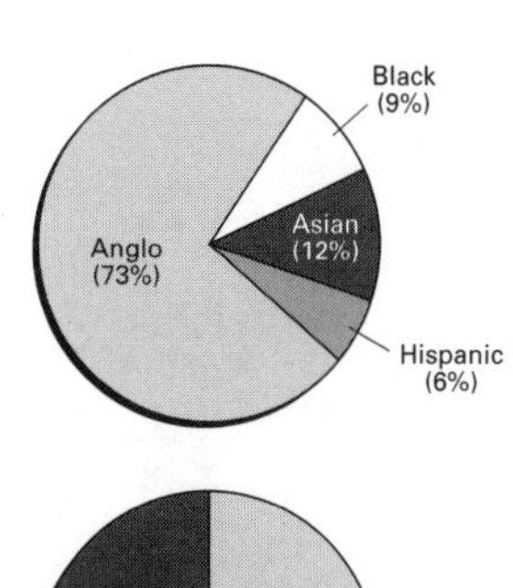


**Population by Gender**

*49%* *Male*
*51%* *Female*

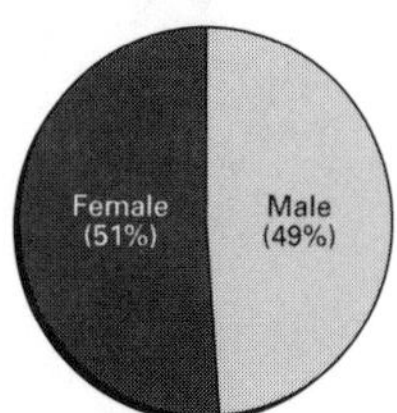

## Population by Age

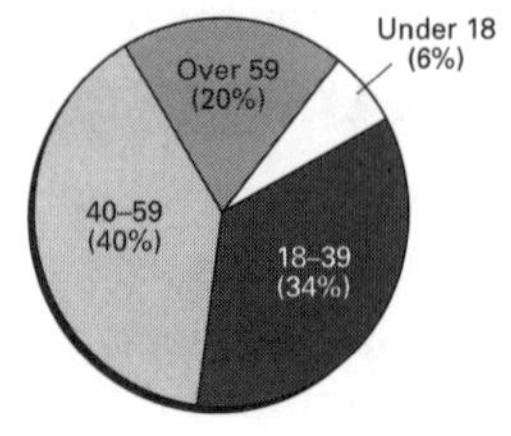


*Median age:* *36*

| | |
|---|---|
| *6%* | *under 18* |
| *34%* | *18–39* |
| *40%* | *40–59* |
| *20%* | *over 59* |

## Average Housing Costs

| | |
|---|---|
| *Low:* | *$189,950* |
| *High:* | *$335,000* |

## Average Rental Costs

| | |
|---|---|
| *Apartment:* | *$640* |
| *2–3-bedroom house:* | *$1,385* |

## Important Places Nearby

### Grocery Stores

**PCC Natural Markets**
*7504 Aurora Avenue N*
*(206) 525-3586*
www.pccnaturalmarkets.com

**Greenlake Market**
*7119 Woodlawn Avenue NE*
*(206) 528-1420*

### Pharmacies

**Bartell Drugs at Greenwood**
*120 North 85th Street*
*Seattle*
*(206) 784-7601*

### Banks

**Key Bank**
*400 Northeast Ravenna Boulevard*
*Seattle*
*(206) 524-8927*
www.key.com

### Hardware Stores

**Chubby & Tubby**
*7906 Aurora Avenue N*
*Seattle*
*(206) 524-1810*

### Hospitals/Emergency Rooms

**University of Washington Medical Center**
*1959 Northeast Pacific Street*
*Seattle*
*(206) 598-3300*

## INTERNATIONAL DISTRICT

In the late nineteenth century, young Chinese men were recruited for Seattle's re-grade and railroad projects. The laborers saved their modest wages until they could send for their families. By the 1930s, a bona fide American Asian community had emerged. In addition to Chinese families, the community was home to Japanese and Filipino immigrants. With Southeast Asians adding to the mix over the next three decades, then-mayor Wes Uhlman changed the name from Chinatown to the more appropriate International District.

Today the area lacks enough buildings to shelter the residents of "the I.D." Absentee landlords own the currently occupied, aging brick

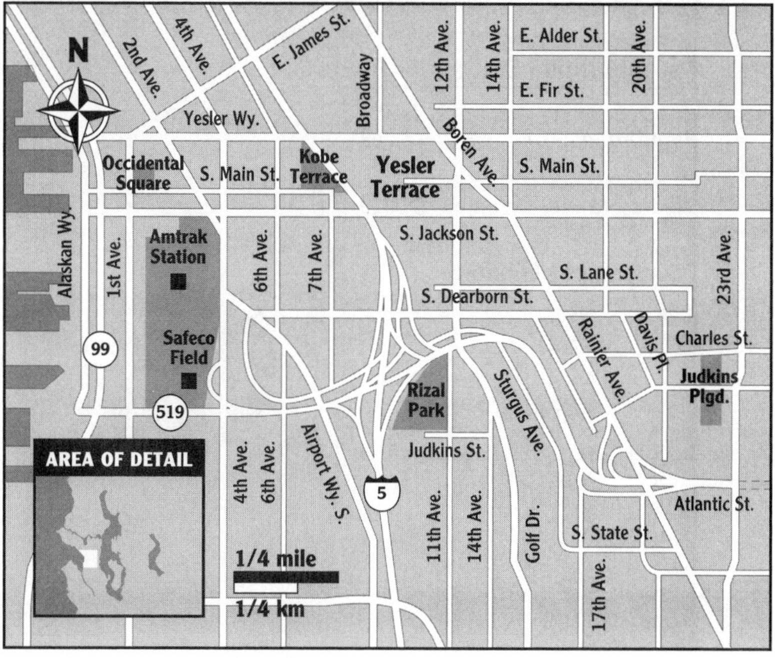

low-rise structures—making them prime targets for deep-pocketed commercial developers. Centered between glitzy downtown Seattle (north) and the port and industrial hub (south), the I.D. is plagued with urban problems. Crime, homelessness, and redevelopment effects are prime concerns of many community activists. Well organized, these groups are making commendable headway into remedying neighborhood ills.

Pavillions and gardens—many with Asian themes—are measurably beautifying the local landscape, and ethnic museums are preserving the diverse cultures of the district. Nippon Kan Theatre showcases Japanese performing arts, and delectable Asian cuisine is found on every street corner. Favorites of locals and visitors are House of Hong and The Four Seas. Uwajimaya, a landmark Japanese grocery store, is nothing less than epic. Herbal shops attract patrons from around the world, literally.

As you might expect, Chinese New Year is a monumental celebration. So is the Harvest Moon Festival. A slew of summer street festivals usher in lion dancers and taiko drummers.

"Kung Hey Fat Choi!"—*May Your Life Be Prosperous*

## Neighborhood Statistical Profile

**Population:** 3,299

**Median family income:** $9,020

**Population by Ethnicity**

*29%* *Anglo*
*13%* *Black*
*52%* *Asian*
*6%* *Hispanic*

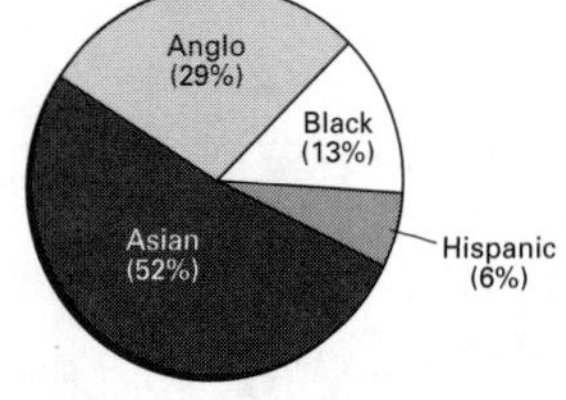

### Population by Gender

*53%* *Male*

*47%* *Female*

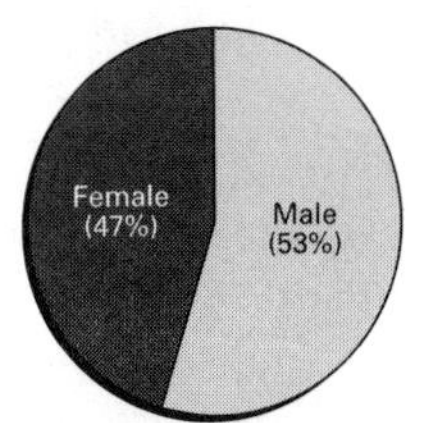


### Population by Age

*Median age:* *45*

*11%* *under 18*

*19%* *18–39*

*48%* *40–59*

*22%* *over 59*

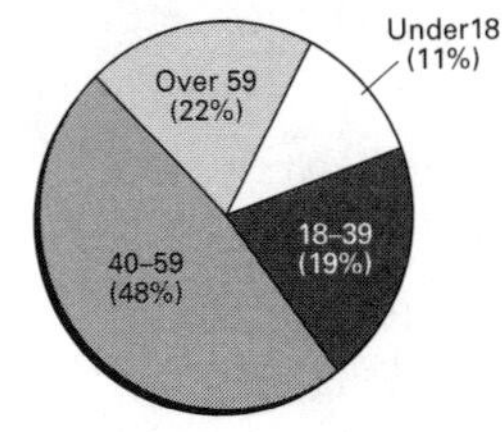


### Average Housing Costs

*Low:* *$69,000*

*High:* *$89,000*

### Average Rental Costs

| | |
|---|---|
| *Apartment:* | *$195* |
| *2–3-bedroom house:* | *n/a* |

## Important Places Nearby

Grocery Stores

**Uwajimaya**
*519 6th Street*
*(206) 624-6248*

**Hop Thanh Supermarket**
*1043 South Jackson Street*
*(206) 322-7473*

Pharmacies

**Luke's Pharmacy**
*611 Maynard Street S*
*Seattle*
*(206) 621-8883*

Banks

**Asia Europe Americas Bank**
*1505 Westlake Avenue N*
*Seattle*
*(206) 217-9350*

**The Bank of Tokyo-Mitsubishi, Ltd.**
*1201 Third Avenue, Suite 1100*
*Seattle*
*(206) 382-6000*

**Farmers Bank of China**
*1201 Third Avenue*
*Seattle*
*(206) 587-2300*

**Korea Exchange Bank**
*900 4th Avenue*
*Seattle*
*(206) 622-7821*

**Washington First International Bank**
*815 South Weller Street*
*Seattle*
*(206) 292-8880*

### Hardware Stores

**The Home Depot**
*2759 Utah Street S*
*Seattle*
*(206) 467-9200*

### Hospitals/Emergency Rooms

**Harborview Medical Center**
*325 9th Avenue*
*Seattle*
*(206) 731-3000*

## LAKE FOREST PARK/LAKE CITY

A lake. A forest. A park. Put them all together and picturesque scenery comes to mind. But don't get your hopes up. Unfortunately, earlier settlements and the town's hilly terrain preclude Lake Forest Park from reaching its full potential.

The neighborhood is really used as a turnstile by outside commuters trying to navigate around the north end of Lake Washington. If you're a "north ender" heading to the Eastside (or vice versa), chances are you'll pass through Lake Forest Park. Eastbound traffic from Edmonds, Woodway, Shoreline, Northgate, Brier, and Mountlake Terrace is funneled through poor little Lake Forest Park. Adding toll booths would incite a civil war, so local police do the next

## LAKE FOREST PARK/LAKE CITY

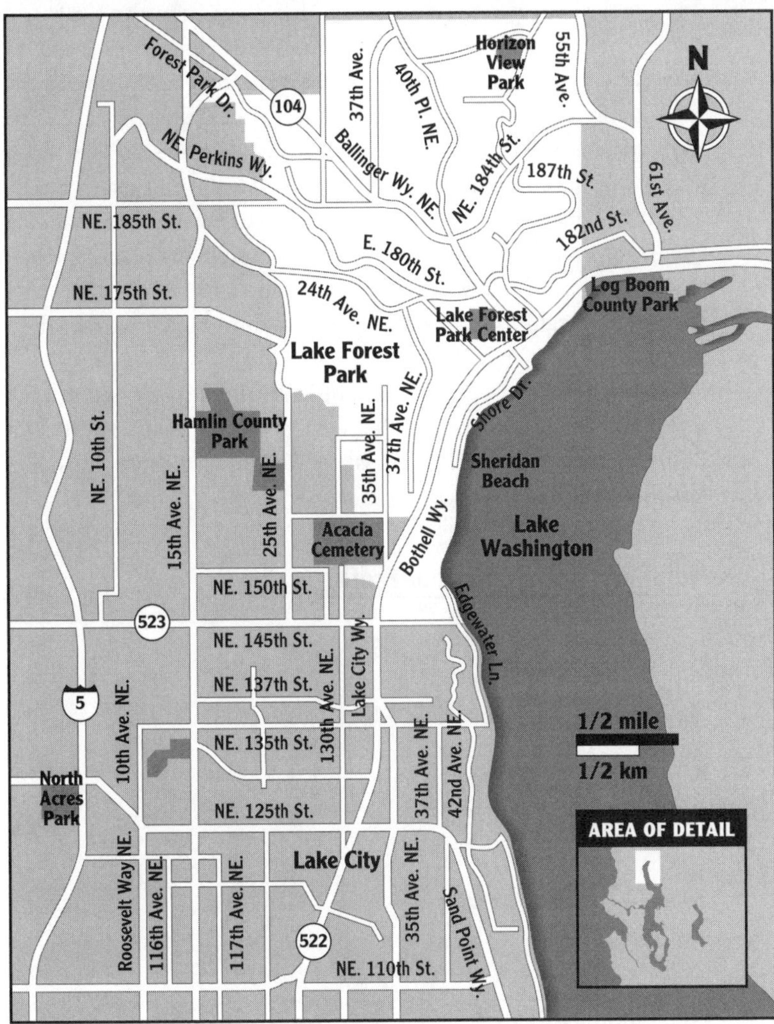


best thing: speed traps. Beware. Speeding tickets may be the tax base of this community. It surely can't be sales tax. There are few stores and no restaurants.

So what does this town have to offer besides hills, traffic, speeding tickets, and no restaurants?

Crooked streets. A few apartment buildings from the 1960s and 1970s. Lots of older, medium-size houses that cling precariously to steep cliffs. Working class residents that have become really good cooks.

Continuing the trend of nice names is neighboring Lake City. Here, too, the advertising is a bit misleading. There's no lake, or at least, none that you can see. The area is flat, old, and plagued with vandalism and burglaries. Houses are smallish and most were built in the 1950s. Some early residents remain, mostly seniors who like the flat, straighter roads. However, most sold out and moved long ago. Current generations of owners are first-time buyers attracted to affordable single-family housing.

There's really just one way out of Lake City. You guessed it, Lake City Way. The road connects the town to North Seattle (west) and Bothell (east) by way of countless stop lights, auto dealerships, and fast-food joints.

## Neighborhood Statistical Profile

**Population:** 21,290

**Median family income:** $50,111

### Population by Ethnicity

| | |
|---|---|
| *78%* | *Anglo* |
| *7%* | *Black* |
| *9%* | *Asian* |
| *6%* | *Hispanic* |

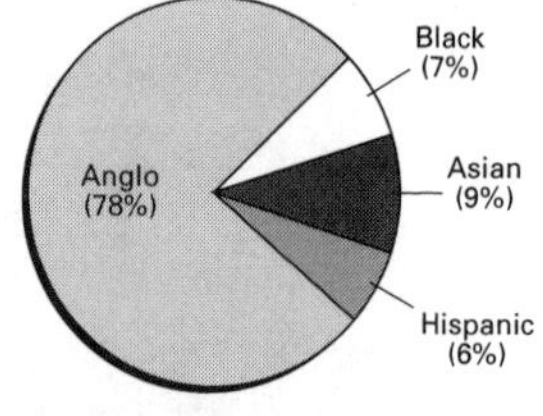


### Population by Gender

| | |
|---|---|
| *49%* | *Male* |
| *51%* | *Female* |

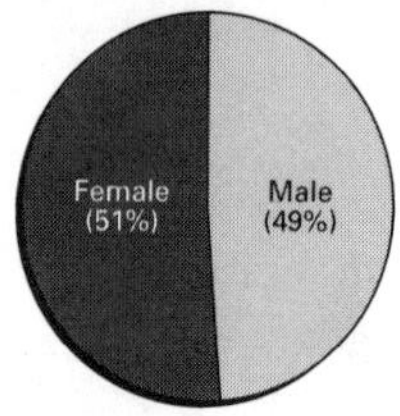

### Population by Age

*Median age:* *37*

| | |
|---|---|
| *10%* | *under 18* |
| *34%* | *18–39* |
| *26%* | *40–59* |
| *30%* | *over 59* |

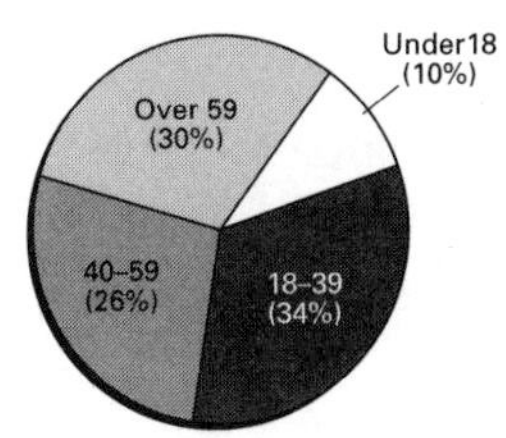


### Average Housing Costs

| | |
|---|---|
| *Low:* | *$259,555* |
| *High:* | *$534,121* |

### Average Rental Costs

| | |
|---|---|
| *Apartment:* | *$598* |
| *2–3-bedroom house:* | *$1,184* |

## Important Places Nearby

Grocery Stores

**Kilimanjaro Market**
*12519 Lake City Way NE*
*(206) 440-1440*

**Lake City Red Apple Market**
*12015 31st Avenue NE*
*(206) 362-7626*

Pharmacies

**Bartell Drugs at Lake City**
*3040 Northeast 127th Street*
*Lake City*
*(206) 362-7572*

Banks

**Washington Mutual**
*17191 Bothell Way NE*
*Lake Forest Park*
*(206) 461-7091*

www.wamu.com

**Washington Mutual**
*12360 Lake City Way NE*
*Lake City*
*(206) 461-4725*

www.wamu.com

Hardware Stores

**Stephenson Ace Hardware**
*9000 Roosevelt Way NE*
*Seattle*
*(206) 522-3324*

**Hospitals/Emergency Rooms**

**Evergreen Hospital Medical Center**
*12040 Northeast 128th Street*
*Kirkland*
*(425) 899-1000*

**Northwest Hospital**
*1550 North 115th Street*
*Seattle*
*(206) 364-0500*

## LAURELHURST

Laurelhurst is the real estate of real estate professionals. Even the name was coined by McLaughlin Realty long ago. Local movers and shakers include prominent developers and heirs of land barons. Town residents—mostly upper-middle class retirees and professional cou-

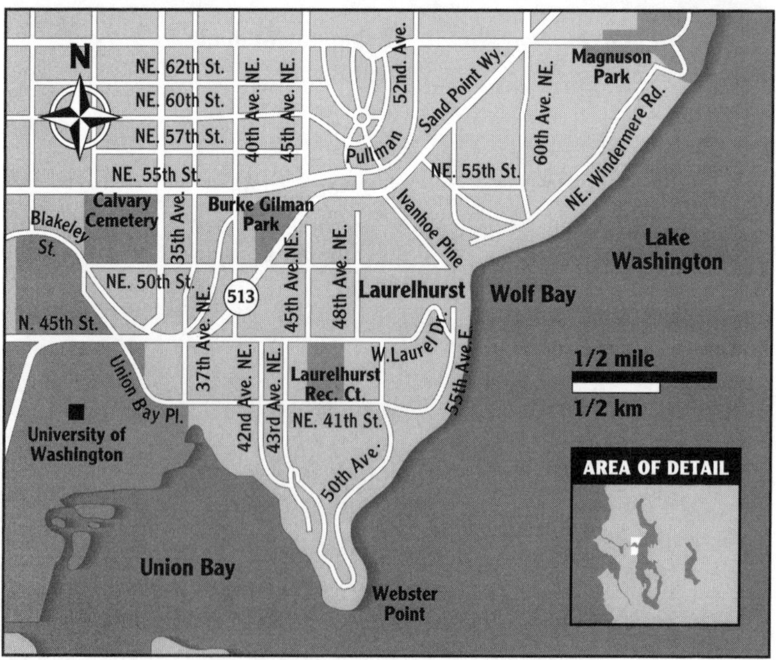

ples with children—not only know land, they know how to preserve it, too. Consider recent foes Children's Hospital and the University of Washington. Even such worthy causes were no match for Laurelhurst's feisty Community Council.

A tour of the neighborhood reveals why residents have been so protective. The houses belong on covers of checkout stand magazines, and the yards are groomed to perfection. Don't expect to see Dad and Junior breaking their backs on a Saturday morning, however. These urban gardens are maintained by surgical crews using scalpels and tweezers, not weed whackers and leaf blowers.

Yuppie storefronts and professional villages define Laurelhurst's exclusionary "business district." As might be expected of a community that lacks only a bronze statue of Martha Stewart, seasonal festivities include a Salmon Bake and Home Tour. Not the most original concepts in the Northwest, but this town has never tried to be different. Staying the same is hard enough.

## Neighborhood Statistical Profile

**Population:** 8,459

**Median family income:** $59,177

### Population by Ethnicity

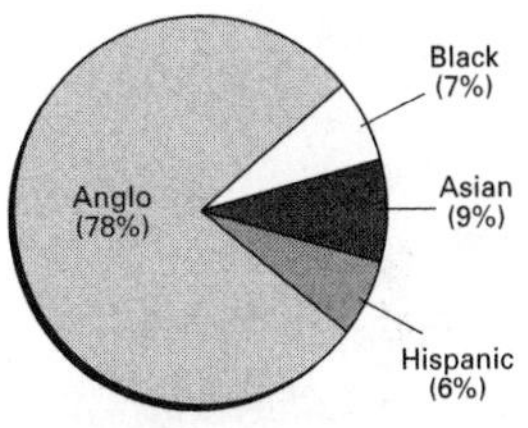


| | |
|---|---|
| *78%* | *Anglo* |
| *7%* | *Black* |
| *9%* | *Asian* |
| *6%* | *Hispanic* |

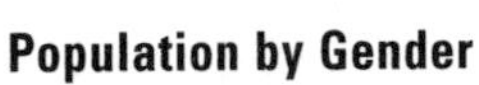

### Population by Gender

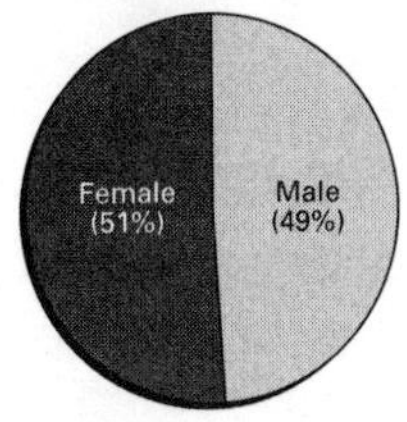


| | |
|---|---|
| *49%* | *Male* |
| *51%* | *Female* |

### Population by Age

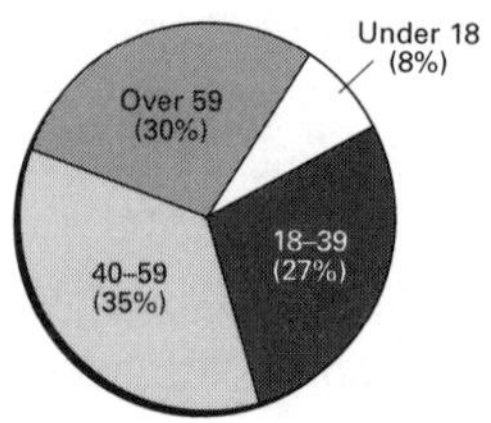


*Median age:* *38*

| | |
|---|---|
| *8%* | *under 18* |
| *27%* | *18–39* |
| *35%* | *40–59* |
| *30%* | *over 59* |

### Average Housing Costs

| | |
|---|---|
| *Low:* | *$345,525* |
| *High:* | *$698,133* |

### Average Rental Costs

| | |
|---|---|
| *Apartment:* | *$565* |
| *2–3-bedroom house:* | *$1,400* |

## Important Places Nearby

Grocery Stores

**Wedgwood Safeway Food & Drug**
*7340 35th Street NE*
*(206) 524-7064*

www.safeway.com

Banks

**Washington Mutual**
*5464 Sand Point Way NE*
*Seattle*
*(206) 461-2575*

www.wamu.com

Pharmacies

**Bartell Drugs at the Village**
*4700 University Village Place NE*
*Seattle*
*(206) 525-0705*

Hardware Store

**Tweedy & Popp Ace Hardware**
*1916 North 45th Street*
*Seattle*
*(206) 632-2290*

**Hospitals/Emergency Rooms**

**University of Washington Medical Center**
*1959 Northeast Pacific Street*
*Seattle*
*(206) 598-3300*

## MADRONA

"The Peaceable Kingdom," it's called, but things weren't always so tranquil in this long-divided town. Back in the 1960s, the Black Panthers occupied headquarters on 34th Avenue and ran military drills in Madrona Playfield.

**MADRONA**

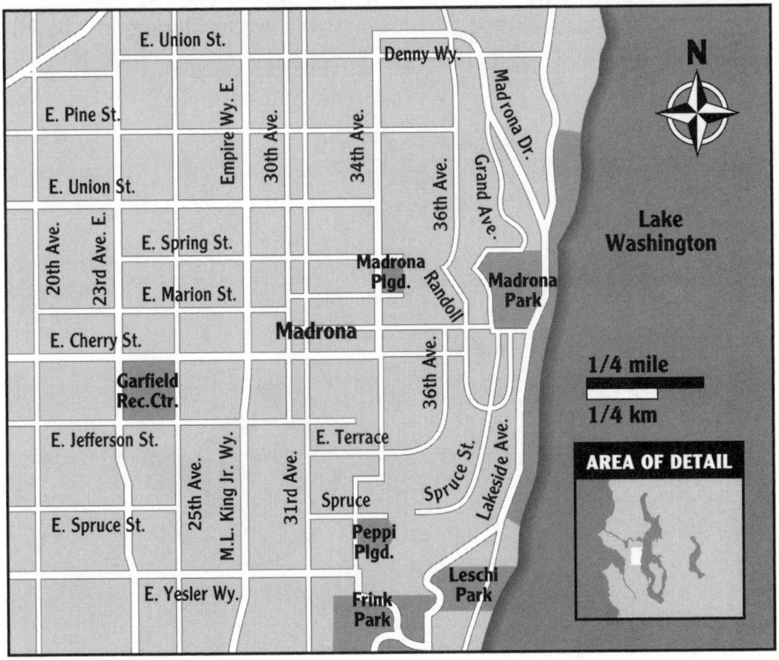

Today, 34th Avenue is still the dividing line between east and west, black and white, and low- and high-rent districts. This street is also the line that separates one kind of crime from another. To the east, offenses consist mainly of burglary and auto theft. The west is wilder, with crimes like aggravated assault, robbery, and rape topping the list.

Various signs, however, point to change for the better. Statistics suggest that the crime tide of the 1980s and early 1990s is ebbing. Community leaders point out that racial lines are starting to blur. Madrona's diversity was problematic in the past, but now serves as inspiration for the town's burgeoning population of artists and writers. Diversity of residential architecture is one of the key ingredients of Madrona's unflappable charm. Adorable bungalows on tree-lined streets appear to be swept from the pages of storybooks. Less cute but more dramatic are lakeside estates that can fetch upwards of $1 million.

Madrona's fashionable west side is so impeccably maintained that September is Neighborhood Cleanup Month. Its April Home Tour is one of the town's premier celebrations. Other annual highlights include the May Fair Community Party.

Madrona's unofficial community center has long been the Hi-Spot, but Cool Hand Luke's may be eclipsing the venerable café.

## Neighborhood Statistical Profile

**Population:** 13,854

**Median family income:** $47,000

### Population by Ethnicity

| | |
|---|---|
| *57%* | *Anglo* |
| *26%* | *Black* |
| *9%* | *Asian* |
| *8%* | *Hispanic* |

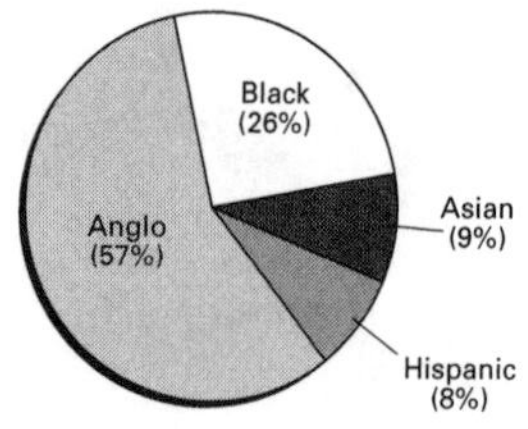

### Population by Gender

*48%* *Male*

*52%* *Female*

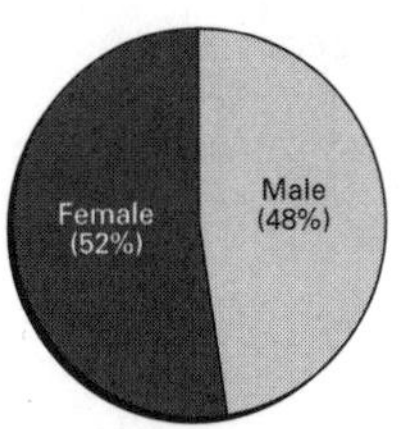


### Population by Age

*Median age:* *34*

*7%* *under 18*

*25%* *18–39*

*39%* *40–59*

*29%* *over 59*

Under 18
(7%)
Over 59
(29%)
18–39
(25%)
40–59
(39%)

### Average Housing Costs

*Low:* *$210,333*

*High:* *$796,666*

### Average Rental Costs

| | |
|---|---|
| *Apartment:* | *$800* |
| *2–3-bedroom house:* | *$2,000* |

## Important Places Nearby

Grocery Stores

**Madrona Homemade Deli Market**
*3309 East Union Street*
*(206) 324-5771*

Pharmacies

**Don Plumlee's Neighborhood Pharmacy**
*4130 East Madison Street*
*Seattle*
*(206) 324-1188*

Banks

**Washington Mutual**
*3820 Rainier Avenue S*
*Seattle*
*(206) 554-7250*

www.wamu.com

Hardware Stores

**Lowe's Hardware & Garden**
*2700 Rainier Street*
*Seattle*
*(206) 760-0832*

**Hospitals/Emergency Rooms**

**Providence Seattle Medical Center**
*500 17th Avenue*
*Seattle*
*(206) 320-2000*

**Swedish Medical Center**
*747 Broadway*
*Seattle*
*(206) 386-6000*

---

## MAGNOLIA

"A rose by any other name is still a rose." Legend has it that a botanically challenged explorer mistook the madrona for a magnolia and, hence, misnamed this charming town. Proud residents cared little about the misnomer, although an effort was launched to rename the community Madrona Bluff. In retaliation, ladies of the Magnolia Chapter Garden Club lobbied residents to plant magnolias. Since 1948 the Buena Vista Garden Club has planted more than fifty such trees, lending credibility to the town's name.

This lovely neighborhood sits on a manmade peninsula, ensuring the isolation that locals crave. There are but three ways to enter or exit Magnolia: West Davis Street, Salmon Bay Interchange, and Magnolia Bridge. Residents consist mainly of white-collar professionals and young families. Perhaps because of its remoteness, Magnolia experiences little crime. Housing ranges from cute bungalows at the foot of the bluff to custom hilltop homes with floor-to-ceiling glass.

Magnolia loves its children. Cherished are Bay View Playground and Discovery Park, where curious youngsters can take guided tours along nature trails. Each August, the town hosts the Magnolia Summer Festival and Kids Parade. The Magnolia Community Center offers an endless list of youth and family activities. Grown-ups aren't neglected, though. The Village Pub is a popular watering hole, and lattes, gourmet take-out, and Scandinavian bakeries are commonplace.

## MAGNOLIA

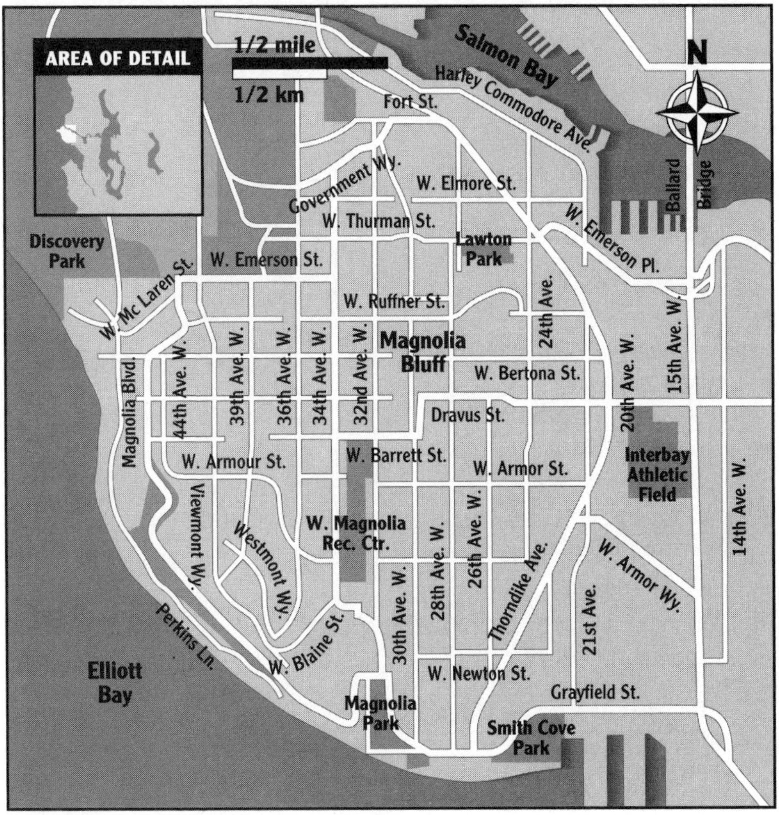

## Neighborhood Statistical Profile

**Population:** 13,109

**Median family income:** $68,000

**Population by Ethnicity**

| | |
|---|---|
| *84%* | *Anglo* |
| *4%* | *Black* |
| *9%* | *Asian* |
| *3%* | *Hispanic* |

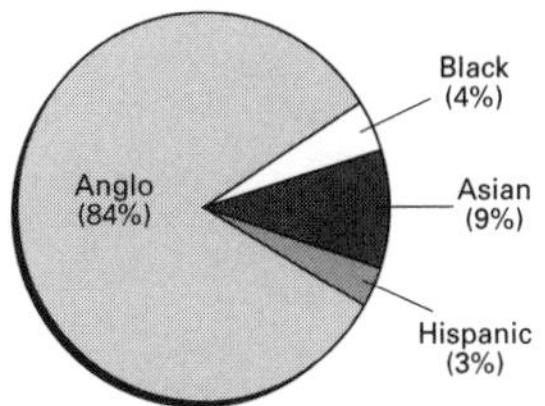

### Population by Gender

*47%* *Male*

*53%* *Female*

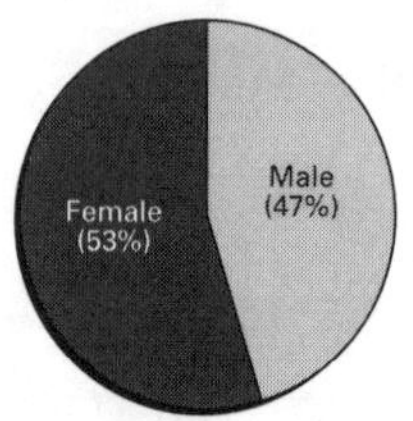


### Population by Age

*Median age:* *39*

*11%* *under 18*

*28%* *18–39*

*29%* *40–59*

*32%* *over 59*

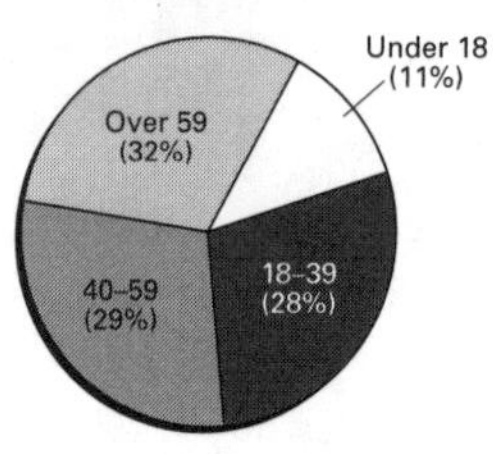


### Average Housing Costs

*Low:* *$235,154*

*High:* *$595,449*

### Average Rental Costs

*Apartment:* *$850*

*2–3-bedroom house:* *$1,800*

## Important Places Nearby

Grocery Stores

**Magnolia Thriftway**
*3830 34th Avenue W*
*(206) 283-2710*

**Quality Food Centers**
*1600 West Dravus Street*
*(206) 283-3600*

www.artsfoodctr.com

Pharmacies

**Bartell Drugs at Magnolia**
*2222 32nd Street W*
*Magnolia*
*(206) 282-2881*

Banks

**Washington Federal Savings**
*3219 West McGraw*
*Seattle*
*(206) 284-5171*

**Hardware Stores**

**Magnolia Ace Hardware**
*2420 32nd Avenue W*
*Seattle*
*(206) 282-1916*

**Hospitals/Emergency Rooms**

**Swedish Medical Center of Ballard**
*5300 Tallman Avenue NW*
*Seattle*
*(206) 782-2700*

## MONTLAKE

This pretty little community of mansionettes and gingerbread houses is reputedly home to cerebral, academic types. Slotted between Washington Park Arboretum and the Museum of History & Industry, it's certainly primed for deep thinking. Some say UW professors inhabit pricey Montlake. I certainly hope so. It's about time we paid our educators what they're worth.

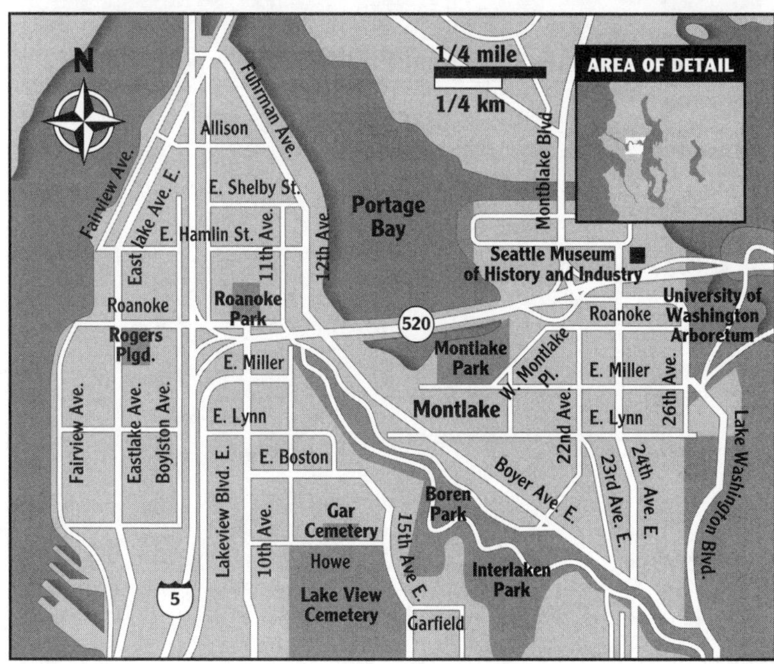

To those only passing through this high I.Q. district, Montlake is synonymous with gridlock. Not the mental gridlock experienced during weekend chess matches at McCurdy Park. The other kind. Traffic and parking around Montlake can fluster even the most formidable minds. Of course, mine snaps like a stale breadstick. But there's good news. The town's design is pedestrian-friendly.

After a day of quantum mechanics and string theory, intellectuals unwind the same way Small Brains do: a mile-high sandwich at The Daily Grind . . . a tall, frosty one at Grady's Pub . . . and a stroll through the Arboretum.

Washington Park Arboretum is like 200 acres of Monet's *Giverney.* (Not bad for a Small Brain, eh?) In full bloom, Azalea Way is beyond adjectives and similes. Foster Island Nature Trail will enchant and delight both young and old. Visitors may partake in an authentic tea ceremony at the park's serene Japanese Garden & Teahouse.

There's very little crime in Montlake itself. The most egregious offense I ever witnessed was the park bench scrawlings of a vandal.

It read, "$E{=}MC^2$."

## Neighborhood Statistical Profile

**Population:** 3,174

**Median family income:** $49,994

**Population by Ethnicity**

| | |
|---|---|
| *89%* | *Anglo* |
| *3%* | *Black* |
| *6%* | *Asian* |
| *2%* | *Hispanic* |

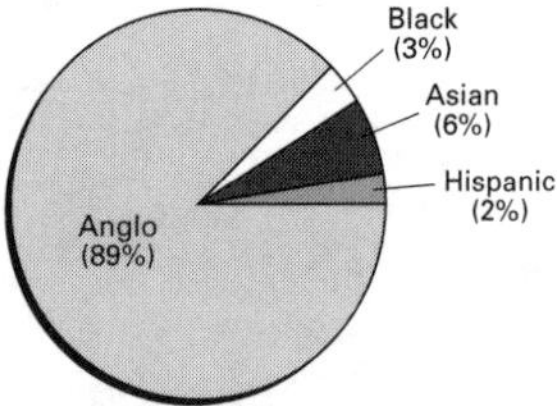

### Population by Gender

*49%* *Male*

*51%* *Female*

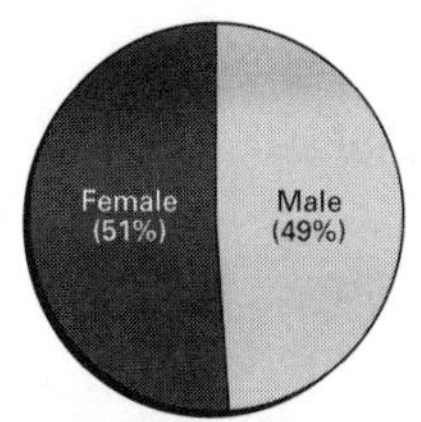


### Population by Age

*Median age:* *38*

*5%* *under 18*

*25%* *18–39*

*42%* *40–59*

*28%* *over 59*

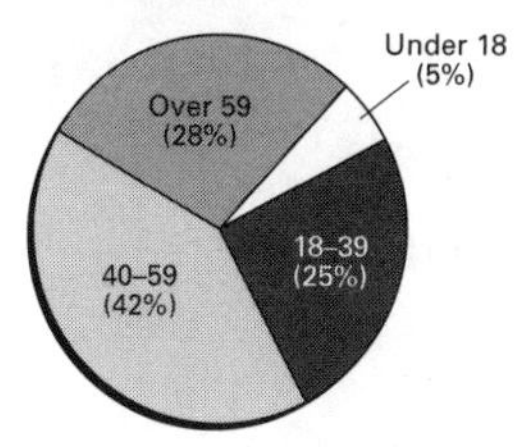


### Average Housing Costs

*Low:* *$340,555*

*High:* *$516,707*

### Average Rental Costs

*Apartment:* *$1,200*

*2–3-bedroom house:* *$2,750*

## Important Places Nearby

Grocery Stores

**Bert's Red Apple Market**
*1801 41st Avenue E*
*(206) 322-1330*

**Beacon Market**
*2500 Beacon Avenue S*
*(206) 323-2050*

Pharmacies

**Wood's Old-Fashioned Rexall Pharmacy**
*271 Northeast 45th Street*
*Seattle*
*(206) 633-4470*

**Banks**

**Washington Mutual**
*4020 East Madison Street*
*Seattle*
*(206) 461-3025*
www.wamu.com

**Hardware Stores**

**Madison Park Hardware**
*1837 42nd Street E*
*Seattle*
*(206) 322-5331*

**Hospitals/Emergency Rooms**

**University of Washington Medical Center**
*1959 Northeast Pacific Street*
*Seattle*
*(206) 598-3300*

---

## QUEEN ANNE

The name is perfect. Hilltop communities are venerable, even regal. Named by the early mill barons for their preferred style of architecture, the city possesses a dignified and distinctly feminine allure. High-pitched roofs, gingerbread details, and inviting porches are trademarks of the Victorian homes that endure as the grand dames of Seattle. Residents on the crown of Queen Anne tend to be fiercely loyal lifelong residents, but stereotypes of "old money" cliques are unwarranted. Nouveau riche types moved in long before *Yahoo!* went public.

Not all of Queen Anne is blue-blooded, though. In lower Queen Anne, you'll find young urbanites and move-up buyers. The north side is the lower-rent district, a hit with students of Seattle Pacific University. To the east, what was once Queen Anne High School is now an ultras-wanky townhouse complex. Heading west toward Interbay you'll find Kinnear Park and the Queen Anne Community Center. You'll also discover a glut of condos and apartments built in the 1980s and 1990s, also popular with young city dwellers. In the center of it all is the "Counterbalance." This area was once dedicated to a gravity-assisted winch that helped trolleys negotiate the steep hill.

Queen Anne is home to 2,500 businesses. Most of them are single proprietorships. Old-fashioned law offices, Ma and Pa grocers, side-

## QUEEN ANNE

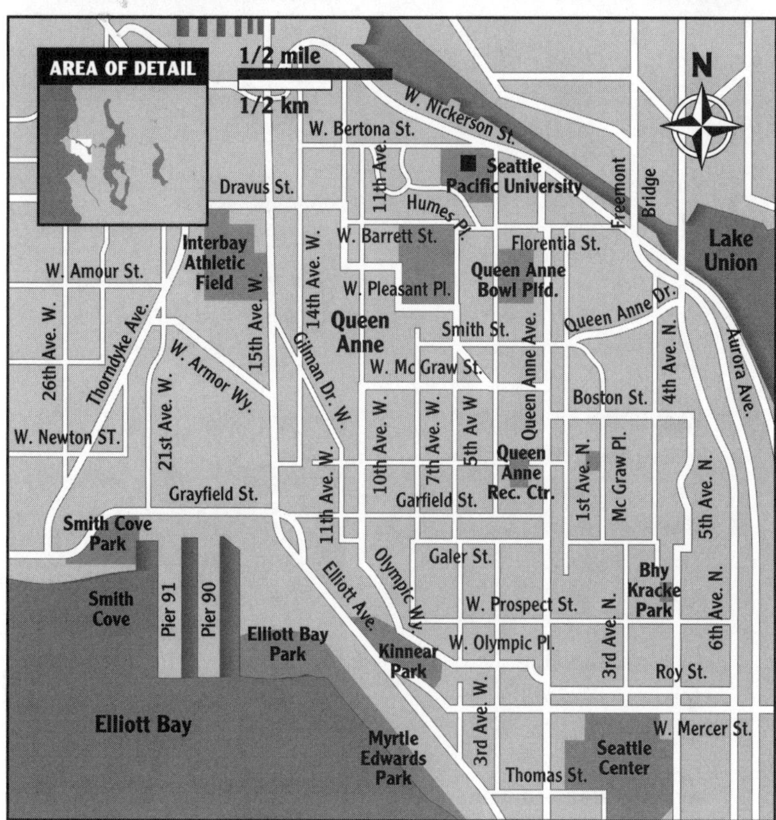


walk bistros, and quaint bookshops give the neighborhood a vintage quality. Hangouts include the Queen Anne Thriftway (a reputed hotspot where singles mingle), "Gigolo Ave" (a.k.a., Bigelow Avenue North, where half-naked runners work up a sweaty sheen), and just about any yuppie café, diner, or Euro bakery.

### Neighborhood Statistical Profile

**Population:** 33,884

**Median family income:** $49,616

## Population by Ethnicity

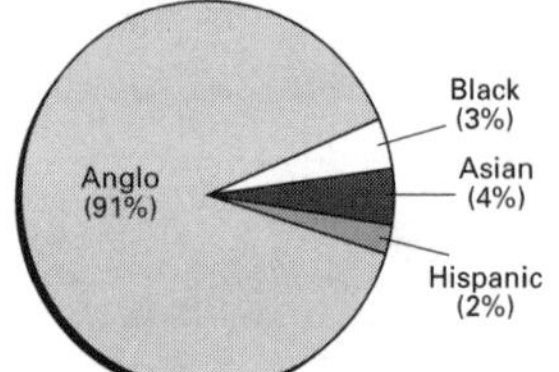


| | |
|---|---|
| *91%* | *Anglo* |
| *3%* | *Black* |
| *4%* | *Asian* |
| *2%* | *Hispanic* |

## Population by Gender

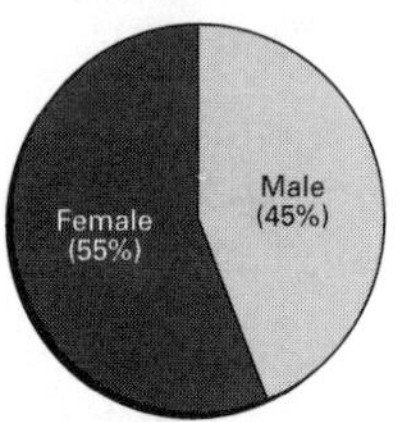


| | |
|---|---|
| *45%* | *Male* |
| *55%* | *Female* |

## Population by Age

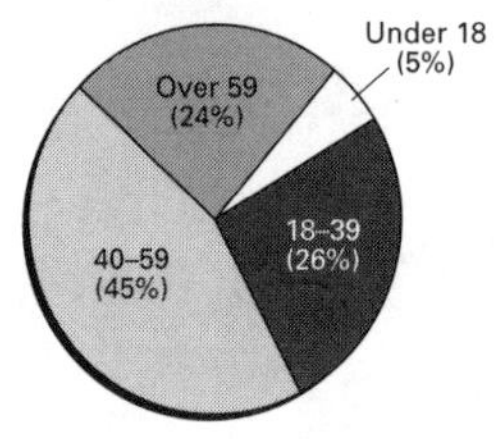


*Median age:* 36

| | |
|---|---|
| *5%* | *under 18* |
| *26%* | *18–39* |
| *45%* | *40–59* |
| *24%* | *over 59* |

## Average Housing Costs

| | |
|---|---|
| *Low:* | *$325,638* |
| *High:* | *$575,722* |

## Average Rental Costs

| | |
|---|---|
| *Apartment:* | *$795* |
| *2–3-bedroom house:* | *$2,750* |

## Important Places Nearby

### Grocery Stores

**Queen Anne Thriftway**
*1908 Queen Anne Avenue N*
*(206) 284-2530*

### Pharmacies

**Bartell Drugs at Queen Anne**
*600 1st Avenue*
*(206) 284-1354*

**Banks**

**HomeStreet Bank**
*1835 Queen Anne Avenue N*
*Seattle*
*(206) 285-5898*
www.homestreetbank.com

**Hardware Stores**

**Five Corners Hardware**
*305 West McGraw Street*
*Seattle*
*(206) 282-5000*

**Hospitals/Emergency Rooms**

**Swedish Medical Center of Ballard**
*5300 Tallman Avenue NW*
*Seattle*
*(206) 782-2700*

**University of Washington Medical Center**
*1959 Northeast Pacific Street*
*Seattle*
*(206) 598-3300*

## UNIVERSITY DISTRICT/UNIVERSITY VILLAGE

Half of the nearly 25,000 residents of the University District are enrolled as students, making it a college town by any standards. Typical of college towns, the U-District is vibrant from September through June.

Village life buzzes around bohemian and avant-garde shops, ethnic bistros, and artsy film festivals. There's Meany Hall, which appeals to culture seekers. The mammoth University Book Store is a literature exchange approaching Amazonian-dot-com proportions.

Unfortunately, not all activities in this neighborhood are culturally enriching. University Way—dubbed "The Ave" by students and strays—is a pipeline for the town's illicit drug trade. But let's be fair. Most street dwellers are not UW enrollees. Caffeine remains the addiction of midnight oil–burning students. Their "fixes" are provided by Espresso Roma and Allegro Espresso Bar. Although crime seems to have crested, the community's senior citizens remain fearful of the streets at night. Much of the U-District, though, is enjoying a rebirth. The popular University Village—an outdoor collection of upscale boutiques and galleries—is a hit with Seattle shoppers.

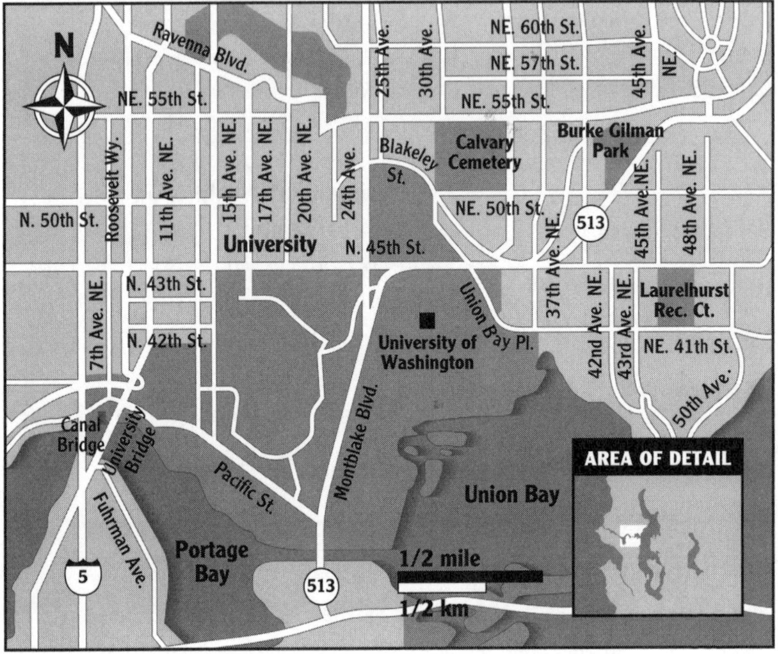


Most dwellings to the south and west are apartments or condominiums. Affordable units appear dated but are preferred by cost-conscious students and retirees. To the north, single-family housing is more common. Homes, too, are aging but affordable.

The U-District is an acquired taste. Those who savor its unique character indulge in local celebrations. Eagerly anticipated is the University Street Fair, which draws enormous crowds. The opening day of boating season spawns a flotilla of outlandishly decorated vessels on nearby Elliot Bay. Hot spots for weekend fun include Giggles Comedy Nite Club and The Big Time Ale House.

## Neighborhood Statistical Profile

**Population:** 24,194

**Median family income:** $18,448

### Population by Ethnicity

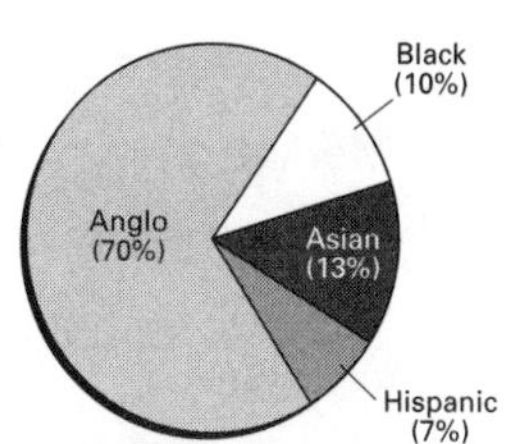


*70%* *Anglo*
*10%* *Black*
*13%* *Asian*
*7%* *Hispanic*

### Population by Gender

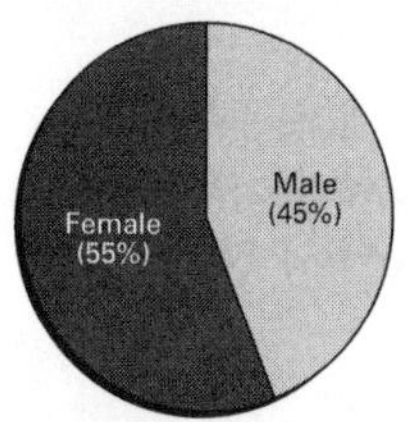


*45%* *Male*
*55%* *Female*

### Population by Age

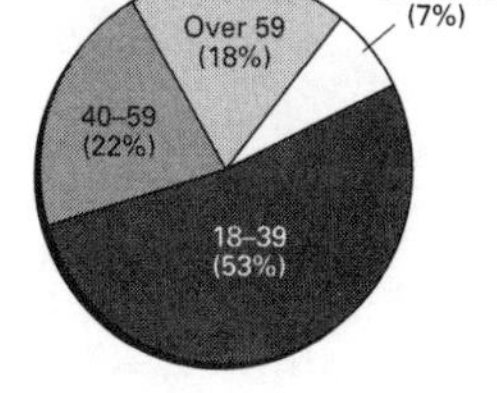


*Median age:* 24
*7%* *under 18*
*53%* *18–39*
*22%* *40–59*
*18%* *over 59*

### Average Housing Costs

*Low:* *$170,000*
*High:* *$269,550*

### Average Rental Costs

*Apartment:* *$555*
*2–3-bedroom house:* *$1,200*

## Important Places Nearby

Grocery Stores

**Aladdin Gyro-Cery**
*4139 University Way NE*
*(206) 632-5253*

**Whole Foods Market**
*1026 Northeast 64th Street*
*(206) 985-1500*
www.wholefoods.com

Pharmacies

**Bartell Drugs at the University**
*4344 University Way NE*
*Seattle*
*(206) 632-3514*

Banks

**Key Bank**
*2690 Northeast University Village Mall*
*Seattle*
*(206) 447-5744*
www.key.com

Hardware Stores

**Hardwick's "Seattle's Oldest" Hardware Store**
*4214 Roosevelt Way NE*
*Seattle*
*(206) 632-1203*

Hospitals/Emergency Rooms

**University of Washington Medical Center**
*1959 Northeast Pacific Street*
*Seattle*
*(206) 598-3300*

## WEST SEATTLE

My grandmother taught me, "If you can't say something nice, don't say anything at all." She never mentioned writing, so it's with a clear conscience that I unleash the power of my keyboard.

The best thing about West Seattle is that it has great views of East Seattle.

## WEST SEATTLE

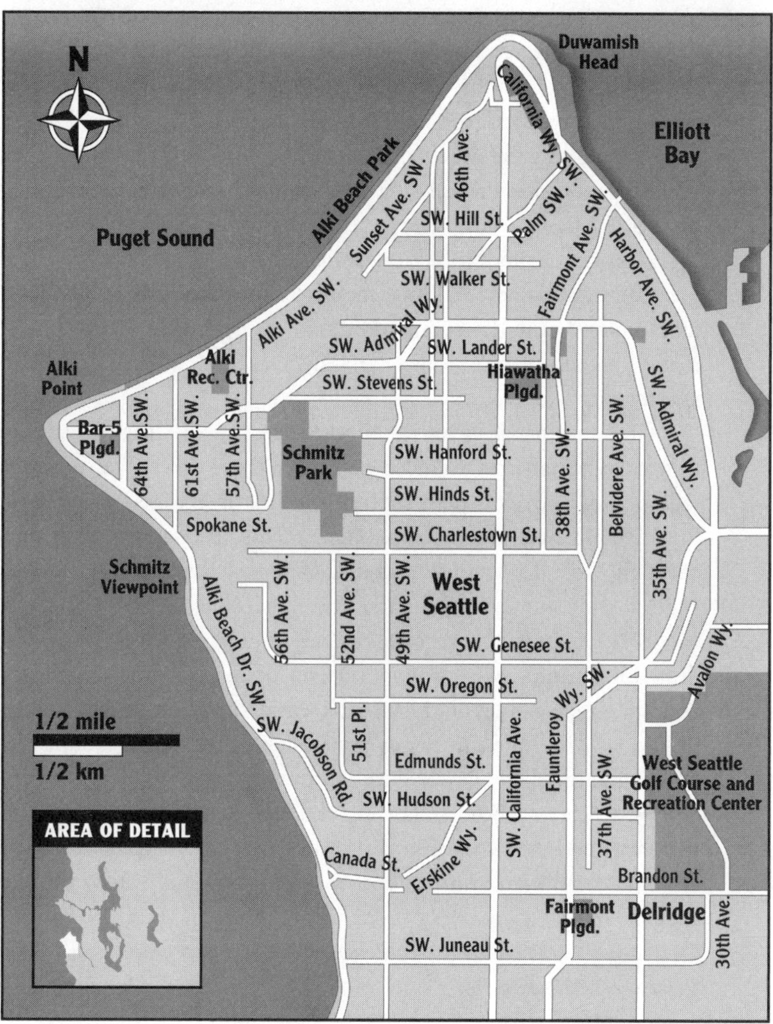


Sure, there's Alki Park and the summer rituals of volleyball and beach bunny parades, but the relative isolation of West Seattle is hardly a tradeoff for three months of fun. A dozen or so historic murals painted on the sides of otherwise unspectacular buildings are the pride of West Seattleites. The landmark Husky Deli is a treasured ingot of the community chest. So are Snubby's and Capers, two other hangouts.

Like any large community this one has nice areas and not-so-nice areas. With water on three sides, you'd expect West Seattle to showcase premium properties. Not so. With the exception of Genesee Hill—a bluff top offering the sweetest cut of real estate—West Seattle has been a hard sell of late. Problem is, the neighborhood crime is nibbling close to the bone.

Motorists entering West Seattle on Fauntleroy Way SW are greeted by antiquated buildings, nondescript storefronts, and lackluster restaurants. Car dealerships dominate the commercial landscape. It may be a good place to buy a car, but I can think of better places to take a test drive.

Grandmother also taught me to focus on the brighter side of things. So let's go back to those views. Oh, those views! The best vantage points from which to capture the Seattle skyline bathing in a Puget Sound sunset are from public lookouts. Just park your car, take a stretch and a deep breath, and soak in the scenery that has been the subject of countless calendars, travel brochures, and postcards. Indoors, you can still appreciate the panorama from a legendary West Seattle institution. Some restaurants are designed around a culinary concept or a chef's reputation. Salty's was designed around a spectacular view. Time melts away as you watch ferries scoot around the Sound and sailplanes gently skim across Elliott Bay.

West Seattle is bordered by Puget Sound to the west, Elliot Bay to the north, and the Duwamish Waterway to the East. Directly south are the cities of Burien and Sea-Tac. Vashon Island and Kitsap County may be reached by ferry from the Fauntleroy Ferry Terminal. Downtown Seattle and the International District are accessed by the West Seattle Freeway.

## Neighborhood Statistical Profile

**Population:** 19,185

**Median family income:** $39,662

### Population by Ethnicity

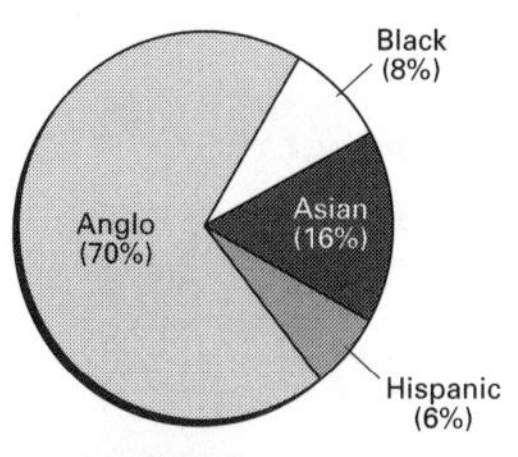


| | |
|---|---|
| *70%* | *Anglo* |
| *8%* | *Black* |
| *16%* | *Asian* |
| *6%* | *Hispanic* |

### Population by Gender

| | |
|---|---|
| *48%* | *Male* |
| *52%* | *Female* |

### Population by Age

*Median age:* *35*

| | |
|---|---|
| *10%* | *under 18* |
| *29%* | *18–39* |
| *32%* | *40–59* |
| *29%* | *over 59* |

### Average Housing Costs

| | |
|---|---|
| *Low:* | *$200,000* |
| *High:* | *$775,000* |

### Average Rental Costs

| | |
|---|---|
| *Apartment:* | *$550* |
| *2–3-bedroom house:* | *$1,350* |

## Important Places Nearby

Grocery Stores

**Heng Heng Supermarket**
*9841 16th Avenue SW*
*(206) 764-1889*

**PCC Natural Markets**
*2749 California Avenue SW*
*(206) 937-8481*

www.pccnaturalmarkets.com

**Pharmacies**

**Westside Pharmacy**
*5401 California Avenue SW*
*West Seattle*
*(206) 937-5722*

**Hardware Stores**

**Alki Lumber & Hardware**
*4422 36th Street SW*
*West Seattle*
*(206) 932-7700*

**Banks**

**First Mutual Bank**
*4520 California Avenue SW*
*West Seattle*
*(206) 932-6299*
www.firstmutual.com

**Hospitals/Emergency Rooms**

**Swedish Medical Center**
*747 Broadway*
*Seattle*
*(206) 386-6000*

## Suburbs

### BELLEVUE

Bellevue used to be strawberry fields forever. Now it's a full-fledged city with all the trimmings, and the flagship of the Greater Eastside. Bellevue is to Seattle what Manhattan is to New York City. A vibrant city within a vibrant city.

In every respect, though, this city is capable of standing alone. Bellevue is home to almost a quarter of the state's hi-tech companies. Shoppers spend more money in Bellevue than in Greater Downtown Seattle: *50 percent* more. With an affluent population of 120,000 residents, it is the state's fourth-largest city and a formidable player in the Northwest economy.

Residential offerings cover all bases. There are single-family homes of varying styles, ages, and prices. Newer houses are featured in large, hillside tracts, as well as small, exclusive plats on the western side of town. Older homes are found in the quiet confines along the city's southern and eastern periphery. Multifamily housing includes the sexy, glass-covered high-rise condominiums of downtown Bellevue. Low-rise condominiums are located along the lakes and

## SEATTLE SUBURBS

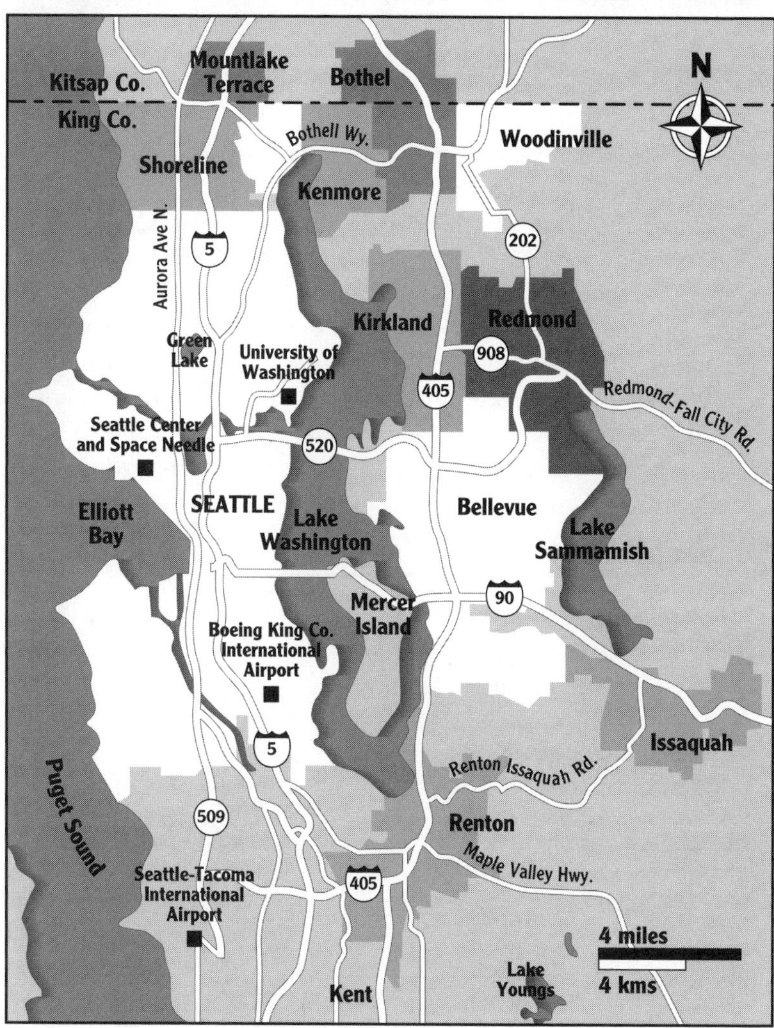


major boulevards. Apartment dwellings can be found anywhere but in the west, where zoning is exclusively single family. Housing isn't cheap on the Eastside, and you pay a premium for Bellevue's convenience and relative safety. The prestige factor tacks on a little, too.

Commuters from downtown and west Bellevue access the I-405 freeway directly and via SR-520. The I-90 is popular with commuters on the eastern side. A major artery connecting east and west is 148th Avenue NE. From Bellevue, a rush-hour commute to downtown Seattle will take forty-five minutes. During off-peak hours, the same trip takes under twenty-five minutes.

The city is very Barbie-and-Ken. By day, it's jammed with suits scurrying from power workouts to power lunches. The retail and financial districts are connected by Northeast Eighth Street, Bellevue Way, and Main Street, and are usually gridlocked. Bellevue Square, the city's retail epicenter, is a way of life.

If the downtown crowds get to be too much, pamper yourself at one of the city's renowned spas or private clubs. Play a round at Bellevue Golf Course or stroll through the tranquil Botanical Gardens at Wilburton Park. If the weather isn't cooperative, visit one of the city's museums or cultural arts centers. You'll thank yourself.

## Neighborhood Statistical Profile

**Population:** 119,655

**Median family income:** $70,421

### Population by Ethnicity

| | |
|---|---|
| *72%* | *Anglo* |
| *8%* | *Black* |
| *16%* | *Asian* |
| *4%* | *Hispanic* |

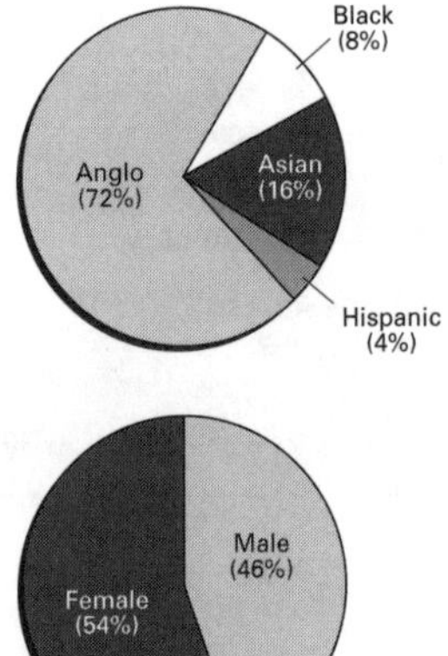

### Population by Gender

| | |
|---|---|
| *46%* | *Male* |
| *54%* | *Female* |

### Population by Age

*Median age:* *38*

*17%* *under 18*

*29%* *18–39*

*36%* *40–59*

*18%* *over 59*

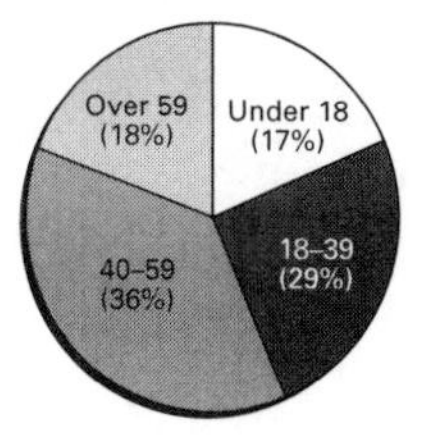


### Average Housing Costs

*Low:* *$245,786*

*High:* *$468,447*

### Average Rental Costs

| | |
|---|---|
| *Apartment:* | *$985* |
| *2–3-bedroom house:* | *$2,200* |

## Important Places Nearby

Grocery Stores

**Bellevue Oriental Mart**
*900 160th Avenue NE*
*(425) 747-1351*

**Larry's Markets**
*699 120th Avenue NE*
*(425) 453-0600*
www.larrysmarkets.com

**Uwajimaya**
*15555 Northeast 24th Street*
*(425) 747-9012*

Pharmacy

**Bartell Drugs at Bellevue Village**
*10116 Northeast 8th Street*
*(425) 454-2468*

Banks

**Pacific Northwest Bank**
*11100 Northeast 8th Street*
*(425) 646-0900*

**Sterling Savings Bank**
*500 108th Avenue NE*
*(425) 454-9212*

**Columbia Bank**
*777 108th Avenue NE*
*(425) 646-9696*
www.columbiabank.com

Hardware Stores

**Lowe's Hardware & Garden**
*11959 Northup Way*
*(425) 646-9031*

Hospitals/Emergency Rooms

**Group Health Eastside Hospital**
*2700 152nd Avenue NE*
*Redmond*
*(425) 883-5151*

**Overlake Hospital Medical Center**
*1035 116th Avenue NE*
*Bellevue*
*(425) 688-5000*

## BOTHELL/KENMORE

A small sign greets motorists entering this slumbering Eastside town from the Interstate-405 freeway. It reads, "*Welcome to Bothell, For a Day or a Lifetime.*" Frankly, I've spent days in Bothell that seemed like a lifetime. But that's because—among other things—I'm a builder. Bothell's not a builder-friendly zone. The town welcomes new housing with the same enthusiasm kindergarten teachers welcome chewing gum. So if you're planning to construct your dream home in this 'burb, hire a builder with the patience of a Zen master.

I'm not saying Bothell is a bad place to live. There's just not a lot to do on a Saturday night. Or a Monday morning. Or a Thursday afternoon. The town's pulse is barely detectable. Ask any of its lifelong residents, and they'll concur . . . that's just the way they like it.

Bothell's proximity to the freeway is a big plus. Getting to the northern towns of Mill Creek and Lynnwood takes only a few minutes on I-405. Southbound motorists will enjoy easy commutes to Kirkland and Bellevue, too. The other major egress is State Route 522, connecting Bothell to the eastern towns of Woodinville and Snohomish. Heading west along Lake City Way is Seattle, by way of Kenmore, and at least a hundred traffic lights.

Bothell's not backward, it's just not in a hurry to leap forward. Like most of the Eastside, the town's public schools and parks are enviable. If backyard barbecues and Little League games are your idea of a satisfying weekend, Bothell may be a good fit. If, however, you prefer a swanky singles scene, keep looking.

## Neighborhood Statistical Profile

**Population:** 21,655

**Median family income:** $54,301

### Population by Ethnicity

*73%* *Anglo*
*9%* *Black*
*11%* *Asian*
*7%* *Hispanic*

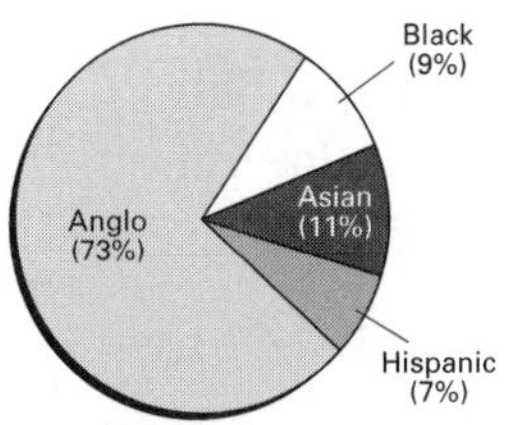


### Population by Gender

*48%* *Male*
*52%* *Female*

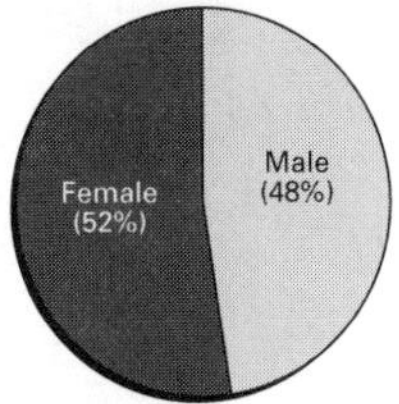


### Population by Age

*Median age:* 35
*16%* *under 18*
*32%* *18–39*
*33%* *40–59*
*19%* *over 59*

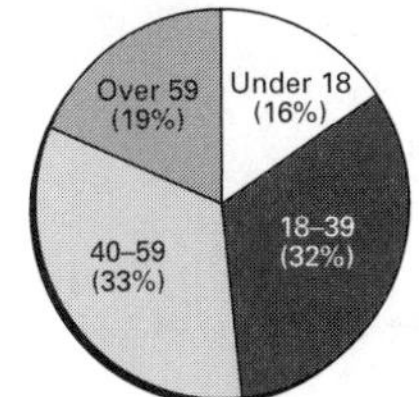


### Average Housing Costs

*Low:* *$199,404*
*High:* *$268,968*

### Average Rental Costs

| | |
|---|---|
| *Apartment:* | *$695* |
| *2–3-bedroom house:* | *$1,652* |

## Important Places Nearby

Grocery Stores

**Safeway Food & Drug**
*18221 Bothell Way NE*
*(425) 486-5652*

www.safeway.com

**Victor's Grocery & Deli**
*11801 Northeast 160th Street*
*(425) 488-0390*

Pharmacy

**Ostrom's Drugs**
*6744 Northeast 181st Street*
*Kenmore*
*(425) 486-7711*

Banks

**Towne Bank**
*10125 Main Street*
*Bothell*
*(425) 398-0559*

**Washington Mutual**
*6701 Northeast 181st Street*
*Kenmore*
*(425) 486-1286*

www.wamu.com

Hardware Store

**The Home Depot**
*18333 120th Avenue NE*
*Bothell*
*(425) 806-9300*

Hospitals/Emergency Rooms

**Evergreen Hospital Medical Center**
*12040 Northeast 128th Street*
*Kirkland*
*(425) 899-1000*

**Northwest Hospital**
*1550 North 115th Street*
*Seattle*
*(206) 364-0500*

## HOLLYWOOD HILL

Lights! Camera! Action! Not exactly, although I once saw a riding instructor with a camcorder. Dismiss any preconceived notions about studio executives "doing lunch" in this town. Hollywood Hill is a quiet community of rolling pastures and winding roads. In the last twenty years, pricey Craftsman style "ranchettes" emerged that peacefully coexist with neighboring horse farms and riding stables. Hollywood Hill exudes an odd but enchanting feeling of rural sophistication. Is it country suburb or elegant farmland? I don't know, but its residents must have the highest per capita vet bills in the county.

Perhaps the best-known landmark is a noble brick structure at the foot of the hill, where Redmond and Woodinville converge. Over the decades the Hollywood Schoolhouse has been a loyal servant to

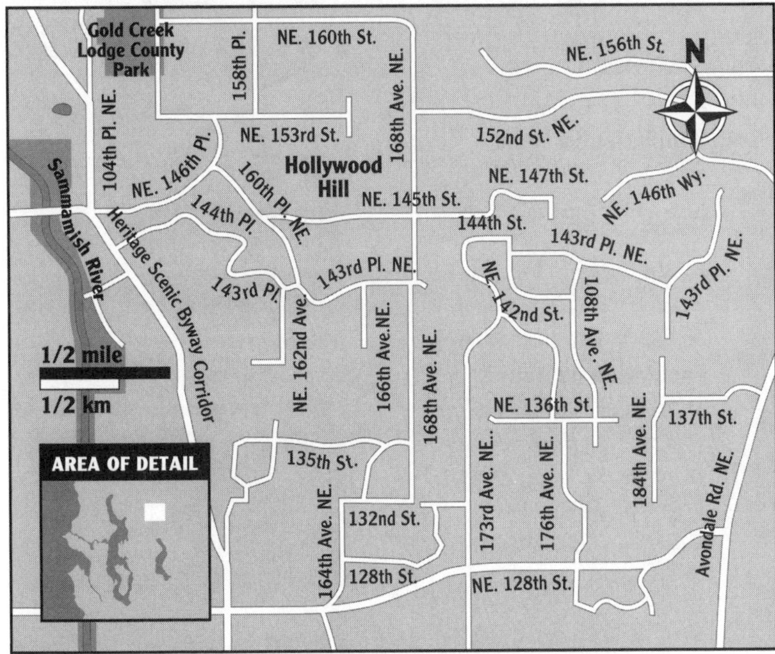

the community. Long dormant as a school, it has doubled as a sanctuary, bowery, and town hall. The historic building is now a museum that hosts gala parties and weddings.

Hollywood Hill can be a problem for commuters with low tolerances for traffic. Even A-to-B navigating requires the bypass finesse of a heart surgeon. Accessing local infrastructure (State Route 522 and I-405) can be tedious.

It's the price you pay for living in the country. Suburb. Country suburb.

## Neighborhood Statistical Profile

**Population:** 4,320

**Median family income:** $71,050

### Population by Ethnicity

| | |
|---|---|
| *94%* | *Anglo* |
| *2%* | *Black* |
| *1%* | *Asian* |
| *3%* | *Hispanic* |

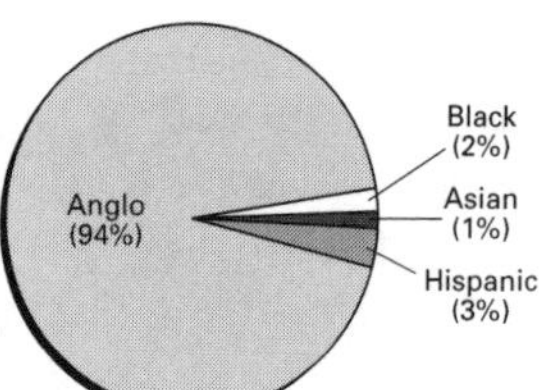


### Population by Gender

| | |
|---|---|
| *49%* | *Male* |
| *51%* | *Female* |

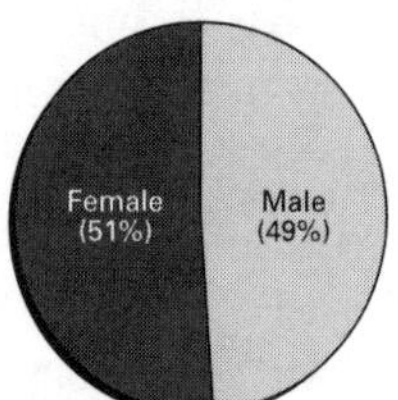


### Population by Age

*Median age:* 34

| | |
|---|---|
| *16%* | *under 18* |
| *24%* | *18–39* |
| *37%* | *40–59* |
| *23%* | *over 59* |

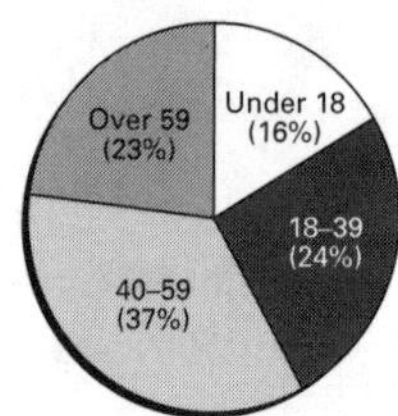

### Average Housing Costs

*Low:* *$298,250*
*High:* *$789,989*

### Average Rental Costs

| | |
|---|---|
| *Apartment:* | *n/a* |
| *2–3-bedroom house:* | *$2,410* |

## Important Places Nearby

Grocery Stores

**Albertson's Food & Drug**
*14019 Woodinville-Duval Road*
*(425) 483-9353*
www.albertsons.com

**Quality Food Centers**
*8867 161st Avenue NE*
*(425) 869-8006*
www.artsfoodctr.com

Pharmacies

**Rite Aid**
*14035 Woodinville-Duvall Road*
*Woodinville*
*(425) 485-6468*

Banks

**Washington Mutual**
*14160 Woodinville-Duvall Road*
*Woodinville*
*(425) 482-1889*
www.wamu.com

Hardware Stores

**McLendon Hardware**
*17705 130th Avenue NE*
*Woodinville*
*(425) 485-1363*

Hospitals/Emergency Rooms

**Evergreen Hospital Medical Center**
*12040 Northeast 128th Street*
*Kirkland*
*(425) 899-1000*

## HUNTS POINT/YARROW POINT

Think boats. Now think *big* boats. Some of the boats on Hunts Point are so huge that people could comfortably live on them. But one glance at the mansions *behind* the yachts confirms that life below deck just wouldn't do. I think the scale of homes in this ultra-exclusive neighborhood is deliberate. Sprawling estates make the yachts look small, a reminder that they're merely toys of the wealthy residents.

Lakefront estates are large and range from neoclassical Mediterranean to contemporary. Their owners are often entertainers, professional athletes, and top executives. Five-car, temperature- controlled garages provide shelter for Humvees and Porsches. In stark contrast, inland homes resting on the crown of the peninsula are smaller and more traditional. What these houses lack in size they

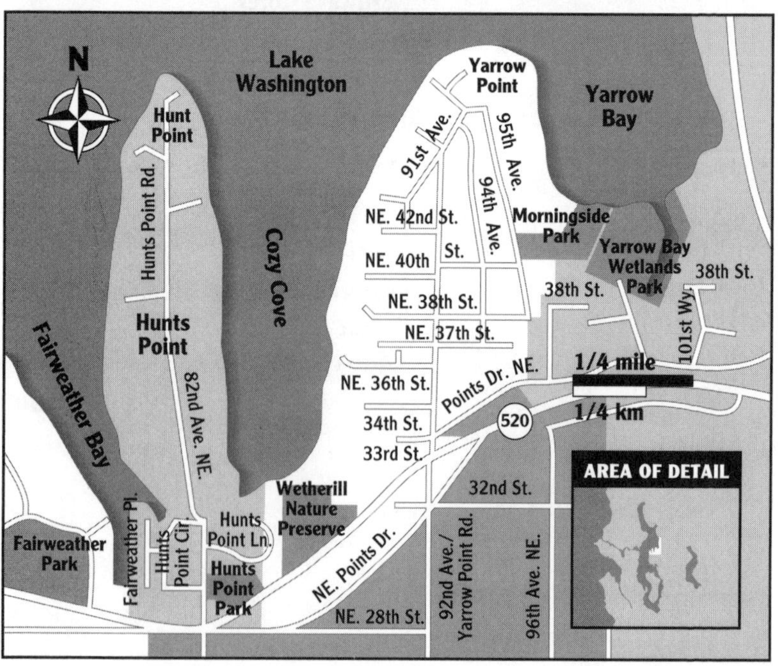

make up for in presentation. As you might expect, older homes remain impeccably manicured. Their owners are often retired professionals who prefer late-model Caddies and Oldsmobiles.

These twin peninsulas are easily accessed by State Route 522, which connects the I-5 and I-405 freeways. Commuting southeast to downtown Bellevue takes only a few minutes. Westerly jaunts to Seattle's financial district can take a half-hour.

If you drive through Hunts Point or Yarrow Bay for aesthetic inspiration, you may be disappointed. The wedge-shaped lots were designed to maximize lakefront footage and minimize exposure of gated entrances. The best and often only views of these spectacular estates are from Lake Washington. For that, you'll need a boat.

One without an inferiority complex.

## Neighborhood Statistical Profile

**Population:** 1,057

**Median family income:** $184,017

### Population by Ethnicity

| | |
|---|---|
| *94%* | *Anglo* |
| *1%* | *Black* |
| *4%* | *Asian* |
| *1%* | *Hispanic* |

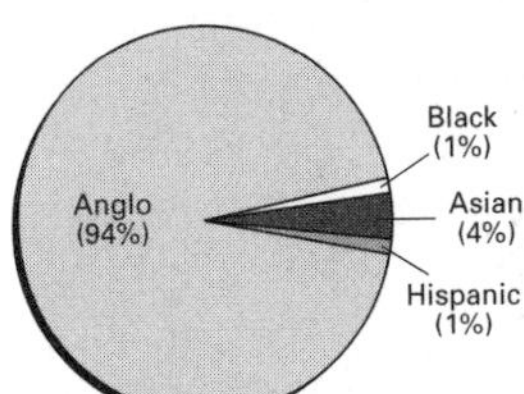


### Population by Gender

| | |
|---|---|
| *46%* | *Male* |
| *54%* | *Female* |

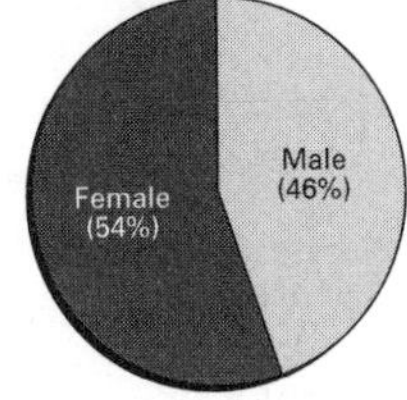

### Population by Age

*Median age: 44*

| | |
|---|---|
| *8%* | *under 18* |
| *14%* | *18–39* |
| *47%* | *40–59* |
| *31%* | *over 59* |

### Average Housing Costs

| | |
|---|---|
| *Low:* | *$550,000* |
| *High:* | *$7,500,000* |

### Average Rental Costs

| | |
|---|---|
| *Apartment:* | *n/a* |
| *2–3-bedroom house:* | *$9,000* |

## Important Places Nearby

Grocery Stores

**Quality Food Centers**
*10116 Northeast 8th Street*
*(425) 455-0870*

www.artsfoodctr.com

**Larry's Markets**
*699 120th Avenue NE*
*(425) 453-0600*

www.larrysmarkets.com

Pharmacies

**Bellegrove Pharmacy**
*1535 116th Avenue NE*
*Bellevue*
*(425) 455- 2123*

Banks

**InterWest Bank**
*6615 132nd Avenue NE*
*Kirkland*
*(425) 558-1100*

www.interwestbank.com

**Pacifica Bank**
*10900 Northeast 4th Street*
*Bellevue*
*(425) 637-1188*

Hardware Store

**Lake Hills Ace Hardware**
*15508 Lake Hills Boulevard*
*Bellevue*
*(425) 401-6802*

**Hospitals/Emergency Rooms**

**Group Health Eastside Hospital**
*2700 152nd Avenue NE*
*Redmond*
*(425) 883-5151*

**Overlake Hospital Medical Center**
*1035 116th Avenue NE*
*Bellevue*
*(425) 688-5000*

## ISSAQUAH

Only a decade or two ago, this was a slumbering little village on the periphery of the Eastside. Issaquah was like the quiet kid sitting in the back of the class. Even neighboring Redmond and Bellevue took little notice. In the 1980s, Californians (and others) arrived. They had cash and wanted houses in the "country." Expensive new developments crept outward from Bellevue in concentric circles. Caught up in the whirlwind of rapid expansion was little Issaquah.

Before long, transplanted professionals—some of whom were cardiovascular surgeons—clogged Seattle-bound arteries. Even Californians, known for high traffic tolerances, grew tired of the commute. So they set up shop close to home, and downtown Issaquah was born.

Is this just another tragic story of urban sprawl? Not really. Issaquah was a late bloomer. It had time to learn from the mistakes of other neighborhoods. The town's heritage has been painstakingly preserved, and its remarkable depots and walking trails escaped the talons of developers. Because of the demographics of new residents, Issaquah's leisure district reflects yuppie values. The requisite sidewalk bistros and curio shops are there, as are chateau-style galleries and espresso parlors.

But it was done well.

This place is very livable. Even cozy. Residents no longer have to venture outward, and the neighborhood's original character is intact. Many of the older buildings have been charmingly renovated. What was once a blacksmith's shop now houses a dental practice. The village barber shop survived, but flattops have yielded to "bowl cuts" and thirteen-year-old soccer players have their hair highlighted before games.

## Neighborhood Statistical Profile

**Population:** 12,892

**Median family income:** $64,844

### Population by Ethnicity

*89%* *Anglo*
*3%* *Black*
*3%* *Asian*
*5%* *Hispanic*

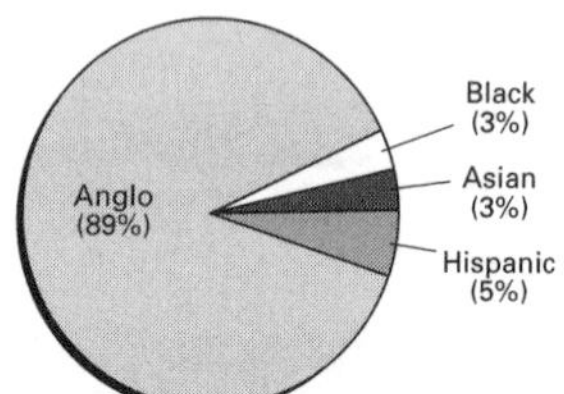


### Population by Gender

*50%* *Male*
*50%* *Female*

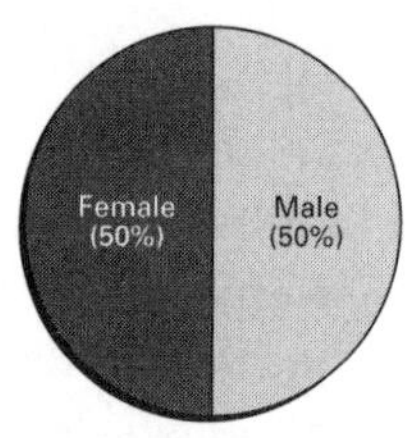


### Population by Age

*Median age:* 33
*16%* *under 18*
*28%* *18–39*
*34%* *40–59*
*22%* *over 59*

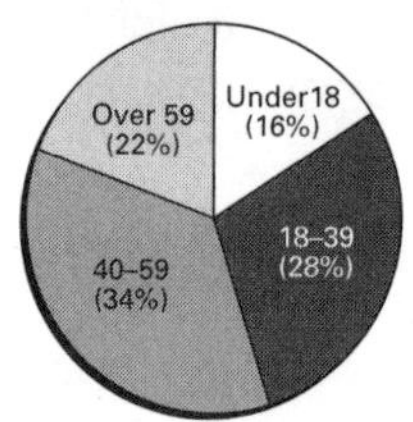


### Average Housing Costs

*Low:* *$289,016*
*High:* *$534,121*

### Average Rental Costs

*Apartment:* *$775*
*2–3-bedroom house:* *$1,835*

## Important Places Nearby

### Grocery Stores

**Tiger Mountain Country Store**
*14331 Issaquah-Hobart Road SE*
*(425) 392-2265*

**PCC Natural Markets**
*1810 12th Avenue NW*
*(425) 369-1222*
www.pccnaturalmarkets.com

**Front Street Market**
*80 Front Street*
*(425) 392-5371*

### Banks

**US Bank**
*1295 Northwest Gilman Boulevard*
*Issaquah*
*(800) 872-2657*
www.usbank.com

**Washington Mutual**
*2950 Issaquah-Pine Lake Road SE*
*Issaquah*
*(425) 391-6949*
www.wamu.com

### Pharmacies

**Rite Aid**
*1065 Northwest Gilman Boulevard*
*Issaquah*
*(425) 392-2865*

### Hardware Stores

**Lowe's Hardware & Garden**
*1625 11th Place NW*
*Issaquah*
*(425) 391-3355*

### Hospitals/Emergency Rooms

**Overlake Hospital Medical Center**
*1035 116th Avenue NE*
*Bellevue*
*(425) 688-5000*

---

## KIRKLAND/JUANITA

This is it. My personal fave. To me, Kirkland has it all. If this town doesn't charm you, it's time to unplug the life support machine. The city is a seamless blend of old and new. Of fast and slow. It's a place

# KIRKLAND/JUANITA

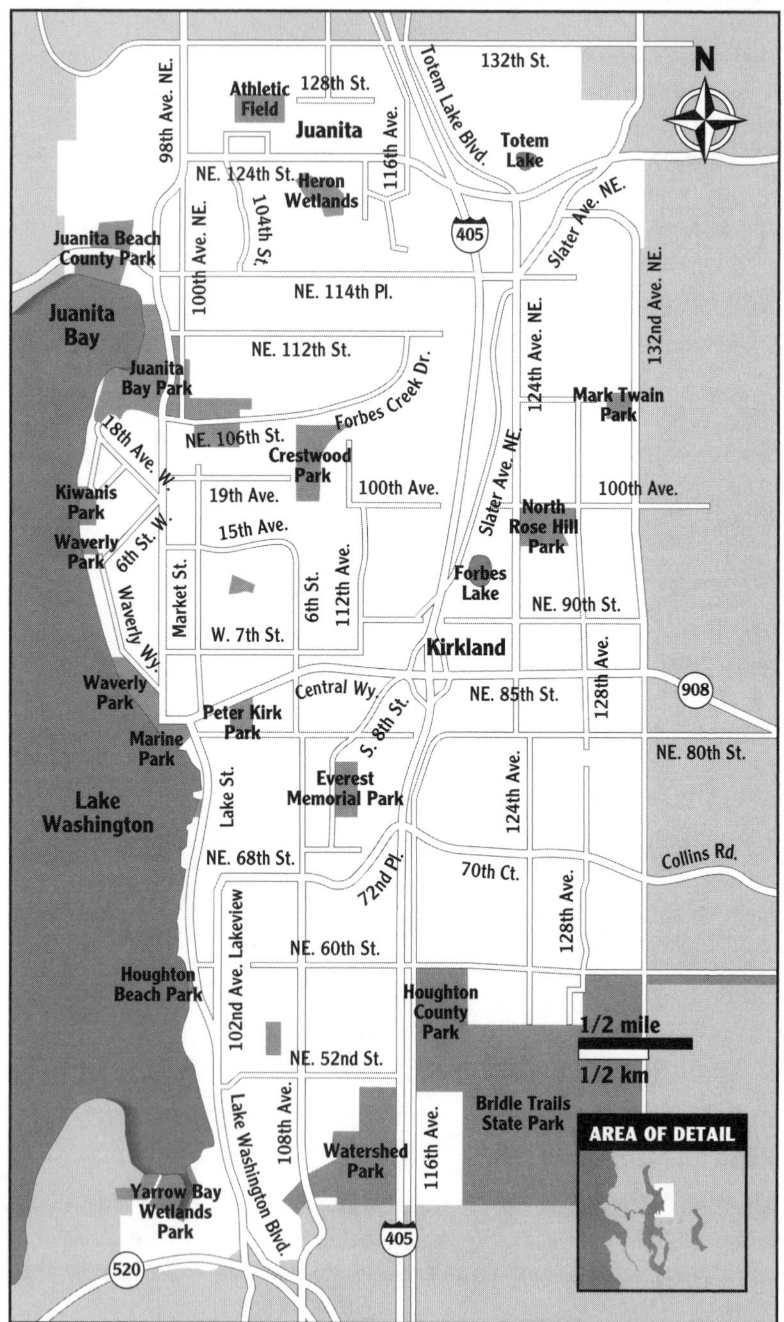

where residents are gracious hosts and visitors are welcomed guests. Kirkland is the sleek Mercedes convertible parked in front of a chic nail salon. It's the 11:00 A.M. power lunch at the yacht club café. But it's also the porch swing creaking in a gentle breeze on a lazy September afternoon. It's kids with pants rolled up trading baseball cards while they dangle their feet in a soothing fountain.

In the winter Kirkland sort of hibernates. Boats are battened down and moored. Dance clubs have no lines. Chocolatiers and art galleries turn their lights off early. Ice cream parlors split bananas and ladel hot fudge for die-hards only. The caffeine culture rises a little later and congregates at yuppie coffeehouses to click away at notebook computers and share sections of the morning paper. During warmer months Kirkland's waterfront restaurants are bustling. Runners, power-walkers, and in-line skaters navigate the sidewalks of Lake Washington Boulevard. Bronzed bodies lounge on the piers at Juanita Bay and the downtown beach parks. On the water, brightly colored jibs and mainsails billow at full mast. And local chatter is about outdoor concerts and summer blockbusters.

After a morning on the lake, tie your skiff or Sea-Doo dockside and enjoy some of the quaint restaurants and signature boutiques along the downtown boulevards. If you run out of cash by nightfall, which is easy to do in Kirkland, roll out a beach towel and enjoy a baseball game under the lights at magnificent Peter Kirk Park.

By now you're probably thinking that Kirkland is an extension of Club Med, a place for hedonists whose rich uncles left them a wad. Not so. Kirkland is home to lots of worker bees and average folk. Recent relaxation of zoning laws and density standards allowed for the development of multifamily condominiums and townhouses. Tasteful condos and apartments did not replace natural terrain, but rather dilapidated buildings along Market Street and Northeast 85th Street. Affordable multifamily housing makes living in Kirkland a dream come true for many people. Height restrictions keep commercial and residential buildings under five stories, preserving the city's views and natural, rolling topography.

Kirkland is surrounded by quality, too. Redmond, Bellevue, Woodinville, Bothell, and Lake Washington make Kirkland a nicely nestled neighborhood.

My only regret? After cresting Rose Hill and beginning a gentle, westward descent into Kirkland, I used to be welcomed by a carved, wooden sign that said simply, "*City of Kirkland.*" It was located in the corner of a knoll where an old horse grazed away the hours of his untroubled life. My children dubbed him Mr. Ed and would bring him carrots, apples, and an occasional sugar cube. To them he was an icon of stability and predictability.

One day, Mr. Ed was gone. His little paradise, framed with a country fence of hewn timber, became tract housing. I scathed the Kirkland City Council for their heartlessness. Later, I discovered that Mr. Ed was rescued by a loving family living one mile away.

For that wonderful old horse it may not be home, but it's still Kirkland.

## Neighborhood Statistical Profile

**Population:** 50,328

**Median family income:** $61,324

### Population by Ethnicity

| | |
|---|---|
| *83%* | *Anglo* |
| *6%* | *Black* |
| *5%* | *Asian* |
| *6%* | *Hispanic* |

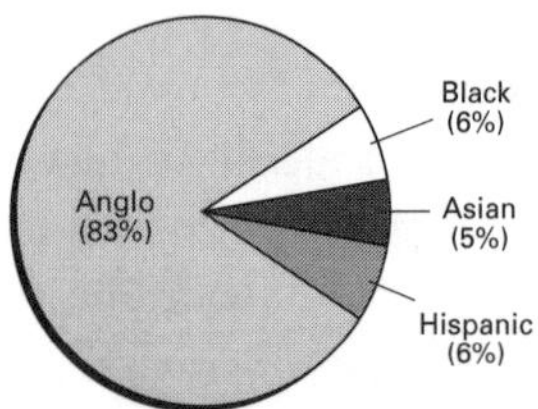


### Population by Gender

| | |
|---|---|
| *50%* | *Male* |
| *50%* | *Female* |

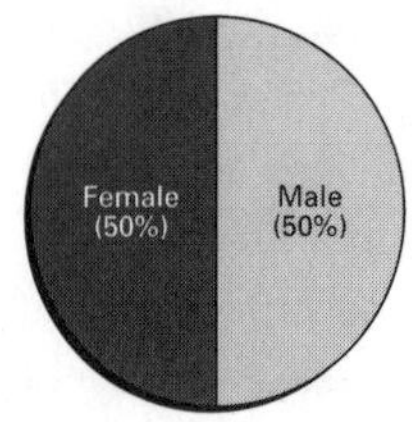

### Population by Age

*Median age:* 34

| | |
|---|---|
| *15%* | *under 18* |
| *26%* | *18–39* |
| *35%* | *40–59* |
| *24%* | *over 59* |

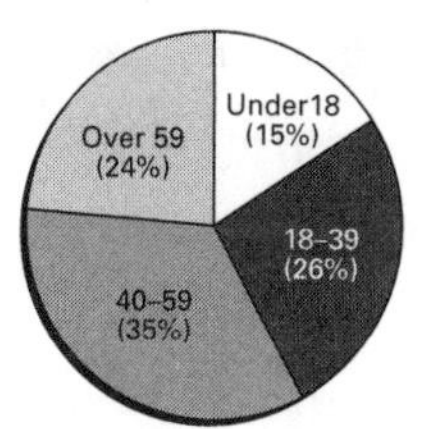


### Average Housing Costs

*Low:* *$259,555*
*High:* *$534,121*

### Average Rental Costs

| | |
|---|---|
| *Apartment:* | *$895* |
| *2–3-bedroom house:* | *$2,660* |

## Important Places Nearby

Grocery Stores

**Bridle Trails Red Apple Market**
*6625 132nd Avenue NE*
*(425) 881-7602*

**Houghton Market**
*10611 Northeast 68th Street*
*(425) 822-9211*

Pharmacies

**Bartell Drugs at Bridle Trails**
*6619 132nd Avenue NE*
*Kirkland*
*(425) 881-5544*

Banks

**Key Bank**
*327 Park Place Center*
*Kirkland*
*(206) 447-3012*
www.key.com

**US Bank**
*13233 100th Avenue NE*
*Juanita*
*(800) 872-2657*
www.usbank.com

Hardware Stores

**Kirkland True Value Hardware**
*424 Kirkland Avenue*
*Kirkland*
*(425) 822-6011*

**Hospitals/Emergency Rooms**

**Evergreen Hospital Medical Center**
*12040 Northeast 128th Street*
*Kirkland*
*(425) 899-1000*

## MEDINA/CLYDE HILL/BEAUX ARTS

This staggeringly exorbitant community and its neighbors Clyde Hill and Beaux Arts are really just extensions of an already extensive Bellevue. However, they extend westward to the coveted shores of Lake Washington. Venturing toward land's edge, real estate prices escalate at a logarithmic rate.

Medina is residential, although some of the houses are of industrial proportions. You won't find a Blockbuster Video in this garden spot. Estates are almost entirely custom-built. Tech zillionaires favor contemporary architecture. *Really* contemporary architecture. Entrepreneurs and retired executives seem to prefer English and Bavarian Tudor or French Country styles. Celebrities and professional athletes lean toward hybrids combining Northwest Traditional with Mediterranean or Cape Cod designs. Inland you'll find smaller, older houses. Many have aged brick or clapboard facades and stately white columns. The flavor is Colonial and Georgian, and reminiscent of the South and Mid-Atlantic coast.

Boats are harbored along private docks, but Medina is not nearly as seafaring as its Hunts Point and Yarrow Bay counterparts. Boulevards wind hypnotically in an attempt to discourage tourist traffic. Excessive roadside landscaping also provides screening from Looky Loos. Most families have grown children, but heirs and "young money" typically send their kids to private schools in Bellevue.

Undeveloped land in Medina is nonexistent, so don't plan on building your dreamhouse here unless you're prepared to swing a wrecking ball. And unless you're relocating with enough cash to rival a small nation, this neighborhood is like a Tony Robbins seminar: for inspirational purposes only.

## MEDINA/CLYDE HILL

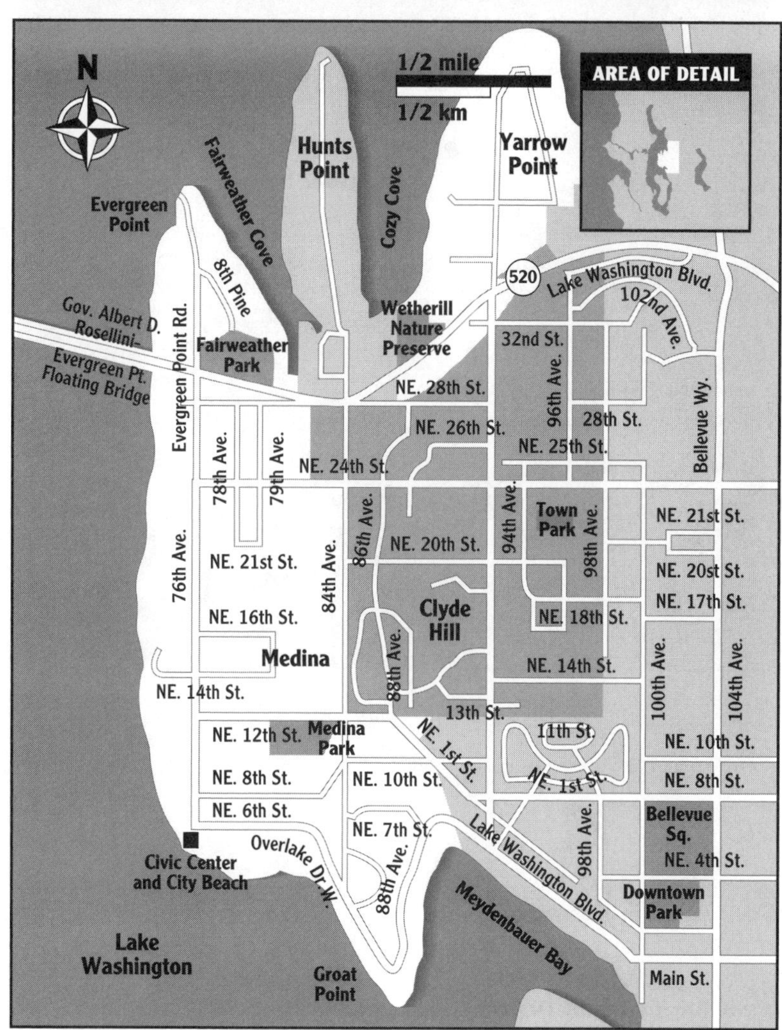


## Neighborhood Statistical Profile

**Population:** 7,344

**Median family income:** $119,315

## BEAUX ARTS VILLAGE

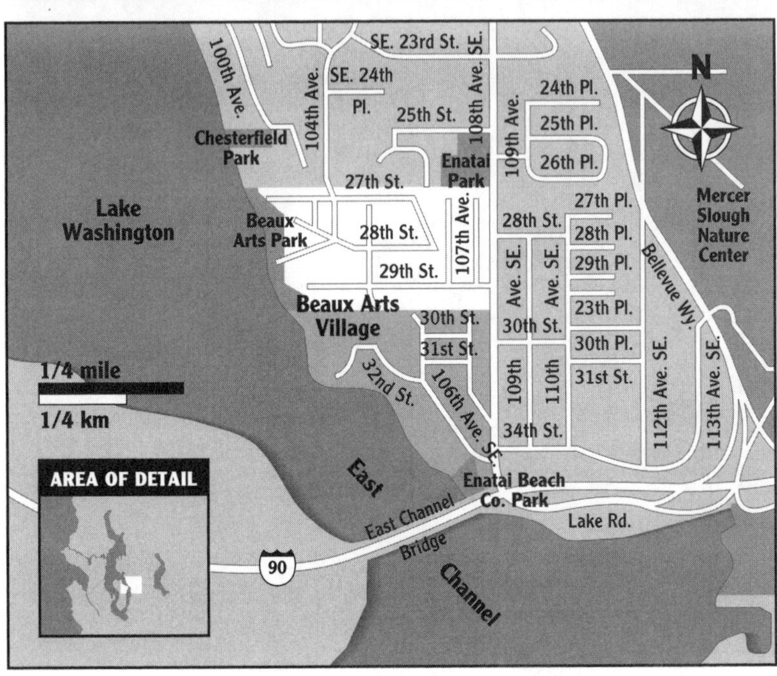


## Population by Ethnicity

| | |
|---|---|
| *96%* | *Anglo* |
| *1%* | *Black* |
| *3%* | *Asian* |
| *0%* | *Hispanic* |

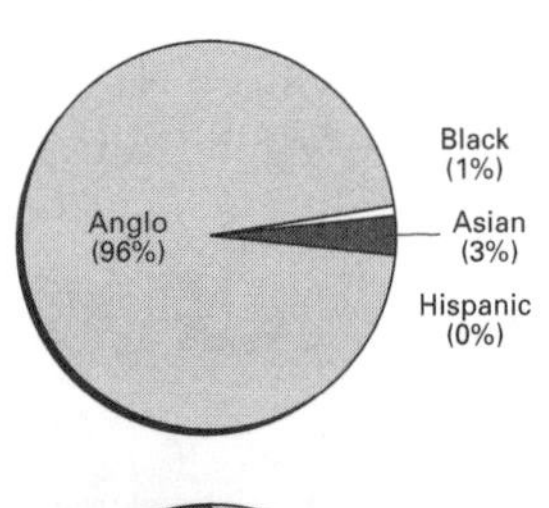

## Population by Gender

| | |
|---|---|
| *46%* | *Male* |
| *54%* | *Female* |

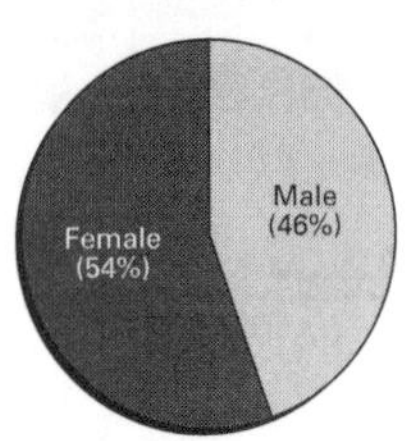

### Population by Age

*Median age: 41*

*7% under 18*

*21% 18–39*

*39% 40–59*

*33% over 59*

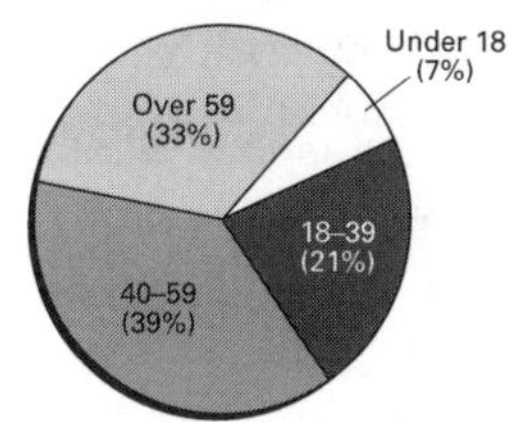


### Average Housing Costs

*Low: $472,200*

*High: $12,000,000*

## Important Places Nearby

Grocery Stores

**Medina Grocery**
*800 Evergreen Point Road*
*(425) 454-3101*

**Larry's Markets**
*699 120th Avenue NE*
*(425) 453-0600*
www.larrysmarkets.com

Pharmacies

**Bartell Drugs at Bellevue North**
*1100 Bellevue Way NE*
*Bellevue*
*(425) 646-9369*

Banks

**Colonial Bank**
*40 Lake Bellevue Drive*
*Bellevue*
*(425) 452-7399*

**Washington Federal Savings**
*3712 150th Avenue SE*
*Bellevue*
*(425) 747-7100*

**First Mutual Bank**
*15635 Northeast 8th Street*
*Bellevue*
*(425) 644-4214*
www.firstmutual.com

Hardware Stores

**Bellevue True Value Hardware**
*1508 145th Place SE*
*Bellevue*
*(425) 746-7560*

**Hospitals/Emergency Rooms**

**Overlake Hospital Medical Center**
*1065 116th Avenue NE*
*Bellevue*
*(425) 688-5000*

---

## MERCER ISLAND

"Mercedes Island," "Merciless Island," "Poverty Rock,"—the monikers for this upscale, five-mile-long suburban island are endless. Expensive housing and high-rent/low-rise office complexes make M.I. the most expensive rock since the Hope Diamond. Views of Seattle are breathtaking. Jaunts to Seattle are a breeze thanks to the I-90 "floating" bridge.

It would be easy to join the legions that poke fun at Mercer Island. But I don't want to. It's really a pleasant place. It's clean and safe, the parks are nice, and the schools are stalwart. Houses are eclectic, ranging from unpretentious Ozzie & Harriet ramblers to contemporary masterpieces. The city council hosts spirited debates about residential zoning variances as titans Nouveau Riche and Old Money collide. You see, narrow waterfront lots are the ire of lifelong residents. As prime lots become depleted (most lots on a small island are prime and deplete quickly), architects wanting to stretch square footage must become increasingly "creative." Height restrictions further constrain designs. Solutions are limited: either a glut of ultracontemporary shoebox homes or "tear-downs." The former are loathed by native islanders, the latter, by preservation societies.

My favorite social commentary about this privileged community concerns manhole covers. They have poetry inscribed on them.

Now *that's* class.

### Neighborhood Statistical Profile

**Population:** 22,874

**Median family income:** $89,011

## MERCER ISLAND

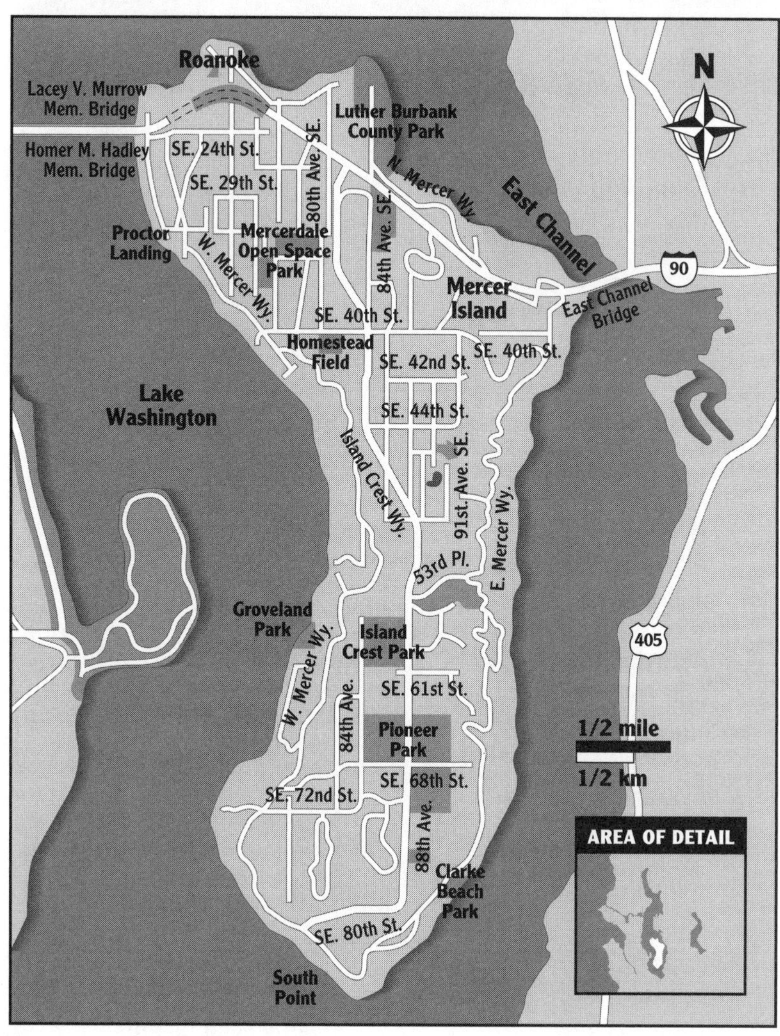

### Population by Ethnicity

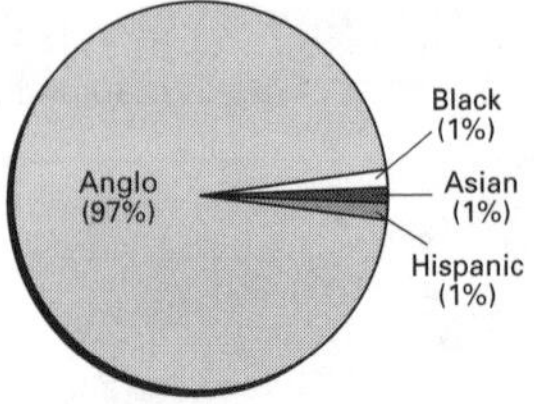


| | |
|---|---|
| *97%* | *Anglo* |
| *1%* | *Black* |
| *1%* | *Asian* |
| *1%* | *Hispanic* |

### Population by Gender

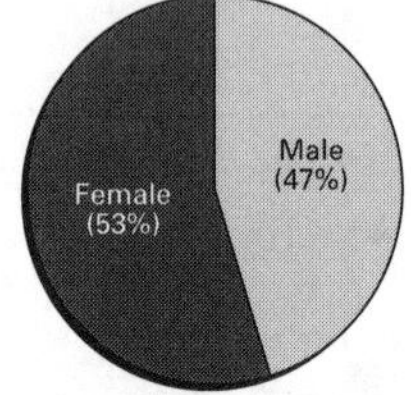


| | |
|---|---|
| *47%* | *Male* |
| *53%* | *Female* |

### Population by Age

*Median age: 40*

| | |
|---|---|
| *11%* | *under 18* |
| *19%* | *18–39* |
| *38%* | *40–59* |
| *32%* | *over 59* |

### Average Housing Costs

| | |
|---|---|
| *Low:* | *$391,466* |
| *High:* | *$949,000* |

### Average Rental Costs

| | |
|---|---|
| *Apartment:* | *$915* |
| *2–3-bedroom house:* | *$2,905* |

## Important Places Nearby

Grocery Stores

**Albertson's Food & Drug Centers**
*2755 77th Street SE*
*(206) 232-0244*

www.albertsons.com

**Quality Food Centers**
*8421 Southeast 68th Street*
*(206) 232-0102*

www.artsfoodctr.com

### Pharmacies

**Rite Aid**
*3023 78th Avenue SE*
*Mercer Island*
*(206) 236-0776*

### Hardware Stores

**True Value Hardware**
*2615 76th Avenue SE*
*Mercer Island*
*(206) 232-7282*

### Banks

**HomeStreet Bank**
*2737 78th Avenue SE*
*Mercer Island*
*(206) 275-1431*
www.homestreetbank.com

**Key Bank**
*2731 77th Avenue SE*
*Mercer Island*
*(206) 447-3041*
www.key.com

### Hospitals/Emergency Rooms

**Overlake Hospital Medical Center**
*1065 116th Avenue NE*
*Bellevue*
*(425) 688-5000*

---

## REDMOND

Let's face it: Microsoft put Redmond on the map. Twenty years before the software behemoth hung its shingle in Redmond, the town had only 1,400 residents. Twenty years after, it was home to 40,000. But there's really much more to this expansive Eastside city than technology campuses. Redmond is a unique weave of high-tech and low-tech industry. It's both urban and rural. For every wireless communications company, there's a family-owned bakery. For every condo complex with fiber optic modem lines, there's a barn with range-roaming horses. Redmond exudes a certain yin and yang quality.

With its Olympic velodrome and hundreds of miles of bike lanes and off-road trails, Redmond has long been the "Bicycle Capital of the Northwest." Now it's for nonpeddlers, too. In the 1990s, downtown Redmond bought into the popular "urban village" concept, which mandates that everything be accessible by foot. New low-rise buildings with cafés and offices on lower floors and townhouses above began to emerge. State-of-the-art health clubs and cinemas soon followed. Then came public parks for everything from modern sculpture to "half-pipe" and "vert" skating. The crown jewel of Redmond city council's master plan is the Redmond Town Center. This quasi-outdoor complex offers limitless shopping and lively dining as well as hotel accommodations.

Redmond meticulously maintains thirty-four public parks. Among them is magnificent Marymoor Park, replete with miniature airport for radio-controlled model aircraft enthusiasts. The town shares the serenity of Lake Sammamish with the adjacent cities of Issaquah and Bellevue. Downtown Seattle is accessed by way of I-405 South and State Route 520 East. Peak hour commutes will take about forty minutes.

## Neighborhood Statistical Profile

**Population:** 51,030

**Median family income:** $66,418

### Population by Ethnicity

| | |
|---|---|
| *86%* | *Anglo* |
| *4%* | *Black* |
| *7%* | *Asian* |
| *3%* | *Hispanic* |

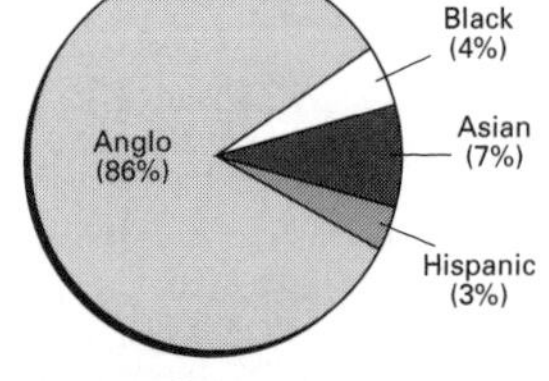


### Population by Gender

| | |
|---|---|
| *52%* | *Male* |
| *48%* | *Female* |

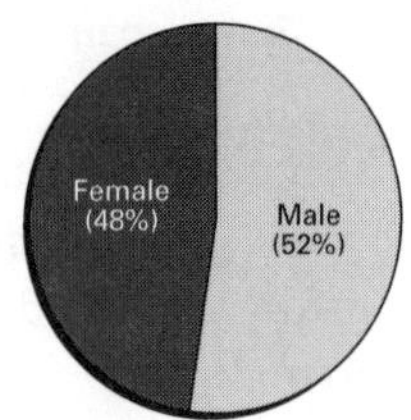

### Population by Age

*Median age: 30*

*17% under 18*

*32% 18–39*

*32% 40–59*

*19% over 59*

Over 59 (19%)
Under 18 (17%)
18–39 (32%)
40–59 (32%)

### Average Housing Costs

*Low: $250,450*

*High: $695,000*

### Average Rental Costs

| | |
|---|---|
| *Apartment:* | *$875* |
| *2–3-bedroom house:* | *$2,525* |

## Important Places Nearby

Grocery Stores

**Chalet Grocery & Deli**
*17980 Redmond Way*
*(425) 885-2771*

**Redmond Country Store**
*7725 159th Place NE*
*(425) 881-4295*

Pharmacies

**Lakeside Drug**
*15840 Redmond Way*
*Redmond*
*(425) 882-1475*

Banks

**InterWest Bank**
*16424 Northeast 79th Street*
*Redmond*
*(425) 885-3388*

www.interwestbank.com

**Washington Federal Savings**
*16200 Redmond Way*
*Redmond*
*(425) 885-4123*

**Redmond National Bank**
*1581 Northeast 85th Street*
*Redmond*
*(425) 881-8111*

**Hardware Stores**

**Lumbermen's**
*17875 Redmond Way*
*(425) 883-0788*

**Hospitals/Emergenct Rooms**

**Group Health Eastside Hospital**
*2700 152nd Avenue NE*
*Redmond*
*(425) 883-5151*

**Evergreen Hospital Medical Center**
*12040 Northeast 128th Street*
*Kirkland*
*(425) 899-1000*

## RENTON

Not everyone in this blue-collar city toils at the Boeing Company. It just seems that way. As goes Boeing, so goes Renton. During the last ten years the airplane manufacturing giant has had steep ascents as well as a few nosedives. There have been record orders for commercial jetliners, but there have also been strikes by the unions of machinists and engineers. Company stock has had more highs and lows than its revered 747s. One thing's for sure: Those Christmas bonuses keep the homogenous and unspectacular city of Renton chugging along.

If Woodinville and Kirkland are French doors to Snohomish County, Renton and Kent are the back gate to Pierce County. There's nothing pretentious about either of these cities. Affordable housing is popular with working-class families and young couples just starting out. Renton's formula is simple: large tracts of generic houses, miles of strip malls, and easy access to Boeing and the I-405 freeway. Where do Rentonites go when an evening of rental videos and teriyaki takeout just won't do? They jump on the 405 North, through the famous "S Turns," and play in the backyards of neighboring Factoria and Bellevue.

## Neighborhood Statistical Profile

**Population:** 66,141

**Median family income:** $44,610

### Population by Ethnicity

*73%* *Anglo*
*8%* *Black*
*12%* *Asian*
*7%* *Hispanic*

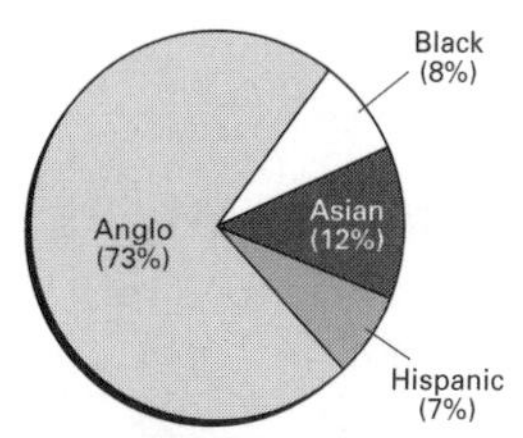


### Population by Gender

*50%* *Male*
*50%* *Female*

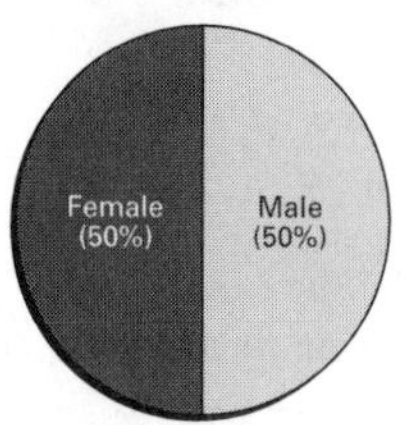


### Population by Age

*Median age:* *31*
*16%* *under 18*
*34%* *18–39*
*33%* *40–59*
*17%* *over 59*

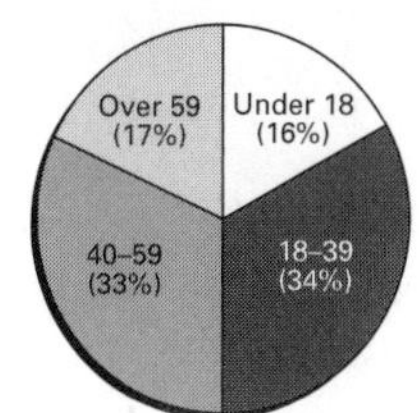


### Average Housing Costs

*Low:* *$165,450*
*High:* *$248,030*

### Average Rental Costs

*Apartment:* *$675*
*2–3-bedroom house:* *$1,375*

## Important Places Nearby

Grocery Stores

**Safeway Food & Drug**
*2725 Northeast Sunset Boulevard*
*(425) 228-5700*
www.safeway.com

**Cedar River Market**
*3418 Southeast 6th Street*
*(425) 228-0758*

Pharmacies

**Walgreens Pharmacy**
*275 Rainier Avenue S*
*Renton*
*(425) 277-0212*

Banks

**Towne Bank**
*54 Rainier Avenue S*
*Renton*
*(425) 254-9934*

**US Bank**
*2950 Northeast Sunset Boulevard*
*Renton*
*(800) 872-2657*
www.usbank.com

Hardware Stores

**McLendon Hardware**
*710 South 2nd Street*
*Renton*
*(425) 235-3555*

Hospitals/Emergency Rooms

**Valley Medical Center**
*400 South 43rd Street*
*Renton*
*(425) 228-3450*

## SHORELINE

The entire western side of this hilly community faces Puget Sound, but don't think it's a snooty waterfront district. Shoreline is refreshingly unpretentious. Residents are working-class folk who enjoy the uniqueness of their neighborhood. Although Shoreline is located directly north of Seattle, much of the urban stress will dissipate by the time you reach the town. Houses are ramblers: small, single-story structures popular with seniors. Young families appreciate Shoreline as one of the few communities close to Seattle that feature lots with large yards.

In the summer this is beach-and-barbecue country. In the winter, it's quiet. Locals are into trucks, campers, and small boats. Parks and recreation centers abound on the west side. Strip malls and multiplex theaters keep people close to home, suiting Shoreline residents just fine. Apartments are common, partly because of the students attending Shoreline's respected community college. Students enrolled in Seattle universities often live in Shoreline to save money and avoid the distractions of the University District.

Splicing through the community are parallel arteries, I-5 and SR 99. Both head north and south, which eases Seattle-bound traffic. East and west traffic is handled by SR 523 (for going around the north end of Lake Washington) and SR 104 (connecting Edmonds and Lake Forest Park). All in all, it's a pretty good design.

All in all, it's a pretty good place to live.

## Neighborhood Statistical Profile

**Population:** 23,975

**Median family income:** $39,415

### Population by Ethnicity

*85%* *Anglo*
*5%* *Black*
*6%* *Asian*
*4%* *Hispanic*

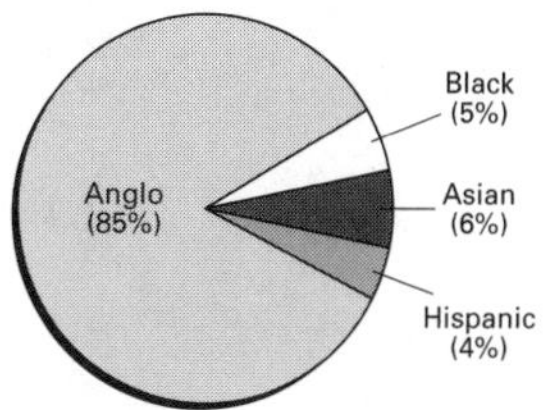


### Population by Gender

*49%* *Male*
*51%* *Female*

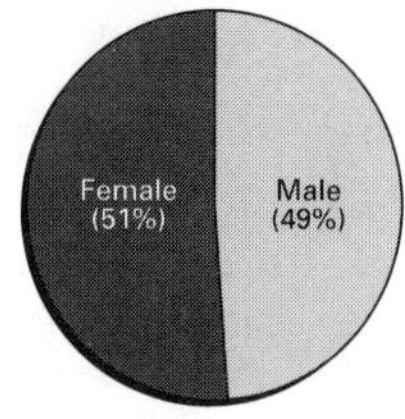

### Population by Age

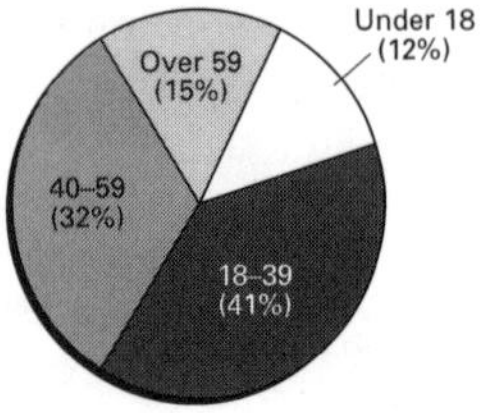

*Median age: 30*

| | |
|---|---|
| *12%* | *under 18* |
| *41%* | *18–39* |
| *32%* | *40–59* |
| *15%* | *over 59* |



### Average Housing Costs

| | |
|---|---|
| *Low:* | *$143,500* |
| *High:* | *$349,000* |

### Average Rental Costs

| | |
|---|---|
| *Apartment:* | *$420* |
| *2–3-bedroom house:* | *$985* |

## Important Places Nearby

Grocery Stores

**Aurora Village Mart**
*20003 Aurora Avenue*
*(206) 533-8115*

**Lupe's Tienda**
*16737 Aurora Avenue N*
*(206) 533-9304*

Pharmacies

**Gateway Pharmacy**
*18320 Midvale Avenue N*
*Shoreline*
*(206) 542-3110*

Banks

**City Bank**
*18840 8th Avenue NW*
*Shoreline*
*(206) 546-5125*
www.citybank.com

Hardware Stores

**The Home Depot**
*1335 North 205th Street*
*Shoreline*
*(206) 546-1900*

Hospitals/Emergency Rooms

**Northwest Hospital**
*1550 North 115th Street*
*Seattle*
*(206) 364-0500*

## WOODINVILLE

As a general rule, if it ends with "ville" it's a two-horse town. Recently Woodinville added a few ponies to the stable. Like neighboring Redmond, this once-pastoral village underwent a large downtown development in the late 1990s. Shopping, trendy ethnic eateries, and the all-important cineplex compose the Woodinville Town Center. This sleepy little village is trying its darnedest to wake up, but a galaxy of Starbucks won't help. Truth is, Woodinville is a family community. And a nice one at that.

By order of the city council, landowners must have at least two acres to subdivide. So don't expect to see tiny cul d' sacs with shoebox-sized duplexes anytime soon. Score: Woodinville 1; twenty-first century 0. Also, thoughtful city planning has kept agricultural, light industrial, and residential zoning at livable proportions. Score: Woodinville 2; twenty-first century 0.

And another thing: Woodinville takes care of its young. Exemplary schools and public libraries attest to the value placed upon education. A new children's repertory theatre headed by Emmy Award–winning actress Peg Phillips (of *Northern Exposure* fame) spotlights the community's artistic values. A world-class winery shares a fertile valley with an eight-field Little League ballpark. An odd combination? Not really. One uses old-school methods to produce some of the finest grapes in the world. The other uses old-school methods to produce some of the finest baseball players in the world.

Score: Woodinville 3; twenty-first century 0.

### Neighborhood Statistical Profile

**Population:** 19,916

**Median family income:** $60,152

### Population by Ethnicity

| | |
|---|---|
| *88%* | *Anglo* |
| *2%* | *Black* |
| *4%* | *Asian* |
| *6%* | *Hispanic* |

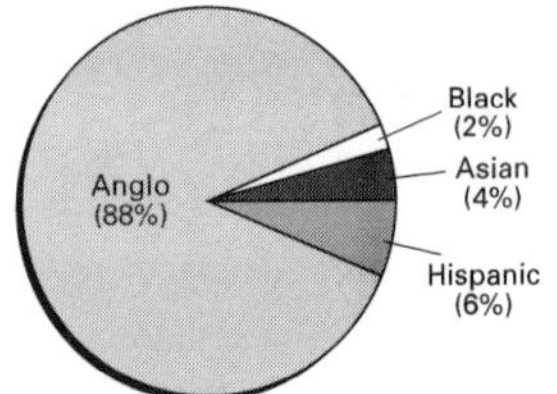


### Population by Gender

| | |
|---|---|
| *49%* | *Male* |
| *51%* | *Female* |

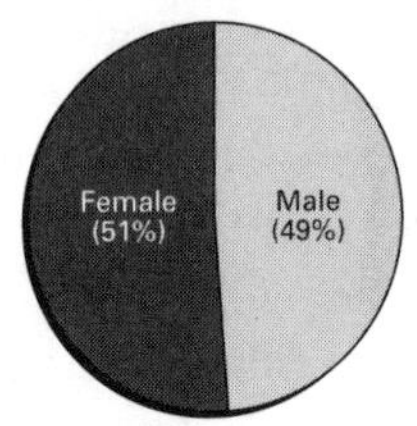


### Population by Age

*Median age:* *34*

| | |
|---|---|
| *14%* | *under 18* |
| *32%* | *18–39* |
| *32%* | *40–59* |
| *22%* | *over 59* |

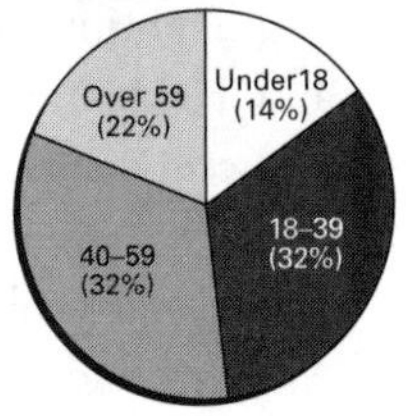


### Average Housing Costs

*Low:* *$225,000*

*High:* *$625,000*

### Average Rental Costs

| | |
|---|---|
| *Apartment:* | *$725* |
| *2–3-bedroom house:* | *$1,650* |

## Important Places Nearby

Grocery Stores

**Albertson's Food & Drug Centers**
*14019 Woodinville-Duvall Road*
*(425) 483-9353*
www.albertsons.com

**Top Food & Drug**
*17641 Garden Way NE*
*(425) 398-6700*

**Trader Joe's**
*12632 120th Avenue NE*
*(425) 823-1685*

### Pharmacies

**Safeway Pharmacy**
*19150 Northeast Woodinville-Duvall Road*
*Woodinville*
*(425) 788-6658*

### Banks

**Towne Bank**
*17530 132nd Avenue NE*
*Woodinville*
*(425) 254-9934*

### Hardware Stores

**McLendon Hardware**
*17705 130th Avenue NE*
*Woodinville*
*(425) 485-1363*

### Hospitals/Emergency Rooms

**Evergreen Hospital Medical Center**
*12040 Northeast 128th Street*
*Kirkland*
*(425) 899-1000*

# CHAPTER 2

# Advice on Finding an Apartment

The American Dream isn't about being an apartment dweller. It's about owning a home. Millions of renters, though, would like to make the American Dream the American Reality. Seduced by low interest rates, tax advantages, and a plethora of home improvement shows on cable television, many tenants feel pressured to join the ranks of home owners. Caveat emptor: One man's dream is another man's nightmare. Home ownership is not for everyone. Is a thirty-year adjustable-rate mortgage all it's cracked up to be? Is real estate the only way to create equity? If you fall prey to "No Money Down" seminar hucksters and their 3:00 A.M. infomercials you might think so.

In this chapter we'll examine apartment life in Seattle. First, let's take a step back.

Days before relocating to Seattle, I negotiated an apartment lease over the phone. It wasn't based upon a previous visit. Or a slick brochure from a property management company. Or even the recommendation of a friend. I reserved the two-bedroom luxury apartment sight unseen, and this was four years before anyone heard of a thing called the Internet. Was I rolling the dice? Not at all. In Washington, real estate contracts—including leases—must be in writing. My verbal lease agreement was neither valid nor enforceable without my signature. More important, I did my homework. Bellevue had every telltale sign of a safe and livable city. To hedge my bet, however, I sought the shortest lease available. After arriving, I simply initialed the addendum and signed the last page.

Even if you plan on buying a home, a short-term lease is smart. A house is a huge investment and responsibility. You needn't be rushed into its purchase. Perhaps an employer has arranged for your temporary residency while you search for or build a new home. If you're relocating without the safety net of an awaiting job, you'll probably have to establish employment and local references before qualifying for a mortgage. In either case it makes sense to be settled and happy in Seattle before delving into home ownership.

Once you've fallen in love with the Emerald City and are ready to take the plunge, there's a lot to consider before you enter into a Purchase & Sale Agreement. For now, we'll focus on apartments and temporary housing.

Renters: 41 percent of Seattle households are rentals

Apartment occupancy rating: 93 percent

## Apartments

Apartment life has its pluses and minuses. Relocating and job hunting can drain your savings account, leaving you with less than a down payment for a house. Consider a garden-variety, three-bedroom home valued at $250,000. A down payment of $40,000 (16 percent) would be required to secure payments of $1,800 on a 30-year fixed-rate mortgage at 8 percent. These monthly payments—all 360 of them—include principal, interest, property taxes, and mortgage insurance. And get this: They total a whopping $648,000! That same $40,000 invested in treasury bills earning 10 percent would yield $698,000 after 30 years. Oh, and to borrow $210,000, the bank will want you to earn at least $60,000 a year.

Apartments in Seattle require much less cash on hand and cater to more modest incomes. A two-bedroom/two-bath unit on the Eastside with full amenities will fetch $1 per square foot, or $1,000 a month. Move-in costs include first month's rent, last month's rent, and a security deposit of around $300. That's $2,300.

The process of renting an apartment is simple and quick. A credit check, driver's license (or state I.D.), and verification of checking and savings accounts are usually all that is needed. Generally, the landlord pays for water service and garbage disposal. The landlord also pays property taxes and insurance, as well as mechanical and landscape maintenance. Payment of electric, telephone, and cable services is usually the responsibility of the tenant. Furthermore, renters are afforded the relief of a federal income tax credit and the protection of Washington State's bulletproof Residential Landlord Tenant Act of 1973.

Former president Jimmy Carter learned that he lost the 1980 election while at Seattle-Tacoma International Airport.

Sounding pretty good? Wait, there's more. The aforementioned "luxury" apartment boasts amenities that include: heated pool, Jacuzzi, exercise room, racquetball courts, entertainment cabana, and nature trails. One can only imagine the mortgage and maintenance costs of a house offering such features.

Before you ink the lease agreement, put the cap back on your pen. I told you there were minuses, remember?

Landlords offer an economical alternative to home ownership for a reason, and it's usually not a charitable heart. It's money. Monthly checks line a landlord's nest, and when it comes time to cash in on income properties, renters' loyalty becomes landlord's equity. Property owners also benefit by the coveted—almost sacred—mortgage interest deduction allowance. Annual interest paid on a mortgage may be deducted from taxable personal income. This is particularly valuable during the early years of a mortgage when principal payments are dwarfed by interest payments. A woman earning $100,000 pays about $40,000 to Uncle Sam. With a $300,000 fixed mortgage at 8 percent, her taxable income becomes $76,000, and her tax burden is reduced to $29,000: a savings of nearly $1,000 a month.

Another benefit of a fixed mortgage is peace of mind. Home owners slumber blissfully knowing that as their income steadily rises, the mortgage payment will stay the same for thirty years. Renters, particularly on month-to-month tenancy, live with the constant fear of rent increases. The 1990s were kind to Seattle's landlords. Between 1993 and 2000, square-foot rates for apartment rental escalated by a staggering 70 percent! Pent-up housing demand also created a "seller's market" in single-family residential markets.

It's not all about ROI (return on investment), though. Apartment life has other drawbacks. Tenants enjoy fewer liberties than homeowners. Apartment complexes enforce by-laws and regulations about pets, use of facilities, and acceptable behavior. If your Golden Retriever, Ringo, likes to take a summer dip in the pool to escape your drum practice, don't consider an apartment. Also, home owners are less transient than renters. Orange and white U-Haul trucks are a common site at apartment complexes. In a single-family environment you get to know your neighbors. Friendships are enduring, and children don't have to watch their friends move away as often.

Lastly, there's "The Club." I'm not talking about something you anchor to your steering wheel. I'm talking about good-standing membership in The Brotherhood & Sisterhood of American Dream Seekers. Mortgage-burning, property-holding, equity-bearing, tax-deducting homeowners bent on refinancing and remodeling at the drop of Alan Greenspan's hat. It's a cozy group of 100-million-plus consumers who keep the cogs of industry oiled and turning. Every renter has known the feeling of filling out a credit application and seeing the little box next to "home owner." *"Hmmm. What would it be like to check it?"*

### Pros

- No down payment
- Lower monthly costs
- Simple and quick

- Low maintenance
- Landlord-tenant law
- Amenities

**Cons**

- No equity
- No interest deduction
- Rent increases
- Less freedom
- Transient neighbors
- Not in "The Club"

**MOVING TIP**

Pack heavier items in small boxes and lighter items in large boxes.

## THINGS TO CONSIDER WHILE LOOKING FOR AN APARTMENT

Resist the temptation to sign the first lease that's shoved across a property manager's desk. There are a lot of apartment units in King County, and only one is most perfectly suited to your unique needs. You must consider the terms of the lease. Price and duration are big ones. Sign the shortest lease possible while you dip your big toe in Northwest culture. Most personal finance counselors agree that rent should be within 25 to 38 percent of gross monthly income. Be candid with yourself. Do you prefer the pulse of the city or the quiet of the 'burbs? Just how temporary is this residency, anyway? Will you need to take on a roommate if you want to build a nest egg or replace your car? If so, can you share a bathroom? Must you maintain a home office? Is there adequate closet space? Are iguanas allowed? Will you really use the StairMaster and the sauna? Can you live with coin-operated laundry without being nickel and dimed to death? Is covered parking included, or will you be scraping frost off your windshield this winter?

Other factors are important, too. Location is paramount.

There are two ways to ponder location. Most people either live where they work, or work where they live. If you're transferring to Seattle, you'll probably want to reside within a forty-five minute commute of downtown. In terms of distance that's only about a fifteen-mile radius. Seattle's freeways are the third-busiest in the nation. If you're relocating unemployed, you may wish to select a neighborhood first and your employment second. Location is about convenience but it's also about happiness. Actual work takes up less than 35 percent of our waking hours. There's more to life. So when considering location, place a premium on proximity to cultural and educational activities, recreation, and entertainment.

## USING A LOCATOR VERSUS LOOKING ON YOUR OWN

You don't need a master's degree to locate apartments in Seattle. But with occupancy rates at 93 percent and new complexes barely keeping up with growth, it's understandable why apartment hunters are turning to newsstand publications, agencies, and the Internet for assistance. This begs the timeless question, "Is it best to hunt alone or with a guide?" There's certainly something romantic about discovering uncharted territory on your own. Queen Isabella of Spain didn't send Columbus off with a copy of *Thomas' Guide to the New World.* Being deluged with information can be overwhelming, though. After seeing several apartments, they start to look alike. They meld into an indistinguishable blur of Formica, sheet vinyl, and plastic blinds. You may be so engrossed in getting from apartment A to apartment B that you fail to grasp a sense of the community. Besides, what better way to familiarize yourself with new surroundings than by casually cruising neighborhoods? Better yet, take a bus. Instead of eyeballing traffic signs you're free to gaze out the window and jot down notes.

On the other hand, you've just uprooted, completed a grueling trip, and you're living out of boxes marked "bare necessities." One more Extra Value Meal or stop at a cash machine and you know your next "residence" will feature padded walls. You need an apartment and you need it now. Apartment finders can save time. In printed form, they're conveniently found at grocery stores and gas stations. Publishers of rental guides make their money by selling advertising space. As a service, professional apartment finders charge a modest fee, often paid by property management companies. Internet apartment finders offer maps and virtual tours of major multifamily complexes. They can answer frequently asked questions and disclose public records of landlord-tenant disputes. Just enter what you're looking for . . .

> Near Bellevue Community College. One-bedroom. 1-1/2 bath. Wood-burning fireplace. Forced-air gas heating. Pool. Enclosed parking. Premium cable. Roommate. Bike path. Bus stop. $700 per month or less.

. . . and a printable list of potential matches is yours at the stroke of a key. Most Internet apartment finders charge about $50 to $75 for six weeks of membership. Some Web sites are subsidized by sponsors and offer free matching services.

## RESOURCES FOR FINDING AN APARTMENT

**Apartment Finders**
*(425) 455-3733*
*No Fee*

***Apartment Guide of Greater Puget Sound***
*11911 Northeast First Street*
*Seattle, WA 98101*
*(425) 454-4431*
www.apartmentguide.com

**Apartment Locators**
*(206) 524-1111*
*$69 Fee*

***Apartments For Rent***
*11711 North Creek Parkway S*
*Bothell, WA 98011*
*(425) 487-2869*
*(800) 235-0080*
*(425) 483-3155 (fax)*
www.aptsforrent.com

***Eastside Journal***
*1705 132nd Avenue NE*
*Bellevue, WA 98009-9230*
*(425) 455-2222*
*(800) 492-2219*
www.eastsidejournal.com

**Oakwood Corporate Housing (Extended Stay)**
*4622 150th Avenue NE*
*Redmond, WA 98052*
*(425) 861-1175*
Employer-Paid Fee

**PlaceFinders**
*905 East Pike Street*
*Seattle, WA 98101*
*(206) 322-5544*
www.placefinders.com
$75 Fee

**City Fact**

Seattle's 23,500 software engineers raked in $6.77 billion, including stock options, in 1998. Individual compensation averaged $287,700.

**Relocation Services (Extended Stay)**
*(800) 990-9292*
*(425) 869-1640*

www.execustay.com

Employer-Paid Fee

***Seattle Post-Intelligencer***
*101 Elliott Avenue W*
*Seattle, WA 98111*
*(206) 448-8000*

www.seattlep-i.com

***Seattle Times***
*Fairview Avenue & John Street*
*Seattle, WA 98111*
*(206) 464-2121*
*(800) 542-0820*

www.seattletimes.com

**US Suites (Extended Stay)**
*(425) 454-4400*

www.ussuites.com

Sublets apartments

For free, twenty-four-hour information about renting apartments, please call (206) 442-2880

- Dial 3045 for tips about using an agency service
- Dial 3046 for information about renter's insurance
- Dial 3047 for a list of questions to ask property managers and landlords
- Dial 3051 to learn more about leases
- Dial 3052 for tips about moving into an apartment

## LIVING ALONE VERSUS HAVING A ROOMMATE

In college I had roommates. Nineteen in four years, to be exact. I haven't had one since. That's not to say my experiences were bad. Actually, as I flipped through my mental Rolodex to arrive at that jaw-dropping figure I smiled, even chuckled. Reflecting on those years brings joy to me. I wasn't endeared to all nineteen of my former roommates, but with them I shared good and bad times and learned a few of life's lessons. Today, several ex-roomies remain close friends of mine. In fact, my goddaughter's parents were once my roommates. On a recent holiday in Pennsylvania I enjoyed brunch with a buddy with whom I roomed seventeen years ago. In the late '70s my sister, Natalie, shared an off-campus house while attending Boston University. To this day, she considers former roomie Laura her dearest friend. Roommates can make life more enriching. Roommates can foster heartfelt and steadfast friendships.

They can also drive you looney.

Whether it be a dormitory or duplex, it's still home. For most people, sharing a home with a virtual stranger is, at best, awkward. And don't think it's simply because the person is unfamiliar. The best of buddies may share a residence only to discover their friendship can't withstand the rigors of cohabitation. If you crave independence and treasure privacy, don't take on a roommate. Sacrifice square footage or amenities in return for affordable solitude.

However, a compatible roommate can make an otherwise out-of-reach apartment a reality. An equitable split of a typical two-bedroom unit and utilities saves each tenant about $6,000 a year. The operative words are *compatible* and *equitable.* The latter is easy if a standard of fairness is maintained. Compatibility is more complex. It cannot be assured through policy. So how do you improve the odds of compatibility? Start with a little introspection. Are you a neat freak? A night owl? Can you put up with country western music? How about kitty litter? Are you tolerant of political opinions? Vegetarians? And then there's the all-important toilet seat: Do you leave it up or down?

Don't expect others to be more tolerant than you. That's Rule Number One of the Roommate Compatibility Code. Once you have a handle on your own idiosyncrasies, make a list of requisites for someone with whom you're willing to share a home. Be fair. Be reasonable.

Then you're ready to solicit the help of an agency, classified advertisements, or an Internet search service.

### Pros of Having a Roommate

- You get companionship
- You can save money
- You can afford a better apartment

### Cons of Having a Roommate

- You sacrifice privacy
- You must learn to share
- You open yourself up to potential conflicts

## ROOMMATE-FINDING RESOURCES

**Gromco Roommate BBS**

www.roommatebbs.com

**My Roommate.com**

www.myroommate.com

**PlaceFinders**

*905 East Pike Street*
*Seattle, WA 98111*
*(206) 322-2233*

**Roommate Access**

www.roommateaccess.com

**Roommate Express-Seattle**

*15100 Southeast 38th Street*
*Bellevue, WA*
*(425) 451-9970*

www.roommateexpress.com

**RoommateFinder**

Info@roommatefinder.com

www.roommatefinder.com

**Roommate Locator.com**

www.roommatelocator.com

**Roommate Service**

www.roommateservice.com

**Roomie Match**

www.roomiematch.com/seattle-roommate

**Seattle Roommate Referral**

*905 East Pike Street*
*Seattle, WA 98111*
*(206) 322-5544*

**SpaceFinders, Inc.**
*300 Vine Street, Suite 16-B*
*Seattle, WA 98111*
*(206) 728-8500*

## Temporary Housing

CITY FACT

Per capita, Seattleites are the most avid moviegoers in the United States.

"Extended stay" is a hybrid concept, blending hotel services with apartment economics. From the outside an extended-stay facility has the no-nonsense look of an airport hotel. Nice, but not fancy. The location annunciates swift access to freeways and business districts. Inside you'll find a quiet lobby and professional, uniformed staff. The mood is serious, but not cold. Dry-cleaning, housekeeping, and room service give guests a feeling of hotel pampering. Weekly rates, however, are more commensurate with residential living. A one-month stay at a plain vanilla hotel approaches $3,500 including Seattle's whopping "Guest Tax" of 14.4 percent. A month at an extended-stay facility tacks only $1,800 onto the expense account, and after thirty days the surtax is lifted.

Temporary housing is also an option. Think of it as "executive apartments." Some complexes are corporate-owned, and each suite is rented on a short-term basis. Other complexes consist of bona fide apartments, some of which are leased by corporations and sublet on a short-term basis. Whether wholly owned or leased and sublet, temporary housing tends to be pricier than extended stay accommodations. They are more roomy and homey, without sacrificing security, office amenities, or maid service. Temporary housing features kitchens, housewares, appliances, and extra bedrooms, if needed. From fully furnished studios to three-bedroom suites, monthly rates range from $1,500 to $3,000.

## LOW-COST ALTERNATIVES

The most economical form of temporary housing is provided by local chapters of the YMCA. Sadly, in 1999 the main Seattle hotel closed its doors. However, the YMCA provides referrals for people seeking alternative resources for temporary housing. In Seattle, the main number for the YMCA is (206) 382-5003.

### Hostels

Often associated with earthy backpackers and students of the global classroom, hostels are funky and inexpensive. They provide an option for passers-through who find themselves in a holding pattern. Commonplace in Europe, only recently have hostels regained popularity in the United States. Credit Generation X and its collective fascination with retro-culture. Urban renewal projects and vintage buildings often host this form of temporary housing. For purposes of economy, hostels encourage bunking and provide communal showers and bathrooms. Part dormitory, part shelter, part urban campground. They're not for everyone, but they're clean, affordable, and—for many people—a rewarding way to travel.

Many hostels belong to international associations and offer reciprocal memberships. Private rooms fetch as much as $45 per night. Shared rooms can be had for as little as $10 to $20. Members receive discounts of about 15 percent. *Australian Backpacker Magazine* recently rated Seattle's Green Tortoise Backpackers Guesthouse as "Best Hostel on the West Coast."

**Ace Hotel**
*2425 First Avenue*
*Seattle*
*(206) 448-4721*

**American International Backpackers Hostel**
*Seattle*
*(206) 720-2965*

**Commodore Hotel Youth Hostel**
*2013 Second Avenue*
*Seattle*
*(206) 448-8868*

**Green Tortoise Backpackers Guesthouse**
*1525 Second Avenue*
*Seattle*
*(206) 340-1222*

**Hostelling International-Seattle/Vashon**
*12119 Southwest Cove Road*
*Vashon Island*
*(206) 463-2592*

**Hostelling International**
*American Youth*
*Hostels/Washington State Council*
*419 Queen Anne N*
*Suite 102*
*(206) 281-7306*

**Hostelling International-Seattle Hostel**
*84 Union Street*
*Seattle*
*(206) 622-5443*

**Panama Hotel**
*605-1/2 South Main Street*
*Seattle*
*(206) 223-9242*

## Extended Stay Facilities

**Accommodations Plus**
*(425) 455-2773*
*(888) 925-0763*

www.aplusnw.com

**Best Western Evergreen Inn**
*13700 Aurora Avenue N*
*Seattle*
*(206) 361-3700*
*(800) 213-6308*

**The Corporate Living Network**
*(425) 450-0830*
*(888) 450-0830*

**ExecuStay**
*18080 Northeast 68th Street*
*Redmond*
*(425) 869-1640*
*(888) 299-8861*

www.execustay.com

**Executive Inn**
*300 10th Avenue*
*Seattle*
*(206) 233-0241*
*(800) 906-6226*

**Extended Stay America**
*Main Street*
*Bellevue*
*(425) 453-8186*

*22520 83rd Avenue S*
*Kent*
*(253) 872-6514*

*3021 196th Street SW*
*Lynnwood*
*(425) 670-2520*

*15451 53rd Avenue S*
*Tukwila*
*(206) 244-2537*

**First Hill Executive Apartment Suites**
*400 Tenth Avenue*
*Seattle*
*(206) 621-9229*
*(800) 571-0848*

**Home-Pac, Incorporated**
*(253) 922-1177*
*(800) 272-1461*
www.home-pac.com

**Homestead Guest Studios**
*3700 132nd Avenue SE*
*Bellevue*
*(425) 865-8680*

*15805 Northeast 28th Street*
*Redmond*
*(425) 885-6675*

*15635 West Valley Highway*
*Tukwila*
*(425) 235-7160*

**Inn at Queen Anne**
*505 First Avenue N*
*(206) 282-7357*
*(800) 952-5043*
www.innatqueenanne.com

**MarQueen Hotel**
*600 Queen Anne Avenue N*
*Seattle*
*(206) 282-7407*
*(888) 445-3706*
www.marqueenhotel.com

**Northwest Suites**
*15446 Bel-Red Road, Suite 110*
*Redmond*
*(425) 861-0500*
*(888) 254-8264*
www.northwestsuites.com

**Quality Inn Suites**
*2224 Eighth Street*
*Seattle*
*(206) 624-6820*
*(800) 437-4867*

**Sorrento Hotel**
*900 Madison Street*
*Seattle*
*(206) 622-6400*

**Stonebrook Suites**
*18124 72nd Avenue S*
*Kent*
*(253) 796-6000*

**8521 Mukilteo Speedway**
*Mukilteo*
*(425) 551-5900*
www.stonebrooksuites.com

**StudioPLUS**
*1431 112th Street SE*
*Everett*
*(425) 337-1341*

*1150 Oakesdale Avenue SW*
*Renton*
*(425) 228-2454*

**University Inn**
*4140 Roosevelt Way NE*
*Seattle*
*(206) 632-5055*
*(800) 733-3855*
www.universityinnseattle.com
univinn@aol.com

**Wimbledon Apartments & Corporate Suites**
*4665 148th Avenue NE, Suite C-104*
*Bellevue*
*(425) 883-6246*
*(800) 717-2562*
www.rent.net/ads/wimbledon
wimblecorp@aol.com

## CITY FACT

Seattle is the centerpiece of a 400-mile, 8-million population corridor from Eugene, Oregon, to Vancouver, British Columbia. This region accounts for a quarter-trillion dollars in annual revenues and would rank as the world's tenth largest economy.

CHAPTER 3

# Advice on Finding a House

My best advice to home buyers is simple and straightforward. "Buy your new home many years ago," I tell them. This sage advice applies to virtually any market, anyplace, anytime. Long-term residential real estate investments rarely sour. They survive the bears and ride the bulls nicely. In Seattle, it seems, housing values just keep spiraling upward, often beyond the reach of singles and young families.

Chapter 2 discussed the difference between what a house sells for and what it actually ends up costing the owner after thirty years of principal, interest, property taxes, and mortgage insurance. Adding routine maintenance to the equation, a $100,000 home purchased in 1970—carrying an $85,000 fixed-rate mortgage at 6 percent—cost its proud owners $250,000 by mortgage burning time. And that's *adjusted* for the prized interest deduction allowance.

People commonly look only at original purchase price and selling price when contemplating their capital gain. Rarely do sellers reflect upon *opportunity costs* and current *replacement cost,* also known as *substitution cost.* Opportunity costs are those foregone by accepting another investment option. Like the T-bills example in chapter 2. Replacement cost is simply the expense of substituting an asset. If you're selling the aforementioned "$100,000 home" for $250,000 and wish to buy a similar home in a comparable neighborhood, plan on spending—you guessed it—$250,000. Then ask yourself where that $150,000 "profit" went. The point is, residential real estate investing turns an actual profit in very few ways:

- Quick Sale: undervalued property purchased and promptly re-sold at fair market value
- Assisted Payments: rental income that accelerates positive equity
- Scaling Down: substituting an expensive house with a more modest house

Quick sales aren't always tied to distressed or foreclosed "fixer-uppers." Just about any property in Seattle during the last decade has provided excellent short-term ROI. Interest rates have remained low, attracting buyers. The supply of new homes has not kept up with demand, satisfying sellers. A win-win, right? Not necessarily. This potent combination of cash supply and a seller's market has catapulted property values into the jet stream. Retired home owners on fixed incomes and young families looking for entry-level home ownership are the forgotten casualties of a robust market. As real estate prices escalate, so do property taxes. For the first time, starter homes in King County are beyond the reach of median-income families.

Who's making a killing in this market? Income property owners. They not only get to ride a property value freight train known as the Seattle Express, but the current housing crunch allows high rental rates and low vacancy rates. Savvy empty-nesters are cashing in big houses and scaling down on square feet, raking in big bucks along the way.

Your house is a critical investment. If you're like most people, your retirement is linked to it. Since the only alternative to buying a home is renting one, the pros and cons of home ownership are similar to the arguments of buying versus renting, discussed in chapter 2. Other things, however, are worth considering before buying a house in Seattle.

## Pros and Cons of Buying a House in Seattle

In recent years, we witnessed fixed-mortgage rates plunge to twenty-five-year lows. Although they've crept up a couple of points, they remain attractive. Historic trends suggest a continuation of increased property values. Also bolstering the argument to buy are government reports that forecast continued economic growth in the Puget Sound region. That's good news, because all this debt will have to be paid down. Lastly, high sales activity has lured more and more lenders into the market. This has driven up competition for mortgages, resulting in an array of buyer-friendly programs and incentives.

**MOVING TIP**

Create a "Must Have" box of absolutely essential items and keep them close to you during the entire move. The Must Have box should contain: a first-aid kit; necessary medication; toiletries; a travel alarm clock; snacks and bottled water; a towel and washcloth; paper plates, towels, and cups; a flashlight with extra batteries; lightbulbs and fuses; a small tool kit; keys to the old and new homes; the television remote control; a good book; and each child's favorite blanket and small toy.

Hang on to your checkbook, though. There's a flip side to this. Newtonian physics suggest that what goes up must come down. After stabilizing, property values might come down. Even tumble. It happened here in the 1970s when Boeing went into a tailspin and had to let go one-third of its workforce. A legendary sign off southbound Interstate-5 proclaimed, "Last One Leaving Seattle Turn Out the Lights." I'd like to add something to Newton's observation. What goes down must come up, and I'm not talking about scuba divers. Interest rates have bottomed out for the current cycle. If you're not locked in under 8 1/4 percent, you may wish to consider an adjustable-rate mortgage. Even an ARM, though, doesn't beat a low fixed-rate.

Remember, too, that in a seller's market, few sellers are willing to make concessions. They don't have to. Discounts, give-backs, seller-carried paper, and options to buy are absent. Like migratory animals, though, they will return.

Also, Seattle developments—even short-plats of three or four homes—are notorious for CCRs (Covenants, Conditions, and Restrictions). These documents are devised by the developer to assure uniformity among builders. CCRs are conveyed with title and enforced by the Homeowner Association after the subdevelopment is sold out. CCRs dictate what home owners can and, more often, *can't* do with their property. Further limitations are placed upon home owners by municipal and county jurisdictions in the form of zoning laws and ordinances. To some people such regulations are an infringement on personal liberties. To others, a small price to pay for joining The Club.

CITY FACT

Thanks to an innovative public arts program, Seattle is home to the seventh largest per capita population of artists in the world.

Lastly, to balance projected growth with the delicate ecosystems that make Washington a place of natural splendor, the controversial Growth Management Act was passed. The regulations are too cumbersome to explain here, but the GMA's broad reach will affect virtually every property owner in the state. How much depends upon the size, location, and native characteristics of the property. If you're planning to develop a lot or invest in acreage, it's advisable that you seek the guidance of a knowledgeable real estate consultant.

**Pros**

- Historically good property values and excellent municipal bond ratings
- Excellent economic growth forecasted for Puget Sound area
- Competitive financing programs and incentives offered by lenders

### Cons

- Market is not predictable
- Seller's market offers few concessions to buyers
- CCRs, zoning laws, ordinances, and Growth Management Act restrict property owners' options

## Things to Consider Before Looking for a House

A good real estate agent will know all the right questions to ask a client. But before you visit a brokerage, drive around town on your own. Get a feel for the city, suburbs, and outlying areas. Familiarize yourself with the different styles of houses. Seattle is a cornucopia of residential architecture. There's the popular Northwest Craftsman look. New England styles like Cape Cod, Nantucket, and Hudson Bay. The techie favorites, Contemporary and Ultra-Contemporary. There's Bavarian Tudor and English Tudor. Neo-Classic Mediterranean. Country French. Swiss Chalet. Victorian. Ranch. Even Pagoda with "Feng Shui" concepts.

Determine whether you like the quaintness of older houses or the freshness of newer ones. Consider traffic patterns and commute times. Note schools, parks, and shopping villages. Be able to articulate specific likes and dislikes to your agent. This keeps wheel-spinning to a minimum. Armed with a checklist of what you're looking for, your agent can present you with the broadest base of potential matches. In turn, this increases the probability that you will find "the perfect home."

At the top of the list should be a realistic price. Do yourself and your agent a favor: submit to prequalification by your preferred lender. This saves time, stress, and embarrassment. Even if you can squeeze a few more dollars out each month, avoid the temptation to overextend yourself. Nothing turns a dream home into a chamber of horrors like straining to meet the mortgage payment every month. Attention first-time buyers: Remember to budget for maintenance. (Hint: average monthly maintenance for a single-family residence is equal to 10 percent of the square footage, converted to dollars.)

Being able to afford a house is one thing; being able to live in it is another. Make sure the house has a livable floor plan not just for now but as your family grows and as you age. Do you really want a formal living room at the expense of a small kitchen or master bedroom? Can the guest bedroom be converted to a nursery someday? Will you always have the back and knees for hiking up two flights of stairs? Is the yard big enough for the dogs? Will the jet ski fit in the garage? Will there be room for a workbench?

**MOVING TIP**

Label your boxes with the room to which their contents are going, not with the room from which they came. This is particularly helpful if you are moving into a larger home. It will cut down on excessive shuffling around once you begin unpacking.

**Things to Consider**

**The House**

- Affordability
- Design
- Livability
- Maintenance
- Duration (buy and sell or buy and retire?)
- Pets
- Hobbies

**The Neighborhood**

- Neighborhood amenities
- School district
- Bus and bike routes
- Safety and security
- Noise level

## LOOKING ON YOUR OWN VERSUS WITH AN AGENT

With the growing popularity of FSBOs ("FIZ-boze")—homes that are For Sale By Owner—a serious question is reverberating throughout the residential real estate industry: "Are agents necessary?"

All real estate contracts in Washington State must be in writing. To enter into contracts such as Agency Agreements and Purchase & Sale Agreements, parties to the contract must be mentally competent and at least eighteen years of age. That's all. You need not be a veteran of real estate transactions. But unless you're a Certified Wheeler-Dealer (CWD), I strongly suggest the services of a competent agent. You're not a native Washingtonian. You're not even a local, yet. You're a relocator, and Washington real estate laws can be "unique." Therefore, my advice is to visit several established brokers and interview a few agents. Select a professional you like and trust. Credentials like Realtor, CRS, GRI, and Relocation Specialist are impressive, but experience and a good track record are crucial. Don't be shy. Ask for references.

Skillful agents are proficient in the art of negotiating. How an offer or counter-offer is presented greatly influences the seller's acceptance or rejection. Savvy agents can save you thousands of dollars, even in a seller's market.

Commissions—usually 6 percent of the selling price—are split equally between the listing broker, listing agent, selling broker, and selling agent (1.5 percent each). Commissions are traditionally paid by the seller at closing. In other words, as a buyer you do not have to pay for your agent's services. The seller does. Another reason to enlist a qualified agent is the Puget Sound Multiple Listing Service. Brokers and their agents have membership access to this massive database that includes the addresses and specifications of every property listed on the index.

The Washington State Department of Licensing maintains rigorous standards for real estate agents. Continuing education classes are mandated. You can be confident that your agent is abreast of the latest real estate laws and trends. Brokers also maintain a "short list" of qualified residential appraisers and home inspectors. They are a good source for remodeling contractors, landscape architects, and interior designers, too.

The process of finding a home can be tedious and disheartening. It can also be efficient and enjoyable. Often, a good agent is the difference.

## Reasons You Need a Real Estate Agent

- You're new to the area
- Agents may negotiate a better deal
- Seller pays your agent's commission

- Agents have access to the PSMLS
- Agents meet rigorous qualification standards
- Brokerages are a good source for referrals:
    - home inspectors
    - landscape architects
    - remodeling contractors
    - interior designers
    - appraisers
    - exterminators
    - title companies
    - escrow officers
- Agents can make the search more enjoyable

## Resources for Finding a House

For assistance with finding and buying a home, call (206) 442-2800.

- Dial 3732 to learn what to look for in a home
- Dial 3733 for help in determining your price range
- Dial 3730 for mortgage options
- Dial 3731 for tips about buying a house

***Eastside Journal***
*1705 132nd Avenue NE*
*Bellevue, WA 98009-9230*
*(800) 492-2219*
www.eastsidejournal.com

***For Sale By Owner***
*(425) 820-3900*
*(800) 760-3500*
www.byownermarket.com

***Harmon Homes***
*11711 Northcreek Parkway South,*
*Suite D-113*
*Bothell, WA 98011*
*(800) 829-7130*
www.harmonhomes.com

***Homes & Land***
*1029 Market Street, Suite A*
*Kirkland, WA 98033*
*(425) 739-6990*
www.homesnland.com

***John L. Scott Homes***
*(206) 230-7608*
www.johnlscott.com

***The Real Estate Book***
*(800) 541-3401*
www.realestatebook.com

***Seattle Post-Intelligencer***
*101 Elliott Avenue W*
*Seattle, Washington 98111*
*(206) 448-8000*
www.seattlep-i.com

***Seattle Times***
*Fairview Avenue and John Street*
*Seattle, WA 98111*
*(206) 464-2121*
*(800) 542-0820*
www.seattletimes.com

CITY FACT

Seattle has become one of the most popular locations in which to film major motion pictures. It is also a favorite setting for bestselling techno-thriller novels and two prime-time television shows.

## INTERNET RESOURCES FOR FINDING A HOME IN THE PUGET SOUND AREA

**About.com**
www.seattle.about.com/citiestowns/pacnwus

This Web site searches newspaper classifieds and multiple listing indices for you, and covers everything from houseplants to houseboats.

**Better Homes & Gardens First-Time Buyer's Guide**
www.ghs.realtor.com

Six easy steps toward purchasing your first home.

### FSBO.com

www.fsbo.com

A large database of properties listed For Sale By Owner.

### Home Buyer's Information Center

www.ourfamilyplace.com/homebuyer

Plenty of Qs & As, checklists, and To Do lists for homebuyers.

### HomePath

www.homepath.com

Fannie Mae sponsored site educates buyers with Starter, Purchase, and Refinance "paths" from A–Z . . . in eight languages.

### Homes.com

www.homes.com

Lots of information about neighborhood comparisons, mortgage calculation, and home improvement ideas.

### HomeSpace.com

www.homespace.com

A great site to shop for lenders as well as home products and services. Thoughtful house hunting and home ownership tips, too.

### HouseHunt.com

www.househunt.com

This is a big one, matching buyers' specifications with homes and mortgages.

### International Home Information Network

www.evergreenweb1234.com

This helpful Web site allows buyers to review résumés of brokers and agents.

**I Own.com**

www.iown.com

Expert opinions about: "rent vs. buy," home shopping, and alternatives to conventional financing.

**Owners.com**

www.owners.com

A great bookmark for daily interest rates and general real estate advice, this unique site also offers listings and virtual tours.

Take family heirlooms, fragile items, and sensitive electronic devices in a car, not the truck.

**Real Estate Seattle**

www.realestateseattle.com

Advice for first-time buyers and sellers in Seattle.

**Seattle Relocation Solutions**

www.debra4homes.com

The most complete real estate services for home buyers relocating to the Greater Puget Sound area. This award-winning Web site showcases the expertise of Seattle's leading relocation authority.

**Seattle Times School Guide**

www.seattletimes.com/schoolguide

A comprehensive guide to schools and school districts within Greater Seattle.

**Washington State Dept. of Transportation**

www.wsdot.wa.gov/regions/northwest/nwflow

Statewide traffic statistics, routing tips, and live Webcam reports help make your commute quick and easy.

SECTION TWO

# Packing Up and Moving Out

*By Monstermoving.com*

CHAPTER 4

# Getting Organized and Planning Your Move

Written for both the beginner and the veteran, this chapter contains information and resources that will help you get ready for your move. If money is foremost on your mind, you'll find a section on budgeting for the move and tips on how to save money throughout the move—as well as a move budget-planning guide. If time is also precious, you'll find time-saving tips and even suggestions for how to get out of town in a hurry. You'll find help with preliminary decisions, the planning process, and packing, as well as tips and advice on uprooting and resettling your family (and your animal companions). A budget worksheet, a set of helpful checklists, and a moving task time line complete the chapter.

## Paying for Your Move

Moving can certainly tap your bank account. How much depends on a number of factors: whether your employer is helping with the cost, how much stuff you have, and how far you are moving.

To get an idea of how much your move will cost, start calling service providers for estimates and begin listing these expenses on the move budget-planning guide provided at the end of this chapter.

If you don't have the money saved, start saving as soon as you can. You should also check out other potential sources of money:

- Income from the sale of your spare car, furniture, or other belongings (hold a garage or yard sale).
- The cleaning and damage deposit on your current rental and any utility deposits. You probably won't be reimbursed until *after* your move, though, so you'll need to pay moving expenses up front in some other way.
- Your employer, who may owe you a payout for vacation time not taken.

## Taxes and Your Move

Did you know that your move may affect your taxes? As you prepare to move, here are some things to consider:

- Next year's taxes. Some of your moving expenses may be tax-deductible. Save your receipts and contact your accountant and the IRS for more information. Visit *www.irs.gov* or call the IRS at (800) 829-3676 for information and to obtain the publication and forms you need.
- State income tax. If your new state collects income tax, you'll want to figure that into your salary and overall cost-of-living calculations. Of course, if your old state collects income tax and your new one doesn't, that's a factor, too, but a happier one—but remember to find out how much, if any, of the current year's income will be taxable in the old state.
- Other income sources. You'll want to consider any other sources of income and whether your new state will tax you on this income. For example, if you are paying federal income tax on an IRA that you rolled over into a Roth IRA, if you move into a state that collects income tax, you may also have to pay state income tax on your rollover IRA.
- After you move or when filing time draws near, consider collecting your receipts and visiting an accountant.

## The Budget Move (Money-Saving Tips)

Here you'll find some suggestions for saving money on your move.

### Saving on Moving Supplies

- Obtain boxes in the cheapest way possible.

  Ask a friend or colleague who has recently moved to give or sell you their boxes.

  Check the classified ads; people sometimes sell all their moving boxes for a flat rate.

  Ask your local grocery or department store for their empty boxes.

  Borrow a tape dispenser instead of buying one.

  Instead of buying bubble wrap, crumple newspaper, plain unused newsprint, or tissue paper to pad breakables.

  Shop around for the cheapest deal on packing tape and other supplies.

  Instead of renting padding blankets from the truck rental company, use your own blankets, linens, and area rugs for padding. (But bear in mind that you may have to launder them when you arrive, which is an expense in itself.)

### Saving on Labor

- If you use professional movers, consider a "you pack, we drive" arrangement, in which you pack boxes, and the moving company loads, moves, and unloads your belongings.
- Call around and compare estimates.
- If you move yourself, round up volunteers to help you load and clean on moving day. It's still customary to reward them with moving-day food and beverages (and maybe a small cash gift). You may also have to volunteer to help them move some day. But you may still save some money compared to hiring professionals.
- Save on child and pet care. Ask family or friends to watch your young children and pets on moving day.

## Saving on Trip Expenses

### Overnight the Night Before You Depart

- Where will you stay the night before you depart? A hotel or motel might be most comfortable and convenient, but you could save a little money if you stay the night with a friend or relative.
- If you have the gear, maybe you'd enjoy unrolling your sleeping bag and "roughing it" on your own floor the night before you leave town. If you do this, try to get hold of a camping sleeping pad or air mattress, which will help you get a good night's sleep and start your move rested and refreshed.

### Overnight on the Road

- Look into hotel and motel discounts along your route. Your automobile club membership may qualify you for a better rate. Check out other possibilities, too—associations such as AARP often line up discounts for their members, as do some credit cards.
- When you call about rates, ask if the hotel or motel includes a light breakfast with your stay.
- If your move travel involves an overnight stay and you're game for camping, check into campgrounds and RV parks along your route. Be sure to ask whether a moving truck is allowed. Some parks have size restrictions; some RV parks may not welcome moving trucks; and some limit the number of vehicles allowed in a campsite.

## Food While Traveling

Food is one of those comfort factors that can help make the upsetting aspects of moving and traveling more acceptable. Eating also gives you a reason to stop and rest, which may be exactly what you or your family needs if you're rushing to get there. Here are a few pointers to consider:

- Try to balance your need to save money with your (and your family's) health and comfort needs.
- Try to have at least one solid, nutritious sit-down meal each day.

- Breakfast can be a budget- and schedule-friendly meal purchased at a grocery or convenience store and eaten on the road: fruit, muffins, and juice, for example.
- Lunch prices at sit-down restaurants are typically cheaper than dinner prices. Consider having a hot lunch and then picnicking in your hotel or motel on supplies from a grocery store.

## Scheduling Your Move

Try to allow yourself at least three months to plan and prepare. This long lead time is especially important if you plan to sell or buy a home or if you are moving during peak moving season (May through September). If you plan to move during peak season, it's vital to reserve two to three months in advance with a professional moving company or truck rental company. The earlier you reserve, the more likely you are to get the dates you want. This is especially important if you're timing your move with a job start date or a house closing date, or are moving yourself and want to load and move on a weekend when your volunteers are off work.

### WHEN IS THE RIGHT TIME TO MOVE?

If your circumstances allow you to decide your move date, you'll want to make it as easy as possible on everyone who is moving:

- Children adjust better if they move between school terms (entering an established class in the middle of a school year can be very difficult).

### THE "GET-OUT-OF-TOWN-IN-A-HURRY" PLAN

First the bad news: Very little about the move process can be shortened. Now the good news: The choices you make might make it possible to move in less time. The three primary resources in a successful move are time, money, and planning. If you're short on time, be prepared to spend more money or become more organized.

Immediately check into the availability of a rental truck or professional moving service. Next, give your landlord notice or arrange for an agent to sell your home. (If you own your home, you may find it harder to leave town in a hurry.) If your employer is paying for your move, ask if it offers corporate-sponsored financing options that will let you buy a new home before you sell your old one. Then consider the following potentially timesaving choices:

- Move less stuff. Of all the moving tasks, packing and unpacking consume the most time. The less you have to deal with, the quicker your move will go. Consider drastically lightening the load by selling or giving away most of your belongings and starting over in your new location. Although buying replacement stuff may drain your pocketbook, you can save some money by picking up some items secondhand at thrift stores and garage sales. (And after all, everything you have *now* is used, isn't it?)
- Make a quick-move plan. Quickly scan through chapters 4 and 5, highlighting helpful information. Use the checklists and the task time line at the end of this chapter to help you.
- Get someone else to do the cleaning. Before you vacate, you'll need to clean. You can be out the door sooner if you hire a professional cleaning company to come and clean everything, top to bottom, including the carpets. Again, the time you save will cost you money—but it may well be worth trading money for time.

## Planning and Organizing

Start a move notebook. This could be as simple as a spiral-bound notepad or as elaborate as a categorized, tabbed binder. Keep track of this notebook. You'll find it invaluable later when the chaos hits. In your notebook, write notes and tape receipts. Of course, keep *this* book with your notebook! You may find the checklists and moving task time lines at the end of this chapter helpful. You may also find it helpful to assign a "do-by" date to each task on the checklist. To help you gauge what you face in the coming weeks, perhaps you will find it useful at this point to scan through the task time lines before reading further.

The section of the Moving Task Time Line that will help you the most at this point is "Decision Making: Weeks 12 to 9," which you'll find at the end of this chapter.

## Preliminary Decisions

Before you even begin to plan your move, there are a number of decisions you'll need to make regarding your current residence, how you will move (do it yourself or hire a professional), and your new area.

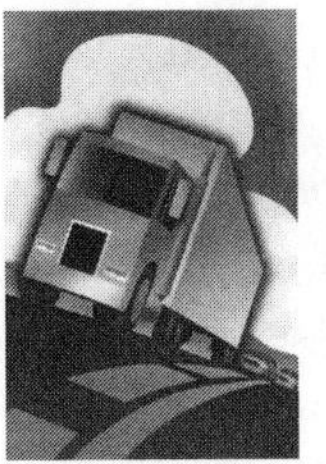

**MOVING TIP**

If you are renting a truck, you'll need to know what size to rent. Here is a general guideline. Because equipment varies, though, ask for advice from the company renting the truck to you.

10-foot truck:
 one to two furnished rooms

14- to 15-foot truck:
 two to three furnished rooms

18- to 20-foot truck:
 four to five furnished rooms

22- to 24-foot truck:
 six to eight furnished rooms

### LEAVING YOUR CURRENT HOME (RENTED PROPERTY)

Leaving a rental unit involves notifying your landlord and fulfilling your contractual obligations. This won't be a problem unless you have a lease agreement that lasts beyond your desired move date.

Your rights and options are dictated by state and local landlord/tenant laws and by your lease agreement. Exit fees can be expensive, depending on the terms of your lease. Here are some tips that may help you get out of a lease gracefully and save a few bucks at the same time.

- Know your rights. Laws governing landlord/tenant agreements and rights vary by state and municipality. Consult state and local law and call and obtain a pamphlet on renter's rights for your state and municipality.
- Review your lease agreement. There's no point in

worrying until you know whether you have anything to worry about—and no use finding out too late that there were things you could have done.

- Look for a way out. Ask your landlord to consider letting you find a replacement tenant to fulfill your lease term (in some areas, this is a right dictated by law). If your move is due to a corporate relocation, your landlord or the property management company *may* be more willing to be flexible with exit fees—especially if you provide a letter from your employer. (And you may be able to get your employer to pick up the cost if you can't get the fees waived.)
- Adjust the timing. If you need to stay a month or two longer than your current lease allows and you don't want to sign for another six months or longer, ask your landlord for a month-to-month agreement lasting until your move date.

## LEAVING YOUR CURRENT HOME (OWNED PROPERTY)

If you own your home, you'll either sell it or rent it out. If you sell, you'll either hire a real estate agent or sell it yourself. If you rent it out, you'll either serve as your own landlord or hire a property management agency to manage the property for you. Here are a few quick pros and cons to help you with the decisions you face.

### Hiring a Selling Agent: Pros

- Your home gets exposure to a wide market audience, especially if the agent you choose participates in a multiple listing service.
- Homes listed with a real estate agent typically sell more quickly.
- Your agent will market your home (prepare and place ads and so on), and will also schedule and manage open houses and showings.
- Your agent will advise you and represent your interest in the business deal of selling, including offers, negotiation, and closing, guiding you through the stacks of paperwork.

### Hiring a Selling Agent: Cons

- Hiring an agent requires signing a contract. If, for whatever reason, you want out, you may find it difficult to break the contract (it's wise to read carefully and sign only a short-term contract. Typical real estate agent contracts are ninety to 120 days in length).
- You pay your agent a fee for the service, typically a percentage of the selling price.

### Selling Your Home Yourself: Pros

- You don't pay an agent's fee.
- You retain more control over showings, open houses, walk-throughs, and so on.

### Selling Your Home Yourself: Cons

- Selling a home takes time. You must arrange your own showings and schedule and conduct your own open houses. Combined with everything else that happens during move preparation (working, interviewing for jobs, finding a new home, planning your move, packing, and so on), you will probably be swamped already. Add home showings (which are based around the buyer's schedule, not yours), and you may find yourself looking for an agent to help you after all.
- You pay for marketing costs, which can add up. Consider the cost of flyers, newspaper ads, or listing your home on a "homes for sale by owner" Web site.
- Since you don't have a real estate agent to represent you in the sale, you may need to hire an attorney at that point, which could take up some of the savings.

## RENTING OUT YOUR PROPERTY

If you prefer to rent out your home, you can turn it over to a property management agency or be your own landlord. The services an agency will perform depend on the agency and your agreement with them. The following table details some of the rental issues you'll need to consider. As you review these, ask yourself how far away you're moving and whether or not you can handle these issues from your new home. Remember that every piece of work you must hire out cuts into the money in your pocket at the end of the month.

### Strategic Financial Issues Related to Renting Out Your Old Home

If your property is located in a desirable neighborhood that is appreciating in value 3 percent or more annually, keeping it may in the long run defray or overcome the cost of management fees. If you rent out your property, it ceases being your primary residence. Find out from your accountant if this will affect your federal or state income taxes or local property taxes (some counties/municipalities give owner-occupied credits that reduce the tax burden). If there is an impact, you'll want to figure the difference into your decision of whether or not to sell and into the total you charge for rent.

| Rental Issue | You As Landlord | Hired Property Manager |
|---|---|---|
| **Vacancy** | You interview candidates, show the property, and choose tenants | The agency finds and selects tenants |
| **Cleaning** | You clean or arrange for cleaning services between tenants | The agency arranges for cleaning services between tenants |
| **Late Rent** | You collect rent and pursue late rent | The agency collects rent and pursues late rent |
| **Rental Income** | The rent you collect is all yours | The agency charges a fee, usually a percentage of the monthly rent |
| **Repairs** | You handle repairs and emergencies or find and hire a contractor to do the work | The agency handles repairs and emergencies |

## Deciding How to Move: Hiring Professionals or Moving Yourself

At first, you may be inclined to handle your own move to save money. But there are other factors to consider, and, depending on your situation, you may actually *save* money if you use professional services. Consider the range of service options some professional companies offer. The right combination could save you some of the headache but still compete with the cost of a do-it-yourself move. For example, some professional moving companies offer a "you pack, we drive" arrangement, in which you pack boxes and the moving company loads, moves, and unloads your belongings. Call around and inquire about rates. Also consider the following list of pros and cons to help you decide what's best for you.

The section of the Moving Task Time Line that will help you the most at this point is "Decision Making: Weeks 12 to 9," which you'll find at the end of this chapter.

### The Pros of Using Pros

- *Time.* You may not have the hours it will take to pack, move, and unpack, but professional movers do—that's their day job.
- *Materials.* The moving company provides boxes and packing materials.*
- *Packing.* The movers pack all boxes (unless your contract states that you will pack).*
- *Loading and Unloading.* The movers load your belongings onto the moving van and unload your belongings at your destination.*
- *Unpacking.* The movers remove packed items from boxes and place items on flat surfaces.*
- *Debris.* The movers dispose of packing debris such as boxes, used tape, and padding.*
- *Experience.* The movers will know just what to do to transport your precious belongings in good condition.
- *Safety.* The movers do the lifting, which could save you a real injury.

Professional moving contracts typically include the services marked with an asterisk (*). Don't count on something unless you know for sure that the contract covers it, though—it's a good idea to ask your mover a lot of questions and read the contract carefully.

### The Cons of Using Pros

- *Administrative chores.* Using professionals requires you to do some up-front work: obtaining estimates, comparing and negotiating prices and move dates, reviewing contracts, and comparing insurance options.
- *Loss of control.* The movers typically take charge of much of the packing and loading process, and you need to adapt to their schedule and procedures.

### The Pros of a Self-Move

- *Control.* You pack, so you decide what items get packed together, how they get packed, and in which box they reside.
- *Cost-cutting.* You may save some money. But as you compare costs, be sure to factor in *all* self-move-related moving and travel costs. These include fuel, tolls, mileage charge on the rented truck, food, and lodging. All these costs increase the longer your trip is.

### The Cons of a Self-Move

- *Risk to your belongings.* Because of inexperience with packing, loading, and padding heavy and unwieldy boxes and furniture, you or your volunteers may inadvertently damage your property.

## OTHER THINGS TO KNOW ABOUT PROFESSIONAL MOVING SERVICES

Your moving company may or may not provide the following services, or may charge extra for performing them. Be sure to ask.

- Disassembling beds or other furniture
- Removing window covering hardware (drapery rods, mini-blinds) or other items from the walls or ceiling

- Disconnecting and installing appliances (dryer, washer, automatic ice maker)
- Disconnecting and installing outside fixtures such as a satellite dish, a hose reel, and so on
- Moving furniture or boxes from one room to another

## MOVING INSURANCE IN A PROFESSIONAL MOVE

By U.S. law, the mover must cover your possessions at $0.60 per pound. This coverage is free. Consider taking out additional coverage, though, because under this minimal coverage, your three-pound antique Tiffany lamp worth hundreds of dollars at auction fetches exactly $1.80 if the moving company breaks it.

Your homeowner's or renter's insurance provider may be willing to advise you on moving insurance options, and the moving company will offer you a number of insurance options. Be sure you understand each option—what it covers and what it costs you. Ask a lot of questions and read everything carefully. No one wishes for mishaps, but it's best to be prepared and well informed should something break or show up missing.

Before buying anything for your new apartment or home, stop and consider what you'll need immediately and what you might be able to do without for a while. You'll spend a lot less if you can afford to wait and look for it on sale or secondhand.

## STORAGE

If you want your moving company to store some or all of your possessions temporarily, inquire about cost and the quality of their facilities:

- Are the facilities heated (or air-conditioned, depending on the time of year that matters to you)?

- Does the moving company own the storage facility or subcontract storage to someone else? If they subcontract, does your contract with the moving company extend to the storage facility company?

### Storage Companies in the Seattle Area

For free twenty-four-hour consumer tips regarding household and commercial storage, call (206) 442-2800.

- press 3825 for information about safeguarding your belongings
- press 3826 to be advised about excluded or illegal items
- press 3827 for tips about using public storage facilities
- press 3828 for suggestions about boxing or crating your belongings

The following companies provide public storage services and facilities in the Greater Seattle area:

**Affordable Self Storage**
*1621 196th Avenue SE*
*Bothell*
*(425) 481-8883*

**A Better Mobile Storage Company**
*6110 West Marginal Way*
*Seattle*
*(800) 662-8810*
www.mobilestorage.com

**Brian & Tony's Mini Storage**
*10805 Roosevelt Way*
*Seattle*
*(206) 364-8777*

**Door to Door Storage**
*6718 216th Street*
*Mercer Island*
*(206) 230-0211*
www.doortodoor.com

**Downtown Self Storage**
*1915 3rd Avenue*
*Seattle*
*(206) 441-3138*

**Hansen Bros. Moving & Storage**
*6860 Coal Creek Parkway*
*Bellevue*
*(425) 255-1451*
www.hansenbros.com

**Kenmore Self Storage**
*18716 68th Avenue NE*
*Kenmore*
*(425) 485-2284*

**Lake City Mini-Storage**
*3116 Northeast 130th Street*
*Lake City*
*(206) 365-3282*

**Magnolia Bridge Self Storage**
*1900 15th Avenue W*
*Fremont*
*(206) 286-6508*

**Mini-Max Storage**
*2656 15th Street W*
*Magnolia*
*(206) 282-7555*

**Money Saver Mini Storage**
*19011 Woodinville/Snohomish Road*
*Woodinville*
*(425) 424-3334*

**Mr. Van Gard Self Storage**
*17828 Midvale Avenue N*
*North Seattle*
*(206) 542-1227*

**Nickerson Street Self Storage**
*1300 West Nickerson Street*
*Queen Anne*
*(206) 285-5800*

**Peoples Storage**
*6908 Northeast 181st Street*
*Kenmore*
*(425) 485-1234*

**PortaBox Storage, Inc.**
*700 Milwaukee Avenue*
*Seattle*
*(206) 623-5039*
www.portabox.com

**Public Storage**
*1515 13th Avenue*
*Capitol Hill*
*(206) 329-6271*
www.publicstorage.com

*12465 Northup Way*
*Bellevue*
*(425) 869-2121*

*5806 221 Plaza SE*
*Issaquah*
*(425) 313-5003*

*20065 15th Avenue NE*
*Lake Forest Park*
*(206) 364-9509*

**Redmond Self Storage**
*17285 Northeast 70th Street*
*Redmond*
*(425) 881-7587*

Before you leave, measure your current home and draw a sketch plan, showing room measurements and furniture placement. Take the plan with you, along with a tape measure and notebook, and draw up similar plans for the house or rental unit you're thinking of choosing. Sketches needn't be very detailed at this stage to help you avoid unpleasant surprises—no point in dragging that California King bed across country if it won't fit in the bedroom.

**Roosevelt Self Storage**
*6910 Roosevelt Way NE*
*Wallingford*
*(206) 526-7030*

**Shurgard Storage**
*2746 Northeast 45th Street*
*Seattle*
*(206) 523-0070*
www.shurgard.com

*14900 Aurora Avenue N*
*Shoreline*
*(206) 363-8515*

**Storage USA**
*1430 North 130th Street*
*Seattle*
*(206) 306-9594*
www.sus.com

**Totem Lake West Self Storage**
*11330 Northeast 124th Street*
*Kirkland*
*(425) 823-9191*

**U-Haul Self-Storage**
*453 Raineer Avenue*
*Renton*
*(206) 772-3106*
www.uhaul.com

## CHOOSING A MOVER

- Start by asking around. Chances are your friends, family, or colleagues will have a personal recommendation.
- Take their recommendations and list them in a notebook, each on a separate sheet. Call these companies to request a

no-obligation, free written estimate—and take notes on your conversation.

- Find out if the company you're talking to offers the services you need. For example, if you want to ship your car, boat, or powered recreational craft in the van along with your household goods, ask if this service is available.
- Do a little investigating. Ask the company to show you its operating license, and call the Better Business Bureau to ask about complaints and outstanding claims.

## GETTING AN ESTIMATE

You need to know what kind of estimate the moving company is giving you. The two most common are "non-binding" and "binding." A *non-binding estimate* (usually free, but potentially less accurate) is one in which the moving company charges you by the hour per worker per truck and quotes you an approximate figure to use in your planning. Depending on circumstances, your final cost could be significantly greater than what shows up in the estimate.

The second type is a *binding estimate,* which you typically pay for. In this type, the professional mover performs a detailed on-site inspection of your belongings and quotes a flat price based on the following:

- The amount of stuff you're moving, whether it is fragile or bulky, and how complicated it is to pack
- Final weight
- Services provided
- Total length of travel

Once you choose a mover, it's a good idea to have a representative visit your home, look at your belongings, and give you a written (binding) estimate. Getting a written estimate may cost you money, but it helps prevent surprises when it comes time to pay the final bill.

You play a big role in making sure that the estimate you receive is accurate. Be sure you show the moving company representative everything you plan to move.

- Remember to take the representative through every closet, out to the garage, into the shed, down to the basement, up into the attic, and to your rented storage facility if you have one.

- Tell the representative about any item you *don't* plan to move (because you plan to get rid of it before you move). Then be sure to follow through and get rid of it so there are no surprises on moving day.
- Point out any vehicles you want to ship in the van along with your household goods, and ask your representative to include the cost in your estimate.

### WHAT MIGHT INCREASE YOUR FINAL BILL

It is reasonable to expect that certain circumstances will unexpectedly increase your final bill, including:

- You do the packing and it's incomplete or done improperly.

## Researching Your New Area

The section of the Moving Task Time Line that will help you the most at this point is "Decision Making: Weeks 12 to 9," which you'll find at the end of this chapter. Other chapters of this book discuss the details of your destination city. Here are some additional move-related tips and resources.

### GENERAL CITY INFORMATION

- Visit your local library and read up on your new area.
- Go online and look for the local newspaper.
- Have a friend or family member mail you a week's worth of newspapers or have a subscription delivered via postal mail.
- Visit *www.monstermoving.com* for easy-to-find city information and links to local services, information, and Web sites.

### JOBS, HOUSING, AND COST OF LIVING

Visit *www.monster.com* for career assistance, and visit *www.monster-moving.com* for links to apartments for rent and real estate and other services, as well as free cost-of-living information.

### CHOOSING SCHOOLS

Selecting schools is of supreme importance for family members who will attend public or private schools.

### Do Your Homework

- Ask your real estate agent to help you find school information and statistics or a list of contacts for home school associations.
- Search the Web.

  Visit *www.2001beyond.com.* There you can compare up to four districts at once. Information on both public and private schools is provided. The extensive twelve-page report provides information on class size, curriculum, interscholastic sports, extracurricular activities, awards, merits, and SAT scores. It also provides the principal's name and phone number for each school in the district. You may need to pay a nominal fee for the twelve-page report (or the cost may be covered by a sponsoring real estate professional, if you don't mind receiving a phone call from an agent).

  Visit *www.monstermoving.com*, which provides links to school information.

### Visit Schools

Arrange to visit schools your children might attend, and bring them along. Your children will pick up on subtleties that you will miss. As you talk with your children about changing schools, try to help them differentiate between their feelings about moving to a new school and area and their feelings about that particular school by asking direct but open-ended questions. (An *open-ended* question is one that invites dialogue because it can't be answered with a simple "yes" or "no"—"What was the best or worst thing you saw there?" for example, or "Which electives looked the most interesting?")

## PLANNING AND TAKING A HOUSE—OR APARTMENT—HUNTING TRIP

Preparing and planning in advance will help you make the most of your trip. Ideally, by this point, you will have narrowed your search to two or three neighborhoods or areas.

- Gather documents and information required for completing a rental application:

  Rental History: Landlord's name, contact information, dates occupied

Personal references: Name and contact information for one or two personal references

Employment information: Current or anticipated employer name and contact info

Bank account number

- Consider compiling all this information into a "Rental Résumé." Even though most landlords won't accept a rental résumé in lieu of a completed application, spending the time up front could be helpful in a market where rentals are scarce. Handing the landlord a rental résumé lets them know you're serious about finding the right place and are professional and organized in how you conduct your affairs.
- Go prepared to pay an application fee and deposits. Deposit the funds in your account and bring your checkbook. Typically, landlords require first and last month's rent and a flat damage and cleaning deposit.
- Take your Move Planning Notebook. List properties you want to visit, one per notebook page. Clip the classified ad and tape it onto the page. Write notes about the property, rent rate, deposit amount, and terms you discuss with the landlord or property manager.

## Planning

Now that you've made pre-move decisions, it's time to plan for the physical move. First, you'll need to organize your moving day. Next, you'll need to prepare to pack.

These are the sections of the Moving Task Time Line that will help you the most at this point:

- "Organizing, Sorting, and Notifying: Weeks 9 to 8"
- "Finalizing Housing Arrangements and Establishing Yourself in Your New Community: Weeks 8 to 6"
- "Making and Confirming Transportation and Travel Plans: Week 6"

- "Uprooting: Weeks 5 to 4"
- "Making and Confirming Moving-Day Plans: Week 3"

You'll find the Moving Task Time Line at the end of this chapter.

## PLANNING FOR MOVING DAY

### The Professional Move: Some Planning Considerations

- Confirm your move dates and finalize any last contract issues.
- Ask what form of payment movers will accept (check, money order, certified check, traveler's checks) and make necessary arrangements.

### The Self-Move: Organizing Volunteers

- Ask friends and relatives to "volunteer" to help you load the truck on moving day.
- Set up shifts, and tactfully let your volunteers know that you are counting on them to arrive on time and stay through their "shift."
- A week or two before moving day, call everyone to remind them.
- Plan on supplying soft drinks and munchies to keep your crew going.

## PLANNING CARE FOR YOUR CHILDREN AND PETS

Moving day will be hectic for you and everyone, and possibly dangerous for your young children. Make plans to take younger children and your pets to someone's home or to a care facility.

## PLANNING YOUR MOVING-DAY TRAVEL

### Driving

- If you will be renting a truck, be prepared to put down a sizable deposit the day you pick up the truck. Some truck rental companies only accept a credit card for this deposit, so go prepared.

- If you belong to an automobile club such as AAA, contact them to obtain maps, suggested routes, alternate routes, rest-stop information, and a trip packet, if they provide this service.
- Visit an online map site such as *www.mapblast.com,* where you'll find not only a map but also door-to-door driving directions and estimated travel times.
- Find out in advance where you should turn in the truck in your new hometown.

### Traveling by Air, Train, or Bus

- Arrange for tickets and boarding passes.
- Speak with the airline to request meals that match dietary restrictions.
- Speak with the airline or the train or bus company to make any special arrangements such as wheelchair accessibility and assistance.
- Plan to dress comfortably.
- If you will be traveling with young children, plan to dress them in bright, distinctive clothing so you can easily identify them in a crowded airport, train station, or bus terminal.

## PREPARING TO PACK: WHAT TO DO WITH THE STUFF YOU HAVE

Moves are complicated, time-consuming, and exhausting. But the process has at least one benefit. A move forces us to consider simplifying our lives by reducing the amount of our personal belongings. If we plan to keep it, we also must pack it, load it, move it, unload it, and unpack it. Here are some suggestions for sifting through your belongings as you prepare for packing.

- Start in one area of your home and go through everything before moving to the next area.
- Ask yourself three questions about each item (sentimental value aside):

    Have we used this in the last year?

    Will we use it in the coming year? For example, if you're moving to a more temperate climate, you might not need all your wool socks and sweaters.

Is there a place for it in the new home? For instance, if your new home has a smaller living room, you might not have room for your big couch or need all your wall decorations.

If you answer "no" to any or all of these questions, you might want to consider selling the item, giving it away, or throwing it out.

## Packing

Here are some tips to help you with one of the most difficult stages of your move—packing.

MOVING TIP

Start packing as soon as you get boxes. Some things you can pack long before the move. For example, off-season holiday decorations and off-season clothes can be boxed right away. The more you do early on, the less there is to do closer to move day, when things are hectic anyway.

- Follow a plan. Pack one room at a time. You may find yourself leaving one or two boxes in each room open to receive those items you use right up until the last minute.
- On the outside of each box, describe the contents and room destination. Be as specific as you can, to make unpacking easier. However, if you are using a professional moving service but doing the packing yourself, consider numbering boxes and creating a separate list of box contents and destinations.
- Put heavy items such as books in small boxes to make them easier to carry.
- Don't put tape on furniture because it may pull off some finish when you remove it.
- As you pack, mark and set aside the items that should go in the truck last (see checklist at the end of this chapter). Mark and set aside your "necessary box" (for a list of items to include in this box, see the checklist at the end of this chapter).

## PACKING FRAGILE ITEMS

- When packing breakable dishes and glasses, use boxes and padding made for these items. You may have to pay a little to buy these boxes, but you're apt to save money in the long run because your dishes are more likely to arrive unbroken. Dishes and plates are best packed on edge (not stacked flat atop each other).
- Pad mirrors, pictures, and larger delicate pieces with sheets and blankets.
- Computers fare best if they are packed in their original boxes. If you don't have these, pack your hardware in a large, sturdy box and surround it with plenty of padding such as plastic bubble pack.
- Use plenty of padding around fragile items.
- Mark "FRAGILE" *on the top and all sides* of boxes of breakables so it's easily seen no matter how a box is stacked.

## WHAT *NOT* TO PACK

- Don't pack hazardous, flammable, combustible, or explosive materials. Empty your gas grill tank and any kerosene heater fuel as well as gasoline in your power yard tools. These materials are not safe in transit.
- Don't pack valuables such as jewelry, collections, important financial and legal documents, and records for the moving van. Keep these with you in your car trunk or your suitcase.

## PACKING AND UNPACKING SAFELY WITH YOUNG CHILDREN

No matter how well you've kid-proofed your home, that only lasts until the moment you start packing. Then things are in disarray and within reach of youngsters. Here are some tips to keep your toddlers and children safe.

- Items your youngsters have seldom or never seen will pique their curiosity, presenting a potential hazard, so consider what you are packing or unpacking. If you stop packing or unpacking and leave the room even for a moment, take your youngsters with you and close the door or put up a child gate.

- Keep box knives and other tools out of a child's reach.
- As you disassemble or reassemble furniture, keep track of screws, bolts, nuts, and small parts.
- Beware of how and where you temporarily place furniture and other items. (That heavy mirror you just took down off the wall—do you lean it up against the wall until you go get the padding material, inviting a curious youngster to pull or climb on it?) For the same reason, consider how high you stack boxes.
- On arriving at your destination, if you can't find someone to baby-sit, set aside a room in your home where your young children can safely play. Set up the TV and VCR and unpack the kids' videos, books, coloring books and crayons or markers, and some toys and snacks.
- Walk through your new home with children and talk about any potential dangers such as a swimming pool or stairs, establishing your safety rules and boundaries.
- If you have young children who are unaccustomed to having stairs in the home, place a gate at the top and one at the bottom. If your child is walking and over toddler age, walk up and down the stairs together a few times holding the railing until they become accustomed to using the stairs.

## Handle with Special Care: Uprooting and Settling the People and Pets in Your Life

The most important advice you can hear is this: Involving children as much as possible will help transform this anxiety-causing, uncertain experience into an exciting adventure. It would take a book to cover this topic comprehensively, but here are some suggestions for making the transition easier:

- *Involve children early.* Ask for their input on decisions and give them age-appropriate tasks such as packing their own belongings and assembling an activity bag to keep them busy while traveling.
- *Don't make empty promises.* Kids can hear the hollow ring when you say, "It'll be just like here. Just give it time," or "You can stay

friends with your friends here." That's true, but you know it's not true in the same way, if you're moving a long distance.

- *Deal with fear of the unknown.* If possible, take children with you to look at potential neighborhoods, homes or apartments, and schools. It may be more expensive and require extra effort, but it will ease the transition and help children begin to make the adjustment.
- *Provide as much information as you can.* If it's not possible to take children with you when you visit new neighborhoods, homes or apartments, and schools, take a camera or video recorder. Your children will appreciate the pictures, and the preview will help them begin the transition. You can also use a map to help them understand the new area and the route you will take to get there.
- *Make time to talk with your children about the move.* Especially listen for—and talk about—the anxieties your children feel. By doing so, you will help them through the move (your primary goal)—and you'll deepen your relationship at the same time, which may be more important in the long run.
- *Share your own anxieties with your children—but be sure to keep an overall positive outlook about the move.* Because most aspects of a move are downers, a negative outlook on your part may shed gloom over the whole experience—including its good aspects. On the other hand, a positive outlook on your part may counteract some of your child's emotional turmoil, uncertainty, and fear.
- *Make it fun.* Give older children a disposable camera and ask them to photograph your move. Once you arrive and are settled in, make time together to create the "moving" chapter of your family photo album.

## HELPING FAMILY MEMBERS MAINTAIN FRIENDSHIPS

Moving doesn't have to end a friendship.

- Give each child a personal address book and have them write the e-mail address, phone number, and postal mail address for each of their friends.

- Stay in touch. E-mail is an easy way. Establish an e-mail address for every family member (if they don't already have one) before you move so they can give it out to friends. Many Web mail services are free and can be accessed from anywhere you can access the Internet. Examples include *www.msn.com, www.usa.net,* and *www.yahoo.com.*
- Make (and follow through with) plans to visit your old hometown within the first year following your move. Visit friends and drive by your old home, through neighborhoods, and past landmarks. This reconnection with dear friends and fond memories will help your family bring finality to the move.

## TRAVELING WITH YOUR PET

- Keep a picture of your pet on your person or in your wallet just in case you get separated from Fido or Fluffy during the move.
- Place identification tags on your pet's collar and pet carrier.
- Take your pet to the vet for an examination just before you move. Ask for advice on moving your particular pet. Specifically ask for advice on how you can help your pet through the move—what you can do before, during, and after the move to help your pet make the transition smoothly.
- Find out if you will need any health certificates for your pet to comply with local regulations in your new home, and obtain them when you visit the vet.

**MOVING TIP**

Save the TV, VCR, kids' videos, and a box of toys to be loaded on the truck last. On arriving at your destination, if you can't find someone to baby-sit, set aside a room in your home where your young children can safely play. Set up the TV and VCR and unpack the kids' videos along with some toys and snacks.

- If your pet is prone to motion sickness or tends to become nervous in reaction to excitement and unfamiliar surroundings, tell your veterinarian, who may prescribe medication for your pet.
- Ask for your pet's health records so you can take them to your new vet.
- If your pet is unusual—say, a ferret or a snake or other reptile—there might be laws in your new city or state regarding the transportation or housing of such an animal. Contact the department of agriculture or a local veterinarian to find out.
- Cats: It's wise to keep your cat indoors for the first two weeks until it recognizes its new surroundings as home.
- Dogs: If appropriate, walk your dog on a leash around your neighborhood to help it become familiar with its new surroundings and learn its way back home.
- If your pet will travel by plane, check with your airline regarding fees and any specific rules and regulations regarding pet transport.
- Your pet will need to travel in an approved carrier (check with your airline regarding acceptable types and sizes).
- Your airline may require a signed certificate of health dated within a certain number of days of the flight. Only your vet can produce this document.

## Move Budget-Planning Guide

### Housing

| | |
|---|---|
| Home repairs | $ ________ |
| Cleaning supplies and services | $ ________ |
| Rental expenses in new city | |
| Application fees (varies—figure $15 to $35 per application) | $ ________ |
| First and last month's rent | $ ________ |
| Damage and security deposit | $ ________ |
| Pet deposit | $ ________ |
| Utility deposits | $ ________ |
| Storage unit rental | $ ________ |
| **Total** | **$** ________ |

### Moving

| | |
|---|---|
| Professional moving services or truck rental | $ ________ |
| Moving supplies | $ ________ |
| Food and beverage for volunteers | $ ________ |
| Tips for professional movers; gifts for volunteers | $ ________ |
| Moving travel: | |
| Airline tickets | $ ________ |
| Fuel | $ ________ |
| Tolls | $ ________ |
| Meals: per meal $______ × ______ meals | $ ________ |
| Hotels: per night $______ × ______ nights | $ ________ |
| **Total** | **$** ________ |

*(continues on next page)*

*(continued from previous page)*

**Other Expenses**

________________________________ $ ________

________________________________ $ ________

________________________________ $ ________

________________________________ $ ________

________________________________ $ ________

________________________________ $ ________

________________________________ $ ________

**Total** .................................... **$** ____________

**GRAND TOTAL** .................................. **$** ____________

## Utilities to Cancel

| Utility | Provider name and phone | Cancel date[1] |
|---|---|---|
| Water and sewer | | |
| Electricity | | |
| Gas | | |
| Phone | | |
| Garbage | | |
| Cable | | |
| Alarm service | | |

1. If you are selling your home, the shutoff of essential services (water, electricity, gas) will depend on the final closing and walk-through. Coordinate with your real estate agent.

## Utilities to Connect

| Utility | Provider name and phone | Service start date | Deposit amount required |
|---|---|---|---|
| Water and sewer | | | |
| Electricity | | | |
| Gas | | | |
| Phone | | | |
| Garbage | | | |
| Cable | | | |
| Alarm service | | | |

## Other Services to Cancel, Transfer, or Restart

| Service | Provider name and phone | Service end date[1] | Service start date[1] |
|---|---|---|---|
| Subscriptions and Memberships | | | |
| Newspaper | | | |
| Memberships (health club and so on) | | | |
| Internet Service Provider | | | |

1. If applicable

*(continues on next page)*

(continued from previous page)

| Other Services to Cancel, Transfer, or Restart | | | |
|---|---|---|---|
| **Service** | **Provider name and phone** | **Service end date**[1] | **Service start date**[1] |
| Government and School | | | |
| Postal mail change of address | | | |
| School records | | | |
| Voter registration | | | |
| Vehicle registration | | | |
| Financial | | | |
| Bank account[2] | | | |
| Direct deposits and withdrawals | | | |
| Safe deposit box | | | |
| Professional | | | |
| Health care (transfer doctors' and dentists' records for each family member)<br>Veterinarian (transfer records)<br>Cleaners (pick up your clothes) | | | |

1. If applicable; 2. Open an account in your new town before closing your existing account.

# Checklists

## MOVING SUPPLIES

### Packing and Unpacking

____ Tape and tape dispenser. (The slightly more expensive gun-style dispenser is a worthwhile investment because its one-handed operation means you don't need a second person to help you hold the box closed while you do the taping.)

____ Boxes. (It's worth it to obtain specialty boxes for your dinnerware, china set, and glasses. Specialty wardrobe boxes that allow your hanging clothes to hang during transport are another big help.)

____ Padding such as bubble wrap.

____ Markers.

____ Scissors or a knife.

____ Big plastic bags.

____ Inventory list and clipboard.

____ Box knife with retractable blade. (Get one for each adult.)

### Loading and Moving

____ Rope. (If nothing else, you'll need it to secure heavy items to the inside wall of the truck.)

____ Padding blankets. (If you use your own, they may get dirty and you'll need bedding when you arrive. Padding is available for rent at most truck rental agencies.)

____ Hand truck or appliance dolly. (Most truck rental agencies have them available for rent.)

____ Padlock for the cargo door.

## THE "NECESSARY BOX"

### Eating

____ Snacks or food. (Pack enough durable items for right before you depart, your travel, and the first day in your new home—and disposable utensils, plates, cups.)

____ Instant coffee, tea bags, and so on.

____ Roll of paper towels and moistened towelettes.

____ Garbage bags.

### Bathing

____ A towel for each person.

____ Soap, shampoo, toothpaste, and any other toiletries.

____ Toilet paper.

### Health Items

____ First aid kit including pain relievers.

____ Prescription medicines.

### Handy to Have

____ List of contact information. (Make sure you can reach relatives, the moving company, the truck driver's cell phone, and so on.)

____ Small tool kit. (You need to be able to take apart and reassemble items that can't be moved whole.)

____ Reclosable plastic bags to hold small parts, screws, bolts.

____ Spare lightbulbs. (Some bulbs in your new home might be burned out or missing.)

____ Nightlight and flashlight.

### OVERNIGHT BAG

____ Enough clothes for the journey plus the first day or two in your new home.

____ Personal toiletries.

### ITEMS FOR KIDS

____ Activities for the trip.

____ Favorite toys and anything else that will help children feel immediately at home in their new room.

## Pet Checklist

____ Food.

____ A bottle of the water your pet is used to drinking.

____ Dishes for food and water.

____ Leash, collar, identification tags.

____ Favorite toy.

____ Medicines.

____ Bed or blanket.

____ Carrier.

____ Paper towels in case of accidents.

____ Plastic bags and a scooper.

____ Litter and litter box for your cat or rabbit.

## Last Items on the Truck

### CLEANING

____ Vacuum cleaner.

____ Cleaning supplies.

### GENERAL

____ Necessary box.

____ Setup for kids' temporary playroom.

____ Other items you'll need the moment you arrive.

## New Home Safety Checklist

### GENERAL

____ Watch out for tripping hazards. They will be plentiful until you get everything unpacked and put away, so be careful, and keep a path clear at all times.

### HEAT, FIRE, ELECTRICAL

____ Be sure nothing gets placed too close to heaters.

____ Test smoke, heat, and carbon monoxide detectors. Find out your fire department's recommendations regarding how many of these devices you should have and where you should place them. If you need more, go buy them (remember to buy batteries) and install them.

____ Find the fuse or breaker box before you need to shut off or reset a circuit.

**WATER**

____ Check the temperature setting on your water heater. For child safety and fuel conservation, experts recommend 120 degrees Fahrenheit.

____ Locate the water shutoff valve in case of a plumbing problem.

---

## Moving Task Time Line

### DECISION MAKING: WEEKS 12 TO 9

____ Consider your moving options (professional versus self-move) and get quotes.

____ If you are being relocated by your company, find out what your company covers and what you will be responsible for doing and paying.

____ Set a move date.

____ Choose your moving company or truck rental agency and reserve the dates.

#### If You Own Your Home

____ Decide whether you want to sell or rent it out.

____ If you decide to sell, choose a real estate agent and put your home on the market or look into, and begin planning for, selling it yourself

____ If you decide to rent out your home, decide whether you want to hire a property management agency or manage the property yourself.

____ Perform (or hire contractors to perform) home repairs.

### If You Currently Rent

____ Notify your landlord of your plans to vacate.

____ Check into cleaning obligations and options.

### Tour Your New City or Town

____ Research your new area at the library or online at *www.monstermoving.com.*

____ Contact a real estate agent or property management agency to help you in your search for new lodgings.

____ Go on a school-hunting and house- or apartment-hunting trip to your new town or city.

### Additional items:

______________________________________________________________

______________________________________________________________

______________________________________________________________

______________________________________________________________

______________________________________________________________

______________________________________________________________

______________________________________________________________

______________________________________________________________

______________________________________________________________

______________________________________________________________

______________________________________________________________

______________________________________________________________

______________________________________________________________

______________________________________________________________

______________________________________________________________

______________________________________________________________

______________________________________________________________

______________________________________________________________

______________________________________________________________

## ORGANIZING, SORTING, AND NOTIFYING: WEEKS 9 TO 8

____ Obtain the post office's change of address kit by calling 1-800-ASK-USPS or visiting your local post office or *www.usps.gov/moversnet/* (where you'll find the form and helpful lists of questions and answers).

____ Complete and send the form.

____ List and notify people, businesses, and organizations who need to know about your move. You may not think of everyone at once, but keep a running list and add people to your list and notify them as you remember them. As you notify them, check them off your list.

____ Start sorting through your belongings to decide what to keep. Make plans to rid yourself of what you don't want: pick a date for a garage sale; call your favorite charity and set a date for them to come pick up donations; call your recycling company to find out what they will accept.

____ For moving insurance purposes, make an inventory of your possessions with their estimated replacement value.

____ If you have high-value items (such as antiques) that you expect to send with the moving company or ship separately, obtain an appraisal.

**Additional items:**

______________________________________________

______________________________________________

______________________________________________

______________________________________________

______________________________________________

______________________________________________

______________________________________________

______________________________________________

______________________________________________

## FINALIZING HOUSING ARRANGEMENTS AND ESTABLISHING YOURSELF IN YOUR NEW COMMUNITY: WEEKS 8 TO 6

____ **Home.** Select your new home and arrange financing; establish a tentative closing date or finalize rental housing arrangements.

____ **Schools.** Find out school calendars and enrollment and immunization requirements.

____ **Insurance.** Contact an agent regarding coverage on your new home and its contents as well as on your automobile.

____ **Finances.** Select a bank, open accounts, and obtain a safe deposit box.

____ **New Home Layout.** Sketch a floor plan of your new home and include room measurements. Determine how your present furniture, appliances, and decor will fit.

____ **Mail.** If you haven't found a new home, rent a post office box for mail forwarding.

____ **Services.** Find out the names and phone numbers of utility providers and what they require from you before they will start service (for example, a deposit, a local reference). (You can list your providers and service start dates on the checklist provided in this chapter.) Schedule service to start a few days before you arrive.

**Additional items:**

______________________________________________

______________________________________________

______________________________________________

______________________________________________

______________________________________________

______________________________________________

______________________________________________

## MAKING AND CONFIRMING TRANSPORTATION AND TRAVEL PLANS: WEEK 6

____ Schedule pick-up and delivery dates with your mover.

____ Make arrangements with your professional car mover.

____ If you need storage, make the arrangements.

____ Confirm your departure date with your real estate agent or landlord.

____ Make your travel arrangements. If you will be flying, book early for cheaper fares.

____ Map your driving trip using *www.mapblast.com* or ask your automobile club for assistance with route and accommodation information.

**Additional items:**

______________________________________________________________

______________________________________________________________

______________________________________________________________

______________________________________________________________

______________________________________________________________

______________________________________________________________

______________________________________________________________

______________________________________________________________

______________________________________________________________

______________________________________________________________

______________________________________________________________

______________________________________________________________

______________________________________________________________

______________________________________________________________

______________________________________________________________

______________________________________________________________

______________________________________________________________

______________________________________________________________

______________________________________________________________

______________________________________________________________

## UPROOTING: WEEKS 5 TO 4

____ Hold your garage sale, or donate items to charity.

____ Gather personal records from all health care providers, your veterinarian, lawyers, accountants, and schools.

____ Notify current utility providers of your disconnect dates and your forwarding address. (You can list your providers and service end dates on the checklist provided in this chapter.)

**Additional items:**

## MAKING AND CONFIRMING MOVING-DAY PLANS: WEEK 3

____ Make arrangements for a sitter for kids and pets on moving day.

____ Call moving-day volunteers to confirm move date and their arrival time.

____ Obtain travelers checks for trip expenses and cashiers or certified check for payment to mover.

____ Have your car serviced if you are driving a long distance.

**Additional items:**

______________________________________________________________

______________________________________________________________

______________________________________________________________

______________________________________________________________

______________________________________________________________

______________________________________________________________

______________________________________________________________

______________________________________________________________

______________________________________________________________

______________________________________________________________

______________________________________________________________

______________________________________________________________

______________________________________________________________

______________________________________________________________

______________________________________________________________

______________________________________________________________

______________________________________________________________

______________________________________________________________

______________________________________________________________

______________________________________________________________

______________________________________________________________

## WEEK 2

____ If you have a pet, take it to the vet for a checkup. For more pet-moving tips, see the section earlier in this chapter on moving with pets.

____ Arrange for transportation of your pet.

____ If you are moving into or out of a high-rise building, contact the property manager and reserve the elevator for moving day.

____ Reserve parking space for the professional moving van or your rental truck. You may need to obtain permission from your rental property manager or from the city.

____ Drain oil and gas from all your power equipment and kerosene from portable heaters.

**Additional items:**

________________________________________
________________________________________
________________________________________
________________________________________
________________________________________
________________________________________
________________________________________
________________________________________
________________________________________
________________________________________
________________________________________
________________________________________
________________________________________
________________________________________
________________________________________
________________________________________
________________________________________
________________________________________

## MOVING WEEK

____ Defrost the freezer.

____ Give away any plants you can't take with you.

____ Pack your luggage and your necessary box for the trip (see the list provided in this chapter).

____ Get everything but the day-to-day essentials packed and ready to go.

**Additional items:**

______________________________________________

______________________________________________

______________________________________________

______________________________________________

______________________________________________

______________________________________________

______________________________________________

______________________________________________

______________________________________________

______________________________________________

______________________________________________

______________________________________________

______________________________________________

______________________________________________

______________________________________________

## MOVING DAY

____ Mark off parking space for the moving van using cones or chairs.

____ See "Moving Day" section of chapter 5 for further to-do items.

CHAPTER 5

# Getting from Here to There: Moving Day and Beyond

This chapter guides you through the next stage in your move: moving day, arriving, unpacking, and settling in. Here you'll find important travel tips for both the self-move and the professional move, information related to a professional car move, and pointers for your first days and weeks in your new home.

## The Professional Move

Early on moving day, reserve a large place for the moving truck to park. Mark off an area with cones or chairs. If you need to obtain parking permission from your apartment complex manager or the local government, do so in advance.

### GUIDE THE MOVERS

Before work starts, walk through the house with the movers and describe the loading order. Show them the items you plan to transport yourself. (It's best if these are piled in one area and clearly marked, maybe even covered with a sheet or blanket until you're ready to pack them in your car.)

Remain on-site to answer the movers' questions and to provide special instructions.

### BEFORE YOU DEPART

Before you hit the road, you will need to take care of some last-minute details:

- Walk through your home to make sure everything was loaded.
- Sign the bill of lading. But first, read it carefully and ask any questions. The bill of lading is a document the government requires movers to complete for the transportation of supplies, materials, and personal property. The mover is required to have a signed copy on hand, and you should keep your copy until the move is complete and any claims are settled.
- Follow the movers to the weigh station. Your bill will be partly based on the weight of your property moved.

### UNLOADING AND MOVING IN

Be sure to take care of these details once the movers arrive at your new home:

- Have your money ready. (Professional movers expect payment in full before your goods are unloaded.)
- Check for damage as items are unpacked and report it right away.
- Unless the company's policy prohibits the acceptance of gratuities, it is customary to tip each mover. $20 is a good amount; you may want to tip more or less based on the service you receive.

## The Self-Move

The following tips should help you organize and guide your help, as well as make the moving day run more smoothly:

- The day before your move, create a task list. Besides the obvious (loading the truck), this list will include tasks such as disconnecting the washer and dryer and taking apart furniture that can't be moved whole.

- Plan to provide beverages and food for your volunteers. Make it easy on yourself and provide popular options such as pizza or sub sandwiches (delivered), chilled soda pop and bottled water (in an ice chest, especially if you're defrosting and cleaning the refrigerator).
- On moving day, remember, you are only one person. So if you need to defrost the freezer or pack last-minute items, choose and appoint someone who knows your plan to oversee the volunteers and answer questions.
- Be sure you have almost everything packed before your help arrives. Last-minute packing creates even more chaos and it's likely that hastily packed items will be damaged during loading or transit.
- If you end up with an even number of people, it's natural for people to work in pairs because they can carry the items that require two people. If you have an odd number of people, the extra person can rotate in to provide for breaks, carry light items alone, or work on tasks you assign.
- Be sure to match a person's physical ability and health with the tasks you assign.
- Appoint the early shift to start on tasks such as disconnecting the washer and dryer and taking apart furniture (such as bed frames) that can't be moved whole.
- Before work starts, walk through the house with your volunteers and describe your loading plan.

**MOVING TIP**

A few weeks before you move, start eating the food in your freezer. Also use up canned food, which is bulky and heavy to move.

- Know your moving truck and how it should be packed for safe handling on the road (ask the truck rental company for directions).
- Load the truck according to the directions your truck rental agency gave you. Tie furniture items (especially tall ones) to the inside wall of the truck. Pack everything together as tightly as possible, realizing that items will still shift somewhat as you travel.

## Move Travel

### GETTING TO SEATTLE

You can arrive in Seattle by land, sea, or air. Land access offers two alternatives: conventional interstate freeway travel, or Amtrak rail service. The Interstate 5 (I-5) is the route of choice for both northbound drivers migrating up the West Coast and southbound drivers arriving from Canada or Alaska. Westward motorists entering from Idaho will likely select the scenic Interstate 90 freeway. Amtrak trains arrive conveniently in downtown Seattle at the historic King Street Station. Of course, Greyhound offers interstate bus transport to their Seattle station on Stewart Street. For information, call (800) 231-2222.

For the maritime set, Seattle is a popular port among cruise-lines. More adventurous mariners may wish to join the 1,500 private vessels which annually navigate through the picturesque San Juan Islands to Puget Sound. For details, contact Port of Seattle (206) 728-3000.

Take a tape measure and your notebook with you. Measure rooms; sketch your new home and write room measurements on your sketch. Before you move, you'll know whether your current furniture will fit and will have a good idea of how it should be arranged.

If you choose air travel, your flight will be one of 400,000 that land annually at Seattle-Tacoma International Airport. "Sea-Tac" is just sixteen miles from downtown Seattle, and there are several routes available. The easiest one exits the Main Terminal parking structure and follows signs directing traffic "To Freeways." Proceed east on State Route 518 (SR 518) to I-5 North. This freeway provides a straight shot to downtown Seattle. The city's "Hotel Row" is best accessed by taking the Seneca Street Exit.

Interstate 405 (I-405) North is the best way to reach the sprawling suburbs of the "eastside." However, it is also possible to get to the eastside by continuing northbound on I-5, passing the Space Needle on your left, to State Route 522 (SR 522) East, and crossing Lake Washington via a "floating bridge."

As with all major airports, Sea-Tac offers taxi, shuttle, limousine, and public and commercial bus services:

Metro Bus: (206) 553-3000

Gray Line Airport Express: (206) 626-6088

Sea-Tac International Taxi Association: (206) 246-9999

SuperShuttle: (206) 622-1424

Airporters: (206) 431-5904

## SELF-MOVE—DRIVING A TRUCK

- A loaded moving truck handles far differently from the typical car. Allow extra space between you and the vehicle you're following. Drive more slowly and decelerate and brake sooner—there's a lot of weight sitting behind you.
- Realize that no one likes to follow a truck. Other drivers may make risky moves to get ahead of you, so watch out for people passing when it's not safe.
- Know your truck's height and look out for low overhangs and tree branches. Especially be aware of filling station overhang height.
- Most accidents in large vehicles occur when backing. Before you back, get out, walk around, and check for obstacles. Allow plenty of maneuvering room and ask someone to help you back. Ask

them to stay within sight of your sideview mirror—and talk over the hand signals they should use as they guide you.

- Stop and rest at least every two hours.
- At every stop, do a walk-around inspection of the truck. Check tires, lights, and the cargo door. (If you're towing a trailer, check trailer tires, door, hitch, and hitch security chain.) Ask your truck rental representative how often you should check the engine oil level.
- At overnight stops, park in a well-lighted area and lock the truck cab. Lock the cargo door with a padlock.

## IF YOU'RE FLYING OR TRAVELING BY TRAIN OR BUS

- Coordinate with the moving van driver so that you arrive at about the same time.
- Plan for the unexpected such as delays, cancellations, or missed connections.
- Keep in touch with the truck driver (by cell phone, if possible), who may also experience delays for any number of reasons: mechanical problems, road construction, storms, or illness.
- Dress comfortably.
- If you are traveling with young children, dress them in bright, distinctive clothing so you can easily identify them in a crowded airport, train station, or bus terminal.

## PROFESSIONAL MOVERS MAY NEED HELP, TOO

Make sure the movers have directions to your new home. Plan your travel so that you will be there to greet them and unlock. Have a backup plan in case one of you gets delayed. It is also a good idea to exchange cell phone numbers with the driver so you can stay in touch in case one of you is delayed.

## TIPS FOR A PROFESSIONAL CAR MOVE

A professional car carrier company can ship your car. Alternatively, your moving company may be able to ship it in the van along with your household goods. Ask around and compare prices.

- Be sure that the gas tanks are no more than one-quarter full.
- It's not wise to pack personal belongings in your transported auto, because insurance typically won't cover those items.
- If your car is damaged in transport, report the damage to the driver or move manager and note it on the inventory sheet. If you don't, the damage won't be eligible for insurance coverage.

## Unpacking and Getting Settled

You made it. Welcome home! With all the boxes and bare walls, it may not feel like home just yet, but it soon will. You're well on your way to getting settled and having life return to normal. As you unpack boxes, arrange the furniture, and hang the pictures, here are a few things to keep in mind:

- Approach unpacking realistically. It's not necessary (and probably not possible) to unpack and arrange everything on the first day.
- Find your cleaning supplies and do any necessary cleaning.
- Consider your family's basic needs (food, rest, bathing) and unpack accordingly:

  Kitchen: Start with the basics; keep less frequently used items in boxes until you decide your room and storage arrangements.

  Bedrooms: Unpack bedding and set up and make beds.

  Bathroom: Because this tends to be a small room with little space for boxes, unpack the basics early and find a place to store the still-packed boxes until you have a chance to finish.

### MAINTAINING NORMALCY . . . STARTING FRESH

During the move and the days following, it's good to keep things feeling as normal as possible. But this can also be a fresh starting point: a time to establish (or reestablish) family rituals and traditions. Beyond the family, this is a time to meet and connect with new neighbors, schoolmates, and your religious or other community.

- Keep regular bedtimes and wake-up times (naps for kids if appropriate).

- If you typically eat dinner together, continue to do this, despite the chaos.
- If you typically have a regular family time—an activity or outing—don't feel bad if you must skip it one week due to move-related chores, but restart this ritual as soon as you can. In fact, your family may appreciate this special time even more in the midst of the upheaval and change.

Rome wasn't built in a day, and neither are friendships. If your move means you have to start over, take heart: persistence and work will pay off over time. Here are a few suggestions for making your first connections with people—both individuals and communities of people—in your new area.

- Encourage family members who need encouragement in making new friends.
- Provide opportunities for building friendships from day one. Take a break from unpacking and knock on doors to meet neighbors. (It's not a good idea to start a friendship by asking for help unloading, though!)
- Get involved in activities your family enjoys and make time in your schedule for people, even though moving and resettling is a hectic and busy time.
- Meet and connect with your religious or other community.

## DISCOVERING YOUR COMMUNITY

Here you'll find suggestions for getting settled in your new surroundings:

- Be sure every family member gets a feel for the neighborhood and main streets; memorizes your new address; learns (or carries) new home, office, and mobile phone numbers; and knows how to contact local emergency personnel including police, fire, and ambulance.
- Go exploring on foot, bike, mass transit, or by car (turn it into a fun outing) and start learning your way around.
- Locate your local post office and police and fire stations, as well as hospitals and gas stations near your home.
- Scout your new neighborhood for shopping areas.
- Register to vote.

- If you have moved to a new state, visit the Department of Motor Vehicles to obtain your driver's license and register your vehicle (see below).
- If you haven't already done so, transfer insurance policies to an agent in your new community.

## IMPORTANT PHONE NUMBERS

### Public Utilities

**Puget Sound Power & Light**
*General Information:*
*(425) 454-6363*

**Seattle City Light**
*General Information:*
*(206) 684-3000*

**Washington Natural Gas (Puget Sound Energy)**
*Service & Accounts:*
*(888) 225-5773*

**Cascade Natural Gas Corporation**
*General Information:*
*(206) 624-3900*

**City of Seattle Water Department**
*General Information:*
*(206) 684-5885*

*Emergency 24-Hour Service:*
*(206) 386-1800*

**King County Department of Natural Resources**
*Water District Information: (206) 296-6519*

**MOVING TIP**

Draw up a detailed plan of your new home, including scale drawings of each room that show each piece of furniture you plan to take with you. Label furniture and boxes as to where they go in the new home, and have copies of the plan to put in each room there. This will give you at least a chance that most of the work of moving in will only need to be done once.

**Seattle Engineering Department**
*General Information: (206) 386-1218*

**Seattle Public Utilities ("Combined Utilities Package")**
*Water, Garbage, Sewer, Electric: (206) 684-3000*

**Seattle Solid Waste Utility**
*General Information: (206) 684-7600*

**Seattle Drainage & Wastewater Utility**
*General Information: (206) 684-7774*

**Hazardous Waste Hotline**
*(206) 296-4692*

## Telecommunications

**AT&T**
*(800) 222-0300*

**AT&T Cable**
*(877) 824-2288*

**Sprint**
*(800) 877-4646*

**GTE**
*(800) 613-9211*

**MCI**
*(800) 950-5555*

**USWest**
*(800) 244-1111*

## Police & Fire Protection (Non-Emergency)

### Police, Sheriff, and State Patrol

Beaux Arts: (425) 454-8580

Bellevue: (425) 452-6917

Bothell (425) 486-1254

Clyde Hill: (425) 454-7187

Hunts Point: (425) 454-1332

Issaquah: (425) 837-3200

King County (Sheriff): (206) 296-3311

Kirkland: (425) 828-1183

Lake Forest Park: (206) 364-8216

Medina: (425) 454-1332

Mercer Island: (206) 236-3500

Redmond: (425) 556-2500

Seattle: (206) 625-5011

Shoreline: (206) 296-3311

University of Washington: (206) 543-9331

Washington State Patrol: (425) 649-4370

Yarrow Point: (425) 454-7187

**MOVING TIP**

Unless company policy prohibits acceptance of gratuities, it is customary to tip each professional mover. $20 is a good amount; you may want to tip more or less based on the service you receive.

If you move yourself, you might also want to give each of your volunteers a gift. Cash or a gift certificate is a nice gesture. Perhaps one of your volunteers is a plant-lover and will cheerfully accept your houseplants as a thank-you gift. It's also a good idea to supply plenty of soft drinks or water and snacks for them!

### King County, Snohomish County, and Unincorporated Fire Districts

Beaux Arts: (425) 452-6892

Bellevue: (425) 452-6892

Bothell (425) 486-1678

Clyde Hill: (425) 452-6892

East Renton: (425) 255-5151

Hunts Point: (425) 452-6892

Juanita: (425) 828-1143

Issaquah: (425) 837-3130

Kenmore: (425) 486-2784

Kirkland: (425) 828-1143

Lake Forest Park: (425) 486-2784

Medina: (425) 452-6892

Mercer Island: (206) 236-3600

Redmond: (425) 556-2200

Seattle: (206) 386-1400

Shoreline: (206) 546-5716

Woodinville: (425) 483-2131

Yarrow Point: (425) 452-6892

### Emergency Services

Emergency Response: Dial 9-1-1

U.S. Coast Guard: (203) 217-6000

FBI (Seattle): (206) 622-0460

Crisis Clinic: (206) 461-3222 (Seattle); (800) 244-5767 (toll free); (206) 461-3219 (TTY only)

Washington Poison Center: (206) 526-2121 (Seattle); (800) 732-6985 (outside Seattle); (206) 517-2394 (TTY only); (800) 572-0638 (TTY outside Seattle)

### Pest Extermination

For free twenty-four-hour consumer tips regarding pest extermination, call (206) 442-2800.

- press 3605 for information about combating termites
- press 3606 to be advised about keeping pests out
- press 3608 for suggestions about choosing a pest control specialist

**Aard Pest Control**
*King County: (206) 575-3319*
*Toll-Free: (800) 359-6860*

**A Complete Pest Control**
*Seattle: (206) 362-2847*
*Eastside: (425) 454-2847*
*Toll-Free: (800) 394-2847*

**Alpha Ecological**
*Bellevue: (425) 451-4416*
*Lynnwood: (425) 774-2833*

**Cascade Pest Control**
*Seattle: (206) 525-0882*
*Bellevue: (425) 641-6264*
*Renton: (425) 255-1045*
www.cascadepest.com

**Critter Control Humane Removal**
*Seattle: (206) 431-6833*
*Bellevue: (425) 688-0188*

**Eden Advanced Pest Technologies**
*Seattle: (206) 587-5338*
*Bellevue: (425) 882-3205*
*Toll-Free: (800) 401-9935*

**MOVING TIP**

Reserve a large place for the moving truck to park on the day you move out. Mark off an area with cones or chairs. If you need to obtain parking permission from your apartment complex manager or the city, do so in advance.

**Good Earth Pest Control**
*Seattle: (206) 523-3473*
*Eastside: (206) 230-0420*
yp.uswestdex.com

**McDonnel Bugless**
*Seattle/Mercer Island: (206) 362-7425*
*Bellevue/Kirkland: (425) 454-2012*

**Orkin**
*Kirkland: (425) 803-0454*
*Mercer Island: (206) 232-7259*
*24-Hours: (800) 800-6754*
www.orkin.com

**Prism Guaranteed Pest Elimination**
*Seattle: (206) 625-9467*
*Eastside: (425) 637-8401*
www.prismservices.com

**Terminix**
*Seattle/Bothell/Kirkland: (425) 487-6643*
*Bellevue/Redmond: (425) 451-7876*
*Mercer Island: (206) 232-4704*
www.terminix.com

**United Exterminating Company**
*Seattle: (206) 632-1270*
*Bellevue/Redmond/Kirkland: (425) 747-1003*
*Bothell/Issaquah/Woodinville: (425) 747-1003*

## VEHICLE REGISTRATION

You must register your vehicle within thirty days of becoming a Washington resident. The minimum traffic fine for residents failing to license their vehicle is a whopping $330, so don't procrastinate! To obtain proper licensure for your vehicle, contact the County Auditor or subagent office nearest you. Subagent offices are privately owned licensing services that operate in concert with the Department of Licensing. If you're bringing a vehicle from another state, the Washington State Patrol will need to physically inspect and verify the Vehicle Identification Number (VIN). The charge for this is $15.

Also, vehicles manufactured since 1968 must pass an emissions test every two years. The charge for this is $12 and must be paid in cash. For more information regarding emissions requirements and the locations of testing centers, please call (800) 272-3780 or visit the Department of Ecology Emissions Web site at *www.wa.gov/ecology/air/emis-1.html*

Before applying for your new Washington vehicle license, make sure to have everything you'll need, including:

- current title and registration (or photocopy of title held by lien-holder)
- a Washington State Patrol inspection certificate
- certification of passing a DOE emissions test, if necessary
- personal photo identification
- an odometer reading if the vehicle is less than ten years old
- an empty scale weight slip (for trucks and trailers)
- cash or check for payment of licensing fees

How much are licensing fees? For passenger vehicles, the base fee is $30. For trucks, the base fee escalates according to declared gross weight, ranging from $35 (4,000 lbs.) to $70 (12,000 lbs.). Ancillary charges may include:

- filing fee, $7
- license service fee, $0.50
- fixed excise tax, $30
- clean air fee, $2
- local fee, $15
- title application fee, $1.25
- emergency medical services fee, $6.50
- decal fee, $0.50
- license plate fee, $7 (per pair)
- licensing subagent's fee, $7.50

So count on spending about $100 for first-time licensing. Personalized "vanity plates" will tack on another $46, and $30 each year thereafter.

Disabled persons may obtain a Parking Privilege Application at any vehicle licensing office or drivers licensing office. The application requires the signature of a medical doctor.

To learn more about the licensing and registration of vehicles, please contact:

**Department of Vehicle Licensing**
*P.O. Box 9909*
*Olympia, WA 98507-8500*

**King County License & Regulatory Service Division**
*500 4th Avenue Suite 401*
*Seattle, WA 98104*
*(206) 296-4000*

**Emissions Testing Hotline**
*(800) 453-4951*

## TAKING CARE OF THE FINANCIAL IMPLICATIONS OF YOUR MOVE

Now that you have arrived, you can take care of some of the financial and tax implications of your move. Here are some things to think about (it's also wise to consult an accountant):

- Some of your moving expenses may be tax-deductible. Prepare for tax filing by collecting receipts from your move. Also contact the Internal Revenue Service to obtain the publication and form you need. Visit *www.irs.gov* or call (800) 829-3676.
- State income tax. If your new state collects income tax, you'll need to file a state income tax form. For help with your relocation-related taxes, visit *www.monstermoving.com* and check out the "Relocation Tax Advisor."
- Other income sources may have tax implications. As you prepare to file, you'll want to consider any other sources of income and whether your new state will tax you on this income. For example, if you are paying federal income tax on an IRA that you rolled over into a Roth IRA and your new state collects income tax, you may also have to pay state income tax on your rollover IRA.

## Home at Last

Once the truck is unloaded, the boxes are unpacked, and the pictures are hung, once you're sleeping in a *bed*—instead of on a loose mattress—you'll dream sweet dreams. Tomorrow, with the stress of this move slipping away behind you and the next move not even a faint glimmer on the horizon of your mind, you'll begin to discover the opportunities and savor the possibilities of your new city, new job, new school—your new home.

SECTION THREE

# Getting to Know Your Town

CHAPTER 6

# What's Around Town

Any jeweler will tell you. The more facets, the more brilliant a gem's sparkle. The Emerald City has lots of facets. Like other great cities—San Francisco, New Orleans, Boston—Seattle is full of character. Some might even say it has a split personality. On one hand, the city represents the hub of the Pacific Rim, an international marketplace with lively trade. On the other hand, it's the flagship of the Great Northwest: where early settlers staked their claim, taming the rugged timberlands. In short, it's the only place I know that has restaurants where you can wash down your salmon sushi with a microbrew called Cougar Mountain Ale.

Cozy seafood parlors and quaint pubs aren't the only places that reveal the town's charm. Seattle's uniqueness permeates virtually every aspect of local culture, including entertainment and recreation. From the crest of Capitol Hill to the First Avenue waterfront, virtually every block reflects the Three As on which Seattleites thrive: academics, arts, and athletics. Where else could one of the finest medical schools in the United States coexist with a Jimi Hendrix museum and a half-billion dollar ballpark? To say that Seattleites are an eclectic bunch is grossly inadequate. We have a monorail that travels one mile, two 70,000-seat football stadiums six miles apart, and a 600-foot Space Needle that still looks like something from the next century.

There's something for everybody in Seattle. Whether you have forty-five minutes to grab a quick bite or a three-day weekend to plan, whether you have loose change or a platinum card in your pocket, you'll find something to do in this chapter. So go ahead. Scribble in the margins. Dog-ear the pages. Paint with your highlighter.

This is your backstage pass to the Emerald City.

## Libraries

**Auburn Library**
*808 9th Street SE*
*Auburn*
*(253) 931-3018*

**Ballard Library**
*5711 24th Avenue NW*
*Ballard*
*(206) 684-4089*

CITY FACT

Seattle's new, state-of-the-art NFL football stadium will open in 2002.

**Bellevue Regional Library**
*1111 110th Avenue NE*
*Bellevue*
*(425) 450-1765*

**Bothell Regional Library**
*18215 98th Avenue NE*
*Bothell*
*(425) 486-7811*

**Burien Library**
*14700 6th Avenue SW*
*Burien*
*(206) 296-5045*

**Everett Public Library**
*2702 Hoyt Avenue*
*Everett*
*(425) 259-8020*

**Federal Way Library**
*848 South 320th Street*
*Federal Way*
*(253) 839-0257*

**Green Lake Library**
*7364 East Green Lake Drive North*
*Seattle*
*(206) 684-7547*

**Issaquah Library**
*120 East Sunset Way*
*Issaquah*
*(425) 392-5430*

**Kent Regional Library**
*212 Second Avenue N*
*Kent*
*(253) 859-3330*

**King County Main Library**
*300 Eighthth Avenue N*
*Seattle*
*(206) 684-6600*

**Kirkland Library**
*308 Kirkland Avenue*
*Kirkland*
*(425) 822-2459*

**Lake City**
*12501 28th Avenue NE*
*Seattle*
*(206) 684-7517*

**Lynnwood Library**
*19200 44th Avenue W*
*Lynnwood*
*(425) 778- 2148*

**Mercer Island Library**
*4400 88th Avenue SE*
*Mercer Island*
*(20) 236-3537*

**North Bend Library**
*115 East Fourth Street*
*North Bend*
*(425) 888-0554*

**Queen Ann Library**
*400 West Garfield Street*
*Queen Anne*
*(206) 386-4227*

**Redmond Library**
*15990 Northeast 85th Street*
*Redmond*
*(425) 885-1861*

**Renton Public Library**
*100 Mill Avenue*
*Renton*
*(425) 235-2610*

**Seattle Public Library**
*1000 Fourth Avenue*
*Seattle*
*(206) 386-4636*

**Tacoma Public Library**
*1102 Tacoma Avenue S*
*Tacoma*
*(253) 591-5607*

**University Library**
*5009 Roosevelt Way NE*
*Seattle*
*(206) 684-4063*

**Vashon Island Library**
*17210 Vashon Highway SW*
*Vashon Island*
*(206) 463-2069*

MOVING TIP

Before leaving, carefully search your attic, basement, and garage. That dusty shoebox just might contain your vintage baseball cards: worth a small fortune.

**West Seattle Library**
*2306 42nd Avenue SW*
*West Seattle*
*(206) 684-7444*

**Woodinville Library**
*17105 Avondale Road NE*
*Woodinville*
*(425) 788-0733*

**King County Library System**

www.kcls.org

webmaster@kcls.org

## Museums

Seattle is a city rich in history, and it has preserved its history well. The museums pay homage to everything from log cabins to spacecraft. Most are free; others charge a modest admission fee.

**Bothell Historical Museum**
*9919 Northeast 180th Street*
*Bothell*
*(425) 486-1889*

Located in The Park at Bothell Landing, this 1893 home showcases exceptional turn-of-the-century furnishings. The Fourth of July Celebration is one of the oldest in America. Outdoor summer concerts at nearby Sammamish River are a popular bonus. Admission is free, but limited to Sundays from 1:00 P.M. to 4:00 P.M., April through mid-December.

**Burke Museum of Natural History**
*University of Washington*
*17th Avenue NE and Northeast 45th Street*
*Seattle*
*(206) 543-5590*

www.washington.edu/burkemuseum

Dinosaur skeletons, a walk-through volcano, and an incredible Ice Age exhibit are just the beginning. Interactive features include a history of the Pacific Rim and one of the country's largest collections of Northwest native art. Open daily from 10:00 A.M. to 5:00 P.M., Thursday until 8:00 P.M. Suggested donations of $5.50 adults, $4 seniors, $2.50 students, under 5 free.

**The Children's Museum**

*305 Harrison Street*
*Seattle*
*(206) 441-1768*

www.thechildrensmuseum.org

Interactive learning and hands-on activities for children ages 1 to 13 make this a popular museum. Discovery Bay, Cog City, Global Village, Time Trek, and Mindscape are just a few exhibits to choose from. Open weekdays from 10:00 A.M. to 5:00 P.M., and weekends from 10:00 A.M. to 6:00 P.M. Located on the lower level of Center House at Seattle Center. $4 adults, $5.50 children 12 and under.

**The Children's Museum of Tacoma**

*936 Broadway*
*Tacoma*
*(253) 627-6031*

www.childrenoftacoma.org

Child-friendly exhibits promote a free exploration of arts and sciences. Close encounters of life experiences capture the imagination of toddler and early elementary students alike. Open Tuesday through Saturday, 10:00 A.M. to 5:00 P.M, Friday until 9:00 P.M. $3 adults, $4 children 3–12, under 3 free.

**Coast Guard Museum Northwest**

*1519 Alaskan Way South*
*Seattle*
*(206) 217- 6993*

An extensive collection of Coast Guard memorabilia, nautical artifacts, and elaborate ship models are displayed. Tours of Coast Guard cutters are offered on weekends. Admission is free. Open Monday, Wednesday, and Friday 9:00 A.M. to 3:00 P.M., and weekends, 1:00 P.M. to 5:00 P.M. Located at Pier 36.

**Gilman Town Hall Museum**

*165 SE Andrews Street*
*Issaquah*
*(425) 392-3500*

www.issaquahhistory.org

Northwest coal magnate L. B. Andrew's collection of ninteenth-century furniture and artifacts is preserved in this museum. You may wish to "do a little time" in the Old Jail, too! Admission is free. Hours vary. Please call for details.

**Issaquah Historic Depot**

*50 Raineer Boulevard NE*
*Issaquah*
*(425) 392-2322*

www.issaquahhistory.org

Listed on the National Register of Historic Places, this museum caters to connoisseurs of railroad memorabilia. Vintage railcars and a World War II troop-train kitchen car are featured. Exhibits also include replicas of historic Burlington Northern routes. Open Saturdays except holiday weekends.

**Log House Museum**

*3003 61st Avenue SW*
*West Seattle*
*(206) 938-5293*

An authentic, turn-of-the-century log house preserves the heritage of the Duwamish and early Northwest settlers. The museum is conveniently located in the tourist village at Alki. Open Thursday, noon to 6:00 P.M., Friday, 10:00 A.M. to 3:00 P.M., and weekends, noon to 3:00 P.M. Donations of $2 for adults and $1 for children are encouraged.

**Marymoor Museum**

*6046 West Lake Sammamish*
*Parkway NE*
*Redmond*
*(425) 885- 3684*

www.marymoormuseum.org

Dedicated to the history of the Greater Eastside, exhibits trace industrial growth from logging to software. The impact of industrial growth on suburban culture is also chronicled. Open Tuesday through Thursday, 11:00 A.M. to 4:00 P.M., Sunday, 1:00 P.M. to 4:00 P.M.

**MOVING TIP**

Family, neighbors, friends, and co-workers make excellent movers. Plan on two persons for every 1,000 square feet of current living space. Double this figure if you are moving to and from two-story structures.

**Meeker Mansion**

*312 Spring Street*
*Puyallup*
*(253) 848-1770*

www.meekermansion.org

The National Register of Historic Places describes this unique house as "an elegant, 1890 Italianate Victorian." It is the meticulously maintained residence of pioneer Ezra Meeker and now the site of special events throughout the year. Open Wednesday through Sunday, 1:00 P.M. to 4:00 P.M. $4 adults, $3 seniors and students, $2 children 11 and under.

**Museum of Flight**

*9404 East Marginal Way S*
*Seattle*
*(206) 764-5720*

www.museumofflight.org

One for the whole family. This museum is a tribute to flight, from Boeing's humble "Red Barn" origin to present-day avionics. Fifty painstakingly preserved aircraft are displayed. Interactive exhibits will challenge kids as well as grown-ups. Don't miss the Great

Gallery. Open every day, 10:00 A.M. to 5:00 P.M., and Thursday, 10:00 A.M. to 9:00 P.M. $9.50 adults, $5 youth, discount for seniors. Free admission on the first Thursday of each month.

**Museum of History & Industry**

*2700 24th Avenue East*
*Seattle*
*(206) 324-1126*

www.seattlehistory.org

A broad perspective of regional life and culture for the entire family. Hands-on learning centers for children, plus exhibits of air and sea transportation, antique cars, and sporting displays. The museum also houses artifacts of the Klondike Gold Rush that started it all. Located near Husky Stadium at the Arboretum, a visit to this museum can fit nicely into other plans. Open Tuesday through Friday, 11:00 A.M. to 5:00 P.M., and weekends, 10:00 A.M. to 5:00 P.M. $5.50 adults, $3 seniors and children 6 to 12, $1 children 5 and under.

CITY FACT

Moody's Investor Service rates Seattle's city bond issues "Aaa," making it one of only ten cities in the United States with such a rating.

**Northwest Railway Museum**

*38625 Southeast King Street*
*Snoqualmie*
*(425) 746-4025*

www.trainmuseum.org

The 1890 Queen Anne–style Snoqualmie Depot is listed on the Washington and National Register of Historic Places. It now houses the museum's rail-car exhibits, restored photograph archives, and railroad memorabilia. The depot remains a junction for Snoqualmie Valley Railroad excursions. Call for times and admission.

### Renton Historical Museum

*235 Mill Avenue S*
*Renton*
*(425) 255- 2330*

rtnmuseum@aol.com

This museum tells the story from Duwamish Indian encampment to coal mining to modern manufacturing. 5,000 photographs and a research library are maintained. Vintage vehicle buffs will appreciate the Ford Model A Coupe and 1927 fire engine. Admission is free; donations are welcome. Open Tuesday through Sunday, 1:00 P.M. to 4:00 P.M.

### Rosalie Whyel Museum of Doll Art

*1116 108th Avenue NE*
*Bellevue*
*(425) 455-1116*

www.dollart.com

Ranked by the International Doll Congress as the world's premier doll collection, this renowned museum will enchant more than just doll enthusiasts. There are 1,500 antique and modern dolls, plus hundreds of miniature houses, teddy bears, and vintage toys. The museum sponsors workshops for collectors and hobbyists. Open Monday through Saturday, 10:00 A.M. to 5:00 P.M., Sunday 1:00 P.M. to 5:00 P.M. $6 adults, $5.50 seniors, $4 youths 5–17, under 5 free.

### Snoqualmie Valley Historical Museum

*320 Bendego Boulevard S*
*North Bend*
*(425) 888-3200*

snoqualmievalleymuseum.org

This museum is dedicated to preserving the history and artifacts of Fall City, North Bend, and Snoqualmie areas. Native American objets d'art and pioneer memorabilia are featured along with historic photographs and logging equipment. Open Thursday through Sunday, 1:00 P.M. to 5:00 P.M., April to October. A donation of at least $1 per person is appreciated.

### Washington State History Museum

*1911 Pacific Avenue*
*Tacoma*
*(888) 238-4373*

www.wshs.org/wshm/home.html

The flagship of the Washington State Historical Society, this museum houses over 100,000 square feet of regional history. Exhibits include an authentic Coast Salish plank house and a full-size Boeing B-17. Hands-on, interactive learning kiosks will delight children. Nearby sites include historic Union Station. Open Tuesday through Saturday, 10:00 A.M. to 5:00 P.M., Sunday, 11:00 A.M. to 5:00 P.M. Admission is free on Thursday. Otherwise, $7 adults, $6.25 seniors, $5 students. Kids under five are free.

## Attractions

Washington has many distinct environments. What other state borders an ocean and features volcanoes, glaciers, a sound, and 14,000-foot peaks? Combine this geographic diversity with vast wildlife reserves, and you have the makings of a natural science mecca.

### Argosy Lake Cruise

*89 Kirkland Avenue*
*Kirkland*
*(206) 623-4252*

www.argosycruises.com

Educational as well as relaxing, Lake Washington cruises are very popular. Argosy's tours depart beautiful Kirkland Marina Park from May to October, weather permitting. Tour selections vary. Call for details.

### Boeing-Everett Tour Center

*I-5 to Exit 189 to Highway 526;*
*head West for 3 miles, follow signs.*
*(800) 464-1476*

www.boeing.com

This popular tour books quickly, but persist: It's worth the effort. Visit the world's largest building and see how 747s, 767s, and 777s are assembled. You can also take a drive along the test-flight line. The tour includes a video cassette. Strict requirements and guidelines apply, so call before visiting. Weekdays tours begin at 9:00 A.M., 10:00 A.M., 11:00 A.M., 1:00 P.M., 2:00 P.M., and 3:00 P.M.

### Cougar Mountain Zoological Park

*19525 Southeast 54th Street*
*Issaquah*
*(425) 391-5508*

www.issaquah.org/zoo/zoo.html

Primarily a teaching facility, the zoo specializes in threatened and endangered species. Programs are designed for schoolchildren and seniors, but everyone is welcome. You get a memorable view of Lake Sammamish and the Cascades, too. Special programs, tours, and events are featured, so call for a detailed schedule. Santa's Reindeer Festival in December is a favorite tradition. March to October, Friday through Sunday, 10:00 A.M. to 5:00 P.M. $6 adults, $5 seniors, $4.50 youth.

### Imax/Omnidome Theater

*Pier 59*
*Alaskan Way and Pike Street*
*Seattle*
*(206) 622-1868*

www.seattleimaxdome.com

The 180-degree dome screen explodes with an Academy Award–winning documentary of the Mount St. Helens eruption. Other acclaimed features include undersea adventures and space exploration. Shows daily. $7 adults, $6.50 seniors, $6 students, $5 children.

### Issaquah State Salmon Hatchery

*125 West Sunset Way*
*Issaquah*
*(425) 391-9094*

www.wa.gov/wdfw/

The exhibits are informative, but a "self-guided tour" is what you'll remember. Get up close and personal with thousands of Coho and Chinook salmon. Mature specimens are released in October as part of Salmon Days Festival. Open daily, twenty-four hours. Admission is free.

**Klondike Gold Rush National Historic Park**
*117 South Main Street*
*Seattle*
*(206) 553-7220*
www.nps.gov/klse/home.html

The park recalls Seattle's early years as an outfitter for the Klondike gold miners. Mining artifacts abound, but don't miss the gold-panning demonstrations and informative presentations. Located in Pioneer Square Historic District. Open 7 days a week, 9:00 A.M. to 5:00 P.M. Admission is free, but donations are appreciated.

**Odyssey, the Maritime Discovery Center**
*Pier 66*
*2205 Alaskan Way*
*Seattle*
*(206) 374-4000*
www.ody.org

Seattle history and industry are inextricably linked to the sea. The curators at Odyssey have developed fifty exhibits examining maritime trade, fishing, and the marine environment. Highly interactive, the Odyssey experience is both educational and entertaining. Try loading a 20-ton container aboard a cargo ship, or navigate a commercial fishing vessel through the challenging Bering Sea. Daily 10:00 A.M. to 5:00 P.M. $6.50 adults, $4 seniors and youth 5–18, children under 5 and members free.

**Pacific Science Center**
*200 Second Avenue N*
*Seattle*
*(206) 443-2001*
www.pacsci.org

Seattle's monument to science is a must-see. The center offers a weekend's worth of "infotainment" with 100 interactive exhibits and virtual reality experiences, a six-story Imax theater, planetarium, and laser concert. It also features a dinosaur exhibit, the Tropical Butterfly House, and live animals.

**Seattle Aquarium**

*1483 Alaskan Way*
*Seattle*
*(206) 386-4300*

www.seattleaquarium.org

With a focus on Puget Sound marine life, this aquarium is considered one of the nation's finest. Spectacular design—including a 400,000-gallon showpiece—and award-winning exhibits make this a favorite among tourists and locals. An outdoor touch-and-feel tidepool will enchant the children. See the world's heaviest captive octopus and the greatest constellation of living seahorses ever assembled, as well as the acclaimed Sound to Mountains exhibit. Daily, 10:00 A.M. to 7:00 P.M. summer, 10:00 A.M. to 5:00 P.M. winter. $8.50 adults, $5.75 6–12, $3.75 children 3–5, under 3 free.

**MOVING TIP**

A month before Moving Day, decide which items you wish to donate, give away, throw away, or sell. You then pack and move as little as possible, but also have a little extra cash and some tax-deductible donations. If you live in an area where more people move in particular seasons—like a university district—other families may want to participate in a garage or yard sale.

**Volunteer Park Conservatory**

*1400 East Galer*
*Seattle*
*(206) 684-4743*

Five climates are maintained in this 1912 Victorian-style conservatory, including tropical jungle and desert environs. Pampered in the elegant glass green house are nearly 2,000 varieties of orchids. Daily 10:00 A.M. to 4:00 P.M. Admission is free.

**Washington Park Arboretum**
*Graham Visitors Center*
*2300 Arboretum Drive E*
*Seattle*
*(206) 543-8800*

**Japanese Tea Garden**
*1502 Lake Washington Boulevard*
*Seattle*
*(206) 684-4725*

www.depts.washington.edu/wpa

A spectacular, 200-acre "living museum" on the shores of Lake Washington is the setting for camellias, hollies, Japanese Maples, and conifers. The collection ranks among the world's largest. Open daily 10:00 A.M. to 4:00 P.M. Admission is free.

CITY FACT

Legendary aviator Charles Lindbergh landed his famous *Spirit of St. Louis* in Seattle on September 13, 1927.

**Woodland Park Zoological Gardens**
*5500 Phinney Avenue N*
*Seattle*
*(206) 684-4800*

www.zoo.org

One of the most highly regarded zoos in the world; at 101-years-old, it's one of the oldest, too. More than 1,000 species of plant life and 300 species of wildlife are beautifully presented in painstakingly engineered environments that occupy 92 acres. The acclaimed African Savanna is unparalleled. Award-winning exhibits include Elephant Forest, Tropical Rain Forest, Trail of Vines, and Northern Trail. Visit one of the finest rose gardens in the world. Open 365 days a year 9:30 A.M. to 6:00 P.M. $8 adults, $7.25 seniors, $5.75 youth, toddlers free.

## Fine Arts

### Bellevue Art Museum

*Bellevue Square*
*Northeast 8th Street and Bellevue Way*
*Bellevue*
*(425) 454-6021*

www.bellevueart.org

Exhibits here showcase regional contemporary art and its relationship with everyday life, along with hands-on opportunities to create and explore art. Monday through Saturday, 10:00 A.M. to 6:00 P.M., Tuesday and Friday, until 8:00 P.M., Sunday, 11:00 A.M. to 5:00 P.M. $3 adults, $2 seniors and students, under 12 free. Second Saturday of each month is free.

### Frye Art Museum

*704 Terry Avenue*
*Seattle*
*(206) 622-9250*

www.fryeart.org

Nineteenth- and twentieth-century European and American representational (realistic) art is the primary focus of the Frye collection. However, Pacific Northwest art is exhibited along with "Earthscape: Artists in Alaska's Copper River Delta." Other offerings include poetry readings, concerts, photographic portfolios, and cine noir. Open Monday through Saturday, 10:00 A.M. to 5:00 P.M., Thursday, until 9:00 P.M., Sunday, noon to 5:00 P.M. Admission and parking are free.

### Henry Art Gallery

*University of Washington*
*15th Avenue NE*
*(206) 543-2280*

www.henryart.org

Modern and contemporary art, research and study facilities, and lecture and film series create a truly comprehensive art experience. Popular touring exhibits and convenient University of Washington campus location are reasons for return visits. Open Tuesday through Sunday, 11:00 A.M. to 5:00 P.M., Thursdays, until 8:00 P.M. Closed holidays. $5 adults, $3.50 seniors, free for high school and college students and children under 13.

### Pilchuck Glass School

www.pilchuck.com

The world's premier glass center founded by the glass guru himself, Dale Chihuly. More than a school or gallery, Pilchuck is the largest and most comprehensive education center for artists working in glass. In its fourth decade, the institution remains an international model for visual arts excellence. Pilchuck is situated on a serene, fifty-four-acre wooded campus in the Cascade foothills overlooking Puget Sound. The school retains an "experimental attitude and international character," showcasing the work of resident master glassblowers. There are three ways to experience Pilchuck: enroll, volunteer, or become a member of Pilchuck Society. For details, call (206) 621-8422.

### Pioneer Square Historic District

*Between First Avenue S and Alaskan Way and Madison Street and Yesler Way*

Enter eight square blocks of a bygone era. Pioneer Square, in the heart of the city, bridges historical architecture and contemporary culture with boutique inns, curio shops, and pubs. It also houses some of the very best galleries in Seattle, spotlighting local artists. Peripheral activities include the Seattle Underground Tour, Bell Street Pier, Safeco Field, and the famed waterfront. Arrive by trolley or horse-drawn carriage, and don't miss the galleries.

### Seattle Art Museum

*100 University Street*
*Seattle*
*(206) 654-3100*

www.seattleartmuseum.org

The world-famous "Hammering Man" statue is an ominous welcome to a fabulous museum. SAM has garnered international recognition for its fine Egyptian sculpture, Northwest Coast native mask collection, and American art. Special events include guest lecturers, family programs, and music and poetry nights. Open Tuesday through Sunday, 10:00 A.M. to 5:00 P.M., Thursday, until 9:00 P.M.. $7 adults, $5 seniors and students, 12 and under free.

## Performing Arts

### A Contemporary Theatre

*700 Union Street*
*Seattle*
*(206) 292-7676*

www.acttheatre.org

Historic Kreielscheimer Place is home of the acclaimed Young ACT Company. This theater offers modern works of drama, comedy, and musicals from May to November. Sister theater The Bullitt Cabaret hosts innovative productions, readings, workshops, and poetry throughout the year. The annual December performances of Charles Dickens's *A Christmas Carol* are a Seattle holiday tradition.

**MOVING TIP**

Feed and water your movers! It's a nice way to show your appreciation, and people tend to work better when they are happy, not hungry. Have pizza and cold pop delivered. This will make the move more of a fun event, and not just a chore.

### Bathhouse Theatre

*7312 West Green Lake Drive N*
*Seattle*
*(206) 524-9108*

Funny name, serious acting. Nestled on the shore of Green Lake, the theater company presents intimate and inventive drama, grounded in European and American tradition but often with contemporary twists. Entering its thirty-first season, Bathhouse Theatre is well established. Count on four to six plays each season.

**Bellevue Chamber Chorus**

*(425) 881-0445*

www.bellevuechamberchorus.net

For lovers of chamber music, this assembly of talent has few equals. The chorus performs throughout Seattle and the eastside.

**Bellevue Philharmonic Orchestra**

*Westminster Chapel*
*13646 Northeast 24th Street*
*(425) 455-4171*

www.bellevuephilharmonic.org

For nearly thirty-four seasons the Bellevue Philharmonic Orchestra has been presenting classical and pop concerts to generations of fans. Don't be surprised if an internationally known guest artist appears.

**Belltown Theatre Center**

*115 Blanchard Street*
*Seattle*
*(206) 781-3470*

Contemporary productions of dramatic literature are featured year-round. After hours, Belltown Theatre Center loosens up for late-night comedy and improvisation. Conveniently located within walking distance of Pike Place Market, there is much to do before and after performances. BTC is also home to the Clay Martin Puppet Theatre.

**CITY FACT**

Seattle incorporated in 1865, when the total population numbered only 350.

**Benaroya Hall**

*200 University Street*
*Seattle*
*(206) 215-4800*

www.seattlesymphony.org

bhmc@benaroyahall.org

This is the premier concert venue in Seattle and the spectacular new home of the Seattle

Symphony, directed by Gerard Schwarz. Its design includes the S. Mark Taper Foundation Auditorium and Recital Hall, with more than 3,000 seats. State-of-the-art sound and lighting are coupled with true elegance to create a perfect environment. Within one block are 5,000 parking stalls.

**Cabaret de Paris**
*Rainier Square*
*1333 Fifth Avenue*
*Seattle*
*(206) 623-4111*

A unique evening awaits fans of Seattle's only cabaret dinner theater. European themes include sensational Parisian song and dance numbers. Owner Annie Agostini has overseen the dinner show since 1967. The cabaret is within walking distance of the Sheraton, Westin, and Four Seasons hotels.

**Civic Light Opera**
*11051 34th Avenue NE*
*Lake City*
*(206) 363-2809*

www.cloonline.org

CLO is entering its twenty-second season of full-length musicals. Each year they perform four outstanding productions. Musical theater workshops for youth are also offered.

**The Empty Space Theatre**
*3509 Fremont Avenue N*
*(206) 547-7500*

www.emptyspace.org

In the historic heart of Seattle's Fremont neighborhood you'll discover this casual, 150-seat theater. Six innovative plays each season include original works as well as classic revivals with unsuspected twists.

**The Fifth Avenue Theatre**
*1308 Fifth Avenue*
*Seattle*
*(206) 625-1900*
www.5thavenuetheatre.org

Since its glorious debut as a vaudeville house in 1926, this theater has thrilled audiences from around the globe. The interior replicates the Throne Room of ancient imperial China's Forbidden City, Beijing. The Fifth Avenue Theatre is a visual delight in every way, hosting concerts, dance performances, lectures, and live broadcasts. The Fifth Avenue Musical Theatre Company, a vehicle for productions, focuses on presenting musicals through subscription series.

**Intiman Theatre Company**
*Seattle Center*
*305 Harrison Street*
*(206) 684-7200*
www.seattlesquare.com/intiman

The company presents world and West Coast premiers of original plays and classics. The six-play season runs from May through December at the Playhouse: an intimate, freshly remodeled, 500-seat venue located in Seattle Center.

**Kirkland Performance Center**
*350 Kirkland Avenue*
*Kirkland*
*(425) 893-9900*
www.kpcenter.org

Sporting a brand-new, 400-seat theater, Kirkland Performance Center hosts an impressive list of events every season. The best of regional music, dance, and drama is spotlighted. Lake Washington waterfront and downtown amenities are within walking distance.

### Kirkland Arts Center

*620 Market Street*
*Kirkland*
*(425) 822-7161*

www.kirklandartscenter.org

The century-old Peter Kirk Building is home to this magnificent center. Ten exhibitions each season focus on regional artists and subjects. Annual happenings include Summerfest at Marina Park and Holiday Arts & Crafts in December.

### Meydenbauer Center

*1110 Northeast 6th Street*
*Bellevue*
*(425) 637-1020*

www.meydenbauer.com

This place has a little bit of everything. From baroque music to "wiggle shows," from stand-up comedy to "inflatable theater," it's provided year-round as part of the Ikea Family Stage performing arts series. The Theater at Meydenbauer Center has over 400 seats from which to marvel at music, dance, drama, and cultural film noir. Part of downtown Bellevue's convention center, a bevy of engaging activities are available.

### Moore Theatre

*1932 2nd Avenue*
*Seattle*
*(206) 443-1744*

www.themoore.com

From avant-garde shows to heavy metal, you're bound to find it at the Moore Theatre. Smack dab in the middle of historic downtown Seattle, peripheral offerings for food and entertainment are plentiful.

**Northwest Chamber Orchestra**
*1305 4th Avenue, Suite 522*
*Seattle*
*(206) 343-0445*

www.wolfenet.com/~nwco

For twenty-eight seasons this orchestra has enchanted music lovers with its repertoire of pre-baroque and contemporary chamber works. Two series will be performed in Benaroya Hall and a third series in the Seattle Asian Art Museum at Volunteer Park. The orchestra is directed by Adam Stern.

MOVING TIP

Drive your rental truck around the block a few times and practice parking. You'll gain confidence and feel more comfortable when navigating highways. When the truck is full, however, it may handle differently, so make a trial run or two around the block after you've finished loading.

**On the Boards**
*100 West Roy Street*
*Seattle*
*(206) 217-9886*

Contemporary dance, music, and drama are featured in this Queen Anne Hill theater. For something different, check out the "multimedia performances." OTB's season is from October through July.

**Pantages Theatre**
*901 Broadway*
*Tacoma*
*(253) 591-5890*

www.broadwaycenter.org

Inspired by a theater in the Palace of Versailles, the eighty-three-year-old Pantages Theatre is the cultural epicenter of Tacoma. The 1,186-seat historic building is home to the Tacoma Opera, Symphony, City Ballet, Philharmonic, and Concert Band.

**Paramount Theatre**

*911 Pine Street*
*Seattle*
*(206) 682-1414*

www.paramount.com

This is the Grande Dame of Seattle stages. Headliners and Broadway touring companies play to full houses year-round. Renovated to its original luster, attending a Paramount Theatre event is like stepping back in time to an era of warm elegance. The Seattle Convention Center is within walking distance, and ample parking is provided by adjacent lots.

**Pacific Northwest Ballet**

*Seattle Center*
*301 Mercer Street*
*Seattle*
*(206) 441-9411*

www.pnb.org

The internationally acclaimed ballet presents a season with seven sensational programs, including the annual classic, *The Nutcracker.* From September through June, the ballet's home is the exquisite Seattle Center Opera House. Shakespeare, Bach, and American contemporary themes are among the favorites of resident and visiting ballet enthusiasts.

**Rialto Theater**

*310 South 9th Street*
*Tacoma*
*(253) 591-5890*

The dramatic Beaux Arts 1918 theater seats 750 patrons. The styling and detail are stunning, and the Northwest Sinfonietta and Tacoma Youth Symphony are guaranteed to sweep you away.

**Sammamish Symphony Orchestra**

*(206) 517-7777*

www.plateau.org/ssoa

Less well known than it ought to be, this orchestra—under the baton of conductor R. Joseph Scott—plays cozy community venues to the delight of audiences in the know. SSO can be found at Eastlake Performing Arts Center, Eastlake High School Auditorium, and Pine Lake Covenant Church, among other venues.

**Seattle Center**

*305 Harrison Street*
*Seattle*
*(206) 684-8582*

www.seattlecenter.com

Classical and contemporary tastes can be satisfied at any of the venues in Seattle Center. Rich in performing arts, the center hosts the Opera House, Bagley Wright Theatre, the Playhouse, and Charlotte Martin Theatre. Seattle Center is the city's most comprehensive platform for cultural arts.

**Seattle Children's Theatre**

*Seattle Center*
*305 Harrison Street*
*Seattle*
*(206) 441-3322*

www.sct.org

This is one of the finest children's theaters in the Puget Sound area. From September to June, Seattle Children's Theatre presents a half-dozen mainstage productions for families and school audiences. Educational outreach programs and drama classes are available. Most theatrical and instructional programs are held in Charlotte Martin and Eve Alvord Theatres, in Seattle Center.

**Seattle Opera**

*321 Mercer Avenue*
*Seattle*
*(206) 689-7676*

www.seattleopera.org

Opera is masterfully presented during the August-through-May season at Seattle Center Opera House. German opera is the cornerstone of the repertory, and guest sopranos and tenors from Metropolitan Opera are frequently spotlighted. This is considered the finest opera assemblage in the Pacific Northwest.

**Seattle Repertory Theatre**

*Seattle Science Center*
*305 Harrison Street*
*(206) 443-2222*

www.seattlerep.org

Spanning a season from October to May, the finest community actors thrill audiences with five mainstage productions in Bagley Wright Theatre and four plays in Leo K. Theatre. Brilliant works range from classical to contemporary.

**Seattle Shakespeare Festival**

*(206) 467-1382*

www.seattleshakes.org

This is Washington State's only professional classical theater, and presents a three-play indoor season from September through April. Performances are staged at the University of Washington Ethnic Cultural Theatre and at the Children's Museum Theatre in Seattle Center.

CITY FACT

Seattle's fastest-growing sport is youth soccer, played nearly year-round on 5,000 acres of public parkland.

**Seattle Symphony**

*Benaroya Hall*
*Second Avenue and University Street*
*Seattle*

www.seattlesymphony.org

Internationally renowned, the Seattle Symphony is one of Seattle's most prized treasures. Performances at the sensational Benaroya Hall are consistently reviewed with strings of superlatives. With over 3,000 seats for weekly performances spanning September to June, you're sure to get a chance to savor the symphony. Approaching its 100th season, the Seattle Symphony is led by Maestro Gerard Schwarz.

**Snoqualmie Falls Forest Theatre**

*6800 David Powell Road*
*Fall City*
*(425) 222-7044*

Combine the uniqueness of outdoor dinner theater with the beauty of the Snoqualmie Falls forest and you have the ingredients for an unforgettable evening. For thirty-five seasons the Snoqualmie Falls Forest Theatre has been offering captivating weekend plays. But the season is short: from June through August. Get your tickets now!

**Tacoma Dome**

*2727 East "D" Street*
*Tacoma*
*(253) 572-3663*

The 23,000 seats are anchored beneath the world's largest wood-domed structure. Adjacent to the Tacoma Dome is the 28,000-square-foot Exhibition Hall, host of the professional hockey franchise Sabercats. You'll also find rock concerts, motor sports, and consumer shows on the schedule. Eleven parking lots accommodate over 3,000 vehicles.

**Tacoma Little Theatre**

*210 North "I" Street*
*Tacoma*
*(253) 272-2281*

www.tacomalittletheatre.com

This community theater's six-show season is infused with music, comedy, and drama. During summer months, a popular youth theater is featured.

**Tacoma Musical Playhouse**

*7116 Sixth Avenue*
*Tacoma*
*(253) 565-6867*

www.tmp.org

Every year this playhouse delights audiences of all ages with a variety of original and vintage productions. Events include four mainstage musicals and three "Musicals in Concert." But the hottest tickets are to the "Musical Murder Mystery Dinners!"

**Valley Community Players**

*231½ Main Avenue S*
*Renton*
*(425) 226-5190*

www.valleycommunityplayers.com

A homegrown repertory featuring original works, sketch comedy and improvisation in a casual environment. Some of the finest grass roots performing arts you'll ever find.

**Village Theatre Company**

*303 Front Street N*
*Issaquah*
*(425) 392-2202*

www.vt.org

Live family entertainment is the focus of this inventive group of local artists. From September through June, Village Theatre Company produces four musicals and a play. Winter performances are held at First Stage Theatre, while summer events can be found at KID-STAGE.

## Restaurants

The Pacific Northwest celebrates international cuisine, and Seattle is the epicurean epicenter of it all. With sweeping panoramas of Puget Sound, the Cascades, and the Emerald City skyline, Seattle presents some of the most captivating and inventive restaurants you'll encounter anywhere. You'll discover that cuisine, motifs, and prices can be light-years apart. One thing's for sure: With names like AroSpace, Area 51, Asteroid Café, Gravity Bar, Sophie's Cosmic Café, and Space Needle Restaurant, Seattle's kitchens and bars can be out of this world.

Great restaurants are where you find them. Like any metropolitan area, Seattle has a concentration of fine eateries. "Restaurant Row" is on First Avenue at the waterfront. But Capitol Hill, Queen Anne, Fremont, Green Lake, Bellevue, and Kirkland also offer distinctive dining districts. Don't limit yourself. Culinary excellence awaits you in the most unexpected places. My favorite restaurant is out in the boonies, in a rustic lodge perched on the edge of a waterfall.

This list is a deliberately mixed bag of goodies. It includes classic Four-Stars. Neighborhood cafés and bistros are in here, too. So are rib joints, chop and chowder houses, griddle parlors, and hot dog stands. There's even a "cereal salon." One criterion guided the selection process: To make the cut they had to be the best of their kind.

### 5 Spot ★

*1502 Queen Anne Avenue N*
*Seattle*
*(206) 285-7768*

A legendary hangout. Working class grub in this kitschy, Brooklynesque diner is creative and tasty. Sweet potato pasta and beef brisket marinated in Coca-Cola and onion soup are reasons why the flannel-and-denim set faithfully line up for more.

**Adriatica ★★★**
*1107 Dexter Avenue N*
*Seattle*
*(206) 285-5000*

www.opentable.com

This Mediterranean treasure is popular among romantics. Neo-Terra Cotta décor gives a feel of cozy elegance. The view may be gone, but the spirit is alive with signature appetizers like calamari with skorthalia and dishes like grilled pork tenderloin with cranberry port sauce.

CITY FACT

On October 21, 1962, President John F. Kennedy abruptly cancelled plans to speak at the closing ceremonies of the Seattle World's Fair, citing a "cold" and the need for "bed rest." This was a ruse. Unbeknownst to the American public, the Cuban Missile Crisis was unfolding, marking the closest the United States and Soviet Union would come to nuclear war.

**Afrikando West African Cuisine ★★**
*2904 First Avenue*
*Seattle*
*(206) 374-9714*

From décor to drinks, from music to menu, this West African restaurant is utterly authentic. Chef/Owner Jacques Sarr is a native of Senegal, and the culinary genius behind such pleasures as Thiebu Djen and Boulette. Sipping Hibiscus-Root Juice to the sultry Wolof rhythm is hypnotic.

**Assagio Ristorante ★★★**
*2010 Fourth Avenue*
*Seattle*
*(206) 441-1399*

Owner Mauro Golmarvi's masterpiece was the 1997 Seattle Reader's Poll pick for "Best Italian Restaurant." This author agrees. The Crimini Mushroom and Cognac Sauce will make you rob a bank for more.

**Avenue One ★★**

*1921 First Avenue*
*Seattle*
*(206) 441-6139*

Not a bistro wannabe, but a real bistro. In the spirit of Escoffier, the French menu is imbued—not corrupted—by Northwest influences. Try for a seat in the back room, with fireplace and bay view.

**Axis ★★**

*2214 First Avenue*
*Seattle*
*(206) 441-9600*

The well-informed service staff will gladly guide you through the American-Asian à la carte offerings. That is, if you can jockey for position at the counter or vie for a booth.

**Ayutthaya Thai ★★**

*727 East Pike Street*
*Seattle*
*(206) 324-8833*

Seattle, it seems, has more Thai restaurants than does Thailand. But there's a crisp, distinct purity about Ayutthaya. The dishes are not a crude amalgamation of sweet, sour, hot, and salty flavors. They're a blend balanced with a chemist's precision.

**Bait House Coffee Shop ★★**

*5517 Seaview Avenue NW*
*Seattle*
*(206) 297-9109*

You can still buy bait in this adorably odd coffee shop, but why take your chances with rod and reel? Homespun soups, salads, lattes, and live jazz await the angler at heart. This catch is just west of the railroad bridge on the way to Shilshole Bay.

**Belltown Billiards ★★**
*90 Blanchard Street*
*Seattle*
*(206) 448-6779*

www.belltown.com

I'd rather pack a fork and spoon than a $2,500 custom cue at this "gentlemen's pool club." Fourteen tables of nine-ball? Just give me a barstool by the kitchen, where they serve perfect linguine and bruschetta 'til late.

**Book Store at the Alexis ★**
*1009 First Avenue*
*Seattle*
*(206) 382-1506*

www.alexishotel.com

Martinis, Melville, and Marinara. Readers and writers aren't the only devotees of this bookstore. Enjoy a letter-perfect drink and appetizer in the stylish comfort of the Alexis Hotel.

**Brasa ★★★**
*2107 Third Avenue*
*Seattle*
*(206) 728-4220*

www.brasa.com

Campagne was the springboard for Tamara Murphy and Bryan Hill's new Mediterranean splash. Stylishly informal, see-and-be-seen crowds gravitate to distinct venues: a lively lounge, romantic dining room, and gallery-level mezzanine. An ambitious but seamless menu connects Foie Gras, Potato Confit Arugula and White-Truffel Oil Pizza to Guinea Hen with Walnut-Oil Mashed Potatoes, Apricots, and Green-Peppercorn Sauce.

**The Brooklyn ★★★**
*1212 Second Avenue*
*Seattle*
*(206) 224-7000*

This Old Seattle–style oyster parlor pulsates with the pinstripe set at lunchtime. Dinner hours are better for savoring dry-aged, corn-fed Angus steaks and Seattle's best salmon. Never are there less than fourteen varieties of fresh oysters.

**Buca Di Beppo ★★**
*4301 200 Street SW*
*Lynnwood*
*(425) 744-7272*

Straight out of New York's Little Italy, this is lively family fare at its best. Homestyle Italian cooking reflects every Nonna's requisites: fresh ingredients and heaping plates. Go late. As patrons leave, the restaurant becomes a "museum" of vintage photographs and papal memorabilia.

**Bungalow Wine Bar & Café ★★**
*2412 North 45th Street*
*Wallingford*
*(206) 632-0254*

A lovely little house is perched atop a tiny poetry shop. Inside are couples and small groups enjoying "novel" wines and "vintage" books. It's cute, casual, and civilized. Never dull. Neatly presented small entrees are delectable, but the cheese plates and housemade soups are without peer.

**Calcutta Grill ★**
*15500 Six Penny Lane*
*Newcastle*
*(425) 793-4646*

www.newcastlegolf.com

The faux-sandstone exterior, polished walnut floors, and rich maple walls evoke thoughts of a Baronial castle. Dramatically enhancing this aura is the view from a 900-foot cliff of The Golf Club at Newcastle. It's purely intentional. So are the corn-fed Angus steaks and oversized pub sandwiches. Casual locals favor the Fisherman's Pie and Smoked Prime Rib. But don't expect to pay a king's ransom. The entrees are under $15, making Calcutta Grill the best bargain since the Louisiana Purchase.

**Campagne ★★★**

*86 Pine Street*
*Seattle*
*(206) 728-2800*

This is bistro minus bustle, French cuisine minus pretension. That equals restaurant perfection in the heart of Pike Place Market. Campagne offers three venues: fine dining in simple, countryside elegance; a fashionable but relaxed bar; and a garden-serene summer courtyard.

**Canlis ★★★**

*2576 Aurora Avenue N*
*Seattle*
*(206) 283-3313*

www.canlis.com

The tranquil Lake Union blufftop is all that remains of this venerable institution. Once tired and trite, the menu has been brilliantly refocused. A wine list slightly longer than *War and Peace* reigns as Seattle's most complete. Nibble on the Grand Marnier Soufflé as you ponder how valets flawlessly match car and driver without a ticket.

**Capitol Club ★★★**

*414 East Pine Street*
*Seattle*
*(206) 325-2149*

Cumin-laced salsa, manchego cheese, and exotic mustards inspire tapas-style feasting at Capitol Club. This modern Moroccan eatery is a magnet for locals, proving that chronically hip urbanites can also be well-nourished.

**Cascadia ★★★**
*2328 First Avenue*
*Seattle*
*(206) 448-8884*

www.cascadiarestaurant.com

Brandishing a "rain window" and garden-grown fruits and veggies, this gem is a glistening monument to all that is the Cascade Region. Sterling silver, mint white linen, and Limoges china telegraph class. If it isn't cultivated between the Cascade Mountains and the Pacific Coastline, it doesn't reach the kitchen. But any sharp corners are smoothed by the supper club notes of the piano and a casual lounge.

Seattleite David Stern invented the Smiley Face.

**Century Ballroom & Café ★★**
*915 East Pine Street*
*Seattle*
*(206) 324-7263*

www.centuryballroom.com

A newly renovated orchestra stage and 3,000-square-foot dance floor create a dazzling centerpiece for this unique café. Combine Latin dining and dance, or wine and waltz at this popular spot.

**Chateau St. Michelle Winery ★★**
*14111 Northeast 145th Street*
*Woodinville*
*(425) 488-3300*

www.chateauste-michelle.com

A picnicker's paradise, Chateau St. Michelle is more than just Washington's largest winery. One hundred manicured acres surround the historic Stimson Mansion and include an outdoor amphitheater. The concert series is a favorite of the wine-and-cheese crowd. Stock your basket at the gourmet shop or bring your own goodies. Tours are free.

### Chestnut Cottage ★

*929 East Front Street*
*Port Angeles*

Scrumptious and lovingly prepared country breakfasts are the specialty of this sleepy little Victorian cottage. Take the ferry.

### Chez Shea ★★★

*94 Pike Street*
*Seattle*
*(206) 467-9990*

www.chezshea.com

An alternative to Seattle's slick scene, this one's unabashedly romantic. Views from the third floor of Corner Market include Elliott Bay and Pike Place Market. The adjoining bistro and lounge offer à la carte selections, while the dining room is prix fixe.

### Costas Opa Greek Restaurant ★★

*3400 Fremont Avenue N*
*Seattle*
*(206) 633-4141*

Owner Costas Antonopoulos does his best to whisk patrons away to Mykonos by serving up authentic Greek Isle cuisine in whitewashed, kitschy surroundings. It's a tantalizingly convincing ploy aided by the flow of retsina and ouzo. But one of the greatest pleasures at Costas Opa is entirely Seattle: watching the Fremont bridge being raised and lowered to Athenian music.

### Crusty Loaf ★

*2123 Queen Anne Avenue N*
*Seattle*
*(206) 282-5623*

Calling the seductions of this quaint little bakery "bread" is like calling Michaelangelo's David "marble." To the delight of loyal legions, Crusty Loaf turns out a menagerie of exotic baked goods. Try the Jalapeño Cheddar Cornbread, Irish Soda Loaf, or Asiago Sourdough Rolls. Coffee cakes and strudel are tasty, but the wafting aroma of

Sticky Buns and Italian Chocolate Roll will make you camp out on the sidewalk for more.

**Cyclops ★★**
*2421 First Avenue*
*Seattle*
*(206) 441-1677*

A bohemian favorite has been resurrected and re-groomed. Cyclops's watchful neon eye rarely blinks at the ultra-hip Ace Hotel. The owners are artists and it's obvious. Creative retro interior and a full-spectrum menu showcase design talent and culinary savvy.

**Dahlia Lounge ★★★**
*1904 Fourth Avenue*
*Seattle*
*(206) 682-4142*

www.tomdouglas.com

Dichotomies abound at this gastronomic landmark. Glamorous but not impersonal. Airy yet intimate. Popular yet subdued. Chic but not showy. Excellent food and service quash any suspicions that a tradeoff is eminent. Anything with the housemade chevre is delightful, but don't leave without sampling the signature Coconut Crème Pie.

**MOVING TIP**

Don't back the truck up to the front door. You may save your movers a few steps, but the wheels on a fully-stocked truck can easily get stuck in soft grass or dirt.

**Daniel's Broiler ★★★**
*10500 Northeast Eighth Street*
*Bellevue*
*(425) 462-4662*

www.schwartzbros.com

A favorite of Eastside pinstripers since 1989, Daniel's is sophisticated but relaxed. A piano and oyster bar add to its surging popularity, but make no mistake: This is a steakhouse that has earned its charbroiled stripes. Cuts are of the prime, corn-fed class expertly cooked under the legendary 1,800-degree broiler.

**Diggity Dog ★**

*5421 Meridian Avenue N*
*Seattle*
*(206) 633-1966*

www.diggitydog.com

Home-ground sausages on fresh-baked buns make this the unofficial tubesteak emporium of Seattle. Bratwurst, Polish, Cajun, and Italian doggies top the list, but try the Hawaiian-Portuguese, Jalapeño, and Cilantro Turkey creations, too. House-made horseradishes and mustards are outstanding.

**Dilettante Chocolates ★**

*416 Broadway E*
*Seattle*
*(206) 329-6463*

www.dilettante.com

It was started by Seattle's first chocolatier and, yes, grandson of the pastry chef to Czar Nicholas II. But that's just history. The present is sweet and the future bright for Dilettante Chocolates. Soups and sandwiches are splendid, but let's face it: We're after chocolate, and this place has the best. Coupe Dilettante Sundae with Dark Chocolate Ephemere Sauce is paradise found.

**Dragonfish Asian Café ★★**

*722 Pine Street*
*Seattle*
*(206) 467-7777*

www.dragonfishcafe.com

Guests of the Paramount Hotel and locals mix at this popular Pan-Asian café. Delicately prepared seafood appetizers and exotic grilled entrees thrill the crowd until late. The Pachinko machine bar serves some of the city's most respected martinis. Try the Wasabe Mary.

**Dulces Latin Bistro ★★**
*1430 34th Avenue*
*Seattle*
*(206) 322-5453*

www.dulceslatinbistro.com

Chef and co-owner Julie Ann Guerrero has earned special license to use the term "Latin." At her gently appointed Madrona bistro, it means just about anything bordering the South Atlantic or Mediterranean. The eclectic becomes electric with Guerrero's artful, inventive blends of herbs, spices, and chilies. Hers are simply the best Dungeness crab cakes in Seattle.

**El Gaucho ★★**
*2505 First Avenue*
*Seattle*
*(206) 728-1337*

www.elgaucho.com

A 1950s supper club that's dedicated to meat and martinis. There are ostrich and venison filets for hard-core carnivores, and Peppercorn New Yorkers in Cognac Sauce and classic chateaubriand for refined beef eaters. The "Baseball-Cut" Top Sirloin and not-so-petite filet mignon are the city's best examples.

**El Greco ★★★**
*219 Broadway E*
*Seattle*
*(206) 328-4604*

Is the Greek food great? Owner Thomas Soukakos hired the chef, then married her. If that doesn't prove she can cook, one visit to El Greco will. Surprise! They also serve the best eggs Benedict in the world.

**Elliott's Oyster House ★★★**
*1201 Alaskan Way*
*Seattle*
*(206) 623-4340*
www.elliottsoysterhouse.com

An extensive remodel and menu re-engineering has catapulted this fish house to the top. Teak, copper, and rough-hewn timbers lend bucolic authenticity, but this is civilized seafood for the discriminating palate. Elliott's trademark 21-foot shellfish bar is Seattle's longest.

**Empress of Desserts ★**
*10246 Main Street*
*Bellevue*
*(425) 451-8616*

The brainchild of Cordon Bleu graduate and renowned pastry chef Leora Ger has been adopted. Don't fear. The new parents, Melissa Walpole and William Singer, are nurturing the little French bakery-café with lots of love. Soups and sandwiches are still glorious, and the desserts and wedding cakes remain peerless. Delivery service is available.

**Flying Fish ★★**
*2234 First Avenue*
*Seattle*
*(206) 728-8595*
www.flyingfishseattle.com

Industry meets gallery at this Pan-Asian seafood boutique. Fresh fish dishes are artfully spiced but tempered with a silky, smoky quality.

**Garage ★★**
*1130 Broadway*
*Seattle*

Yes, it was once a real garage. Grease monkeys have since evolved into trendy pool sharks at this hyper-hip bar/café/Nine Ball parlor. "International homestyle" fare provides late-night delectables and draws Seattle's rock 'n' jock celebs. This place is so cool the number isn't published.

**Gee Whiz ★**
*1925 Fifth Avenue*
*Seattle*
*(206) 441-0511*

"The World's First and Only Cereal Salon." Deep, white porcelain bowls are filled with the cereals you never outgrow. Rumor has it that the unpretentious eatery stocks 100 brands.

**The Georgian Room ★★★**
*411 University Street*
*Seattle*
*(206) 621-7889*
www.fourseasons.com

Established in 1924, this grande dame of the Four Seasons Olympic Hotel offers fine dining in Italian Renaissance style. The flawless interior and superb service will impress those with the bluest of blood. Wild game delicacies dominate the menu, but lighter seafood entrees are available.

**Hardened Artery ★**
*106 First Avenue N*
*Seattle*
*(206) 284-5003*

Go ahead. Throw caution to the wind and check your calorie counter at the door. This joint's about burgers and barbecue. Seasonal art shows will lower your diastolic and live music will restore your heartbeat.

**The Herbfarm Restaurant ★★★**
*195 Northeast Gilman Boulevard*
*Issaquah*
*(206) 784-2222*
www.theherbfarm.com

What was once a front-yard chive stand is now an herbal theme park. Herb shops, seventeen gardens, and a cooking school create lovely framework. The focal point, though, is a nine-course masterpiece you'll never forget. Dinner takes at least four hours, and costs $130 per person.

**The Hunt Club ★★★**

*Fireside Room at the Sorrento*
*900 Madison Street*
*Seattle*
*(206) 622-6400*

www.hotelsorrento.com

Mahogany, steaks and chops, and suits. Everything you'd expect of a "men's club restaurant." However, the intimacy of the Fireside Room and summer romance of the outdoor Piazza Capri draw young couples and special celebrations.

**I Love Sushi ★★**

*11818 Northeast Eighth Street*
*Bellevue*
*(425) 454-5706*

www.ilovesushi.co

The fish is like velvet at Tadashi Sato's Bellevue restaurant. If it were any fresher you'd need a permit to get it to your plate. Lively chatter and friendly chefs are the litmus test of a sushi bar, and this one passes with flying colors. Bargains like Flame Broiled Fish Cheeks and Chawan Mushi (yummy steamed custard) elevate I Love Sushi to stand-alone status on the Eastside.

**Icon Grill ★★★**

*1933 Fifth Avenue*
*Seattle*
*(206) 441-6330*

Gary Dethleff is a leading Seattle interior designer with over 200 restaurants on his résumé. Now he's added one to his portfolio. As owner, Dethleff had carte blanche to go crazy. And he did, unleashing a creative fury and culinary genius that is Icon. The menu is "down-home eclectic." Must-haves include Yellow Pepper Soup with Cashew Salsa, Bacon-Wrapped Meatloaf, and Texas Funeral Fudge Cake.

**Jitterbug ★**
*2114 North 45th Street*
*Seattle*
*(206) 547-6313*

Make it a retro evening. Catch a movie at the art-deco landmark Guild 45th Theatre, then hop across the street to nostalgic Jitterbug. Critique the film over a stack of the anytime-is-a-good-time Gingerbread Waffles.

CITY FACT

The Seattle suburb of Redmond is home to the headquarters of Microsoft Corporation. It is also the "Bicycle Capital of the Northwest."

**Judy Fu's Snappy Dragon ★★**
*8917 Roosevelt Way NE*
*Seattle*
*(206) 528-5575*

She's Seattle's undisputed Godmother of Mandarin Home Cooking, and the brains behind Pandasia, Black Pearl, and now her very own Snappy Dragon. So well trained, her understudies succeed with their own Mandarin ventures. Fu insists on hand-formed noodles, rolls, and dumplings. That's why the most coveted seats in the house are at the Jiao-Zi Dumpling Bar.

**Kell's Irish Restaurant & Pub ★★**
*1916 Post Alley*
*Seattle*
*(206) 728-1916*
www.kellsirish.com

The McAleeses fled war-torn Belfast and opened Seattle's premier Irish pub in 1983. Tucked into a cranny of Pike Place Market's Upper Post Alley, this treasure's worth the hunt. The Steak and Kidney Pie is splendid, but the Irish Stew is downright sacred.

### Kidd Valley Hamburger Company ★

*5910 Lake Washington Boulevard NE*
*Kirkland*
*(425) 827-5858*

www.ivars.net

Edging out such institutions as Bellevue Burgermaster, University District Dick's, and Downtown Hamburger Mary's, Kirkland's Kidd Valley on scenic Lake Washington Boulevard gets the nod. Sure, the grilled-to-order burgers, homemade fresh fruit shakes, and french fried mushrooms are killer, but the beachfront location is enchanting. Seeing a yacht drop anchor and the crew jet-ski to shore for a bag of burgers is not uncommon.

### Kingfish Café ★★

*602 19th Avenue E*
*Seattle*
*(206) 320-8757*

Nix the reservation idea. They're not taken. Everybody waits, even celebrities. That's the rule. Most people in line aren't first-timers. The upscale soul food is simply that good. The Buttermilk Fried Chicken with Apple Cider Collard Greens is dreamy. So is the Griddle Catfish with Fried Green Tomatoes in Chipotle Mayo. It's leisurely Southern dining made even better with occasional tracks by Gladys Knight and Anita Bakker.

### Le Gourmand ★★★

*425 Northwest Market Street*
*Seattle*
*(206) 784-3463*

The owner is the executive chef. Fresh fruits, vegetables, and herbs are grown in a garden just outside the kitchen, and are often picked upon ordering. How can you go wrong? You can't. Not with Bruce Naftaly's expert fusion of French techniques and local stock. The prix fixe menu is surprisingly reasonable, considering dressings of Chardonnay vinaigrette, Champagne and Chevril Beurre Blanc, Cognac, and mounds of caviar.

**Longshoreman's Daughter ★**
*3510 Fremont Place N*
*Seattle*
*(206) 633-5169*

The name's blue collar but this earthy, funky little place is no greasy truck stop. The food is natural and wholesome, never bland or drab. Pan-Fried Udon Noodles, Freshwater Prawns, and the always-clever Ravioli of the Day keep bringin' 'em back.

**Lush Life ★★**
*2331 Second Avenue*
*Seattle*
*(206) 441-9842*

Sister restaurant of Marco's Supperclub, Lush Life whispers with the restrained sensuality of a speakeasy. Patrons enter through a courtyard gate, evoking a feeling of being personally invited. Inside, this sense of belonging endures with warm hospitality. Nightly specials deserve accolades. Try the lobster risotto or gin-and-juniper marinated double-thick pork chops.

**Metropolitan Grill ★★★**
*820 Second Avenue*
*Seattle*
*(206) 624-3287*

Power lunches by day, relaxed sophistication by night. The Met's salads, soups, and shellfish rank at the top of Seattle's offerings. Connoisseur cuts of prime meat and city-style seafood satiates the urbanite appetite.

**Mistral ★★★**
*113 Blanchard Street*
*Seattle*
*(206) 770-7799*

"Mistral" refers to a blustery winter wind. The restaurant's pristine starkness is engaging: nicely reversing the more-is-more trend. This minimalist concept is limited only to interior appointments, which are soothing in their sterile whiteness. Service and menu, however, are anything but minimal. Chefs are impeccably schooled and their creations provide irrefutable proof. Neo-French entrees are decidedly original and wholly satisfying.

**Monsoon ★★**
*615 19th Avenue E*
*Seattle*
*(206) 325-2111*

The best Vietnamese cuisine in Seattle. Abandoning the brothy staples of the northern border, Monsoon's Saigonese menu draws from fresh vegetables and herbs indigenous to South Vietnam. Tastes and textures are compelling studies in contrast. Flavors collaborate instead of compete, and every bite holds rewards.

**Morton's ★★★**
*1511 Sixth Avenue*
*Seattle*
*(206) 223-0550*

www.mortons.com

Time rinses away as guests are whisked back to an era of steaks, cigars, and Sinatra. Tuxedo-clad waiters ensure butler-like service and make Morton's a magnificently marbled cut above typical steak and chop houses.

MOVING TIP

Keep items designated for commercial storage together, either in the front or rear of the truck, depending on whether the first stop is your new home or the storage facility.

**Nappy Griddle ★**
*3224 Rainier Avenue S*
*Seattle*
*(206) 723-5459*

If it can be flipped, it's on the menu. And breakfast items aren't the only lip-smackin' highlights featured at the Griddle. Frog legs, gizzards, catfish, oysters . . . if it fries, it flies. The Super Nappy Burger is topped with a split hot link, a wedge of pepperjack, and a fried egg. You may want to order a slice of Sweet Potato Pie to go.

**Nell's ★★★**
*6804 East Greenlake Way N*
*Seattle*
*(206) 524-4044*

The chef's the owner, and he named the place after his wife. Maybe that explains why sous maestro Philip Mihalski has poured his heart and soul into this instant classic. Upscale Northwest cuisine is the fare, and the menu is poetic.

**Nikko ★★★**
*1900 Fifth Avenue*
*Seattle*
*(206) 322-4641*

Dapper Japanese executives staying at the Westin Hotel dine at this lavishly appointed, Kaiseki-style restaurant. That's your first clue that Takeyuki Suetsugu's Nikko is for real. Your second clue is the wafting aroma of succulent fish and fresh meats sizzling on the teppan grill. The interior combines Scandi-chic with traditional Japanese.

**Noodle Ranch ★**
*2228 Second Avenue*
*Seattle*
*(206) 728-0463*

The hippest of Seattle's Pan-Asian noodle houses, the Ranch covers all bases. The interior, music, and service are stratospheric. And, oh, those wonderful, wiggly noodles! Try the Mekong Bowl, saving room for homemade tropical ice cream.

**Osteria la Spiga ★**
*1401 Broadway*
*Seattle*
*(206) 323-8881*

"Osteria" means inn. "La Spiga" refers to the supple heart of the wheat stalk. This Harvard Market restaurant, owned by Pietro and Sabrina Borghesi, presents piadina and crescione from their native Romagna. And that means authentic Northern Italian–Adriatic Coast sandwiches. Only two piadina-crescione restaurants exist in America.

**Pig & Whistle ★★**
*8412 Greenwood Avenue N*
*Seattle*
*(206) 782-6044*

The Blue Plate Specials keep coming and the cider brews keep flowing at this diner-meets-tavern. Food here is quick, cheap, and mouthwatering. The secret's out back, in the form of a 1940s-style smoker. Jerk prawns and baby back ribs are nice follow-ups to the white bean chili. Don't wimp out before a slab of Dense Bourbon Chocolate Pie.

**CITY FACT**

Seattle was the first city to deploy "bicycle cops."

**Pink Door ★★**
*1919 Post Alley*
*Seattle*
*(206) 443-3241*

Behind a ravaged pink door, wedged between gold columns imbedded in stone, you'll find a stunning rooftop view of Puget Sound. You'll also encounter luscious food and occasional cabaret and live music. The interior runs from Italian provincial to English gothic, just like the menu. Don't be afraid to sample such antipasti as bagna cauda and tapanada, then shift to grilled quail or lamb shank.

**Rain Dancer ★★**
*4217 University Way NE*
*Seattle*
*(206) 634-2433*
www.rain/dancer.com

This heady Native American eatery is located on the fringe of the University of Washington, near campus theater venues. It's perfect for an original, inexpensive meal before showtime and very vegetarian-friendly. Favorites of regulars include five-spice duck sandwich with apricot relish and Santa Fe grilled cheeses with black bean and spicy maize salsa.

**Salish Lodge & Spa ★★★**
*6501 Railroad Avenue SE*
*Snoqualmie*
*(425) 888-2556*

www.salish.com

This is it. The author's favorite. A rustic but stately lodge nestled in sleepy hills and perched beside the fury of Snoqualmie Falls. The waterfall—100 feet higher than Niagara—inspires a raging Northwest cuisine. Exquisite cuts of meat are house-carved and fresh fish filets are house-smoked, both to perfection. Sommelier Randall Austin has crafted a wine list of more than 600 varieties. It's the envy of connoisseurs around the globe. In winter, the Lodge is comfy, warm, and private. In summer, it is airy and lively. Treat yourself to a weekend.

**Salumi ★**
*309 Third Avenue S*
*Seattle*
*(206) 621-8772*

Restaurant know-how is in the genes. Shopkeeper Armandino Batali cures rare prosciuttos, copas, and Tuscan finnochiona the way his Italian ancestors did for centuries. His grandfather, Angelo Merlino, established Seattle's first Italian grocer in 1903. Batali's son, Mario, is a celebrity chef in New York. Salumi is more than Seattle's best homemade sausages and cured-meat sandwiches. Homespun salads, soups, and take-home suppers are painstakingly concocted.

**Santa Fe Café ★★**
*5910 Phinney Avenue N*
*Seattle*
*(206) 783-9755*

The city's first New Mexican restaurant is still its best. Trendy Tex-Mex places came and went, but this genuine Santa Fe kitchen has flourished over two decades. Why? The little things: spicy beer, blue and red tortillas, and savory guacamole are the best examples in town. Sherry-laced chili sauces and garlic custards elevate colorful dishes to new heights. Cleanse the palate with tequila sherbet and plow into a truffle torte with lime caramel sauce.

**Sapphire Kitchen and Bar ★★**

*1625 Queen Anne Avenue N*
*Seattle*
*(206) 281-1931*

"Little Plates" offer huge tastes at Sapphire, the latest addition to the Queen Anne neighborhood dining scene. Ruiz Redé brings his unique mix of Moroccan, Castillian, and Greek influences to this sultry suburban restaurant, which is drawing urbanites, too.

**Sazerac ★★**

*1101 Fourth Avenue*
*Seattle*
*(206) 624-7755*

www.kimptongroup.com

New Orleans minus the debauchery. Woven into the charm of Hotel Monaco is this upscale Creole restaurant. Colorful and giddy, Sazerac's interior reflects a lighthearted approach to dining. Taste sensations from the kitchen are equally delightful. Skillet-roasted mussels melt in the mouth, and Cajun stand-bys like gumbo and jambalaya are deftly delivered. Sauces are spirited, never harsh.

**MOVING TIP**

Encourage your children to pack their own clothing and toys. However, when the truck is being loaded and unloaded, have a relative, close friend, or trusted babysitter keep the children away from the action.

**City Fact**

Rome wasn't built in a day. Neither was Seattle. But both cities were built on seven hills.

**Shorty's ★**

*2222 Second Avenue*
*Seattle*
*(206) 441-5449*

www.shortydog.com

You don't have to go to Coney Island to get a good 'dog. Shorty's kielbasas, Germans, New York koshers, and Italian hotties are to die for. Wash one down with an ice-cold Lucky Stubby for a buck. Who's Shorty? He's the owner's dog. Yes, he is one of those weiner dogs.

**Six Degrees ★★**

*121 Park Lane*
*Kirkland*
*(425) 803-1766*

www.info@sixdegrees.com

The name sounds frigid, but this re-invented sidewalk tavern is warm and inviting. Butcher-block tables are perfect pedestals for the hearty American fare of succulent rotisserie hens, juicy center-cut New York steaks, and smoky chops. Two-dozen local brews and an impressive wine list complete a simple but remarkable dining experience.

**Spirit of Washington Dinner Train ★★★**

*625 South Fourth Street*
*Renton*

www.columbiawinery.com/train

All aboard for one of the most fascinating and novel dining experiences in Washington. Savvy tourists, nostalgia buffs, and romantic couples keep the reservation line ringing year-round. This four-hour odyssey covers forty-five miles of scenic Puget Sound landscape with a lovely stop at the Columbia Winery. Vintage railcars and white-clad servers recall the taming of the west and an era of transcontinental luxury. Gourmet cuisine and wines are as spectacular as the sights from your picture window. Parlor seating is fine, but the second-floor dome is wrapped in glass for a breathtaking panoramic view.

**Ugly Mug Café ★**
*1309 Northeast 43rd Street*
*Seattle*
*(206) 547-3219*

It didn't take a team of nerdy UW math professors to come up with this workable equation: a straightforward menu; crafted with quality ingredients; served in a comfortable setting; at a reasonable price. There's nothing difficult about the meatloaf sandwich, either. It's probably the best you'll ever eat.

## The Bar and Club Scene

**Area 51**
*165 South Washington Street*
*Seattle*

Small twenty-one-and-over club for dancing nondrinkers.

**AROSpace**
*925 East Pike Street*
*Seattle*
*(206) 320-0424*

Live and DJ, plus food, drink, and avant-garde art exhibits.

**The Backdoor Ultra Lounge**
*503 Third Avenue*
*Seattle*
*(206) 622-7665*
www.backdoorlounge.com

Rat Pack cocktails and board games in a cozy, dim hangout for rockers.

**Ballard Firehouse**
*5429 Russell Avenue NW*
*Ballard*
*(206) 784-3516*

Showcases touring artists, including Where Are They Now bands.

**The Baltic Room**
*1207 Pine Street*
*Seattle*
*(206) 625-4444*

Piano jazz around a fireplace for beer-and-wine singles.

**Bohemian Backstage**
*111 Yesler Way*
*Seattle*
*(206) 447-1514*

Live bands, dancing, and boutique brews draw funky mixed crowds.

**MOVING TIP**

Don't forget to make proper arrangements for the transfer of your medical records. Your physician, dentist, optometrist, and veterinarian will have files containing prescriptions, dental x-rays, and immunization history. Contact the American Medical Records Association to determine your state's procedure.

**Comedy Underground**
*222 South Main Street*
*Seattle*
*(206) 628-0303*
www.comedyunderground.com

Premier outpost for stand-up comics: stars and up-and-comers alike.

**Doc Maynard's, Club Zazu, & Underground Tours**
*610 First Avenue*
*Seattle*
*(206) 682-4646*

Mainstays for single "wildlife" seeking local rock bands, microbrews, or a cool private tour of Seattle's real underground.

**The Drink**
*2245 Eastgate Avenue E*
*Seattle*
*(206) 860-0284*

Cigar-friendly dance and comedy club with a well-stocked bar for singles.

**DV8**
*131 Taylor Avenue N*
*Seattle*
*(206) 448-0888*

Diverse crowd dancing to live and DJ-spun club hits and hip-hop.

**Giggles**
*5220 Roosevelt Way NE*
*Seattle*
*(206) 526-5653*

"TV clean" comedy from rising stars to headliners.

**Goldies on 45th**
*2121 North 45th Street*
*Seattle*
*(206) 632-3453*

Beer, loud music, pinball, beer, sports bar, pool, beer, darts, beer.

**Gravity Bar**
*415 Broadway E*
*Seattle*
*(206) 325-7186*

It's a bar all right: a smoke-free juice-and-veggie bar for healthy hipsters.

**Jazz Alley**
*2033 Sixth Avenue*
*Seattle*
*(206) 441-9729*

Elite jazz club hosts "Earshot" and books greats like Branford Marsalis.

**Jillian's Billiard Club**
*731 Westlake Avenue N*
*Seattle*
*(206) 223-0300*

Thirty-one regulation Brunswick Gold Crown III tables, Ping-Pong, darts, and video tournaments, all in a kid-friendly atmosphere.

**Old Timer's**
*620 First Avenue*
*Seattle*
*(206) 623-9800*

Even young 'ns will take to the live blues and food and drink of the South.

**Parkers Casino & Nightclub**
*17001 Aurora Avenue N*
*Seattle*
*(206) 542-9491*

A landmark roadhouse with limited gaming, Parkers is a standard coach stop for legendary recording artists in the twilight of their careers.

**Polly Esther's**
*332 Fifth Avenue N*
*Seattle*
*(206) 441-1970*

www.pollyesthers.com

Two dance floors, two decades, one vibe: retro.

**ReBar**
*1114 Howell Street*
*Seattle*
*(206) 323-0388*

Experimental live music and theater, as well as familiar DJ-spun tunes.

**RKCNDY**
*1812 Yale Avenue*
*Seattle*
*(206) 667-0219*

All ages gather to watch hot local acts and touring small-venue rockers.

**Romper Room**
*106 First Avenue N*
*Seattle*
*(206) 284-5003*

Surrounded by black light and fluorescent-painted knickknacks, the DJ spins everything from twang to funk.

**Shark Club**
*52 Lake Shore Plaza*
*Kirkland*
*(425) 803-3003*

Billiards, burgers, beer, and a beat: all for surprisingly few dollars.

**Showbox Music Club & House of Blues**
*1426 First Avenue*
*Seattle*
*(206) 628-3151*

Ornate, roomy lounge is perfect venue for touring bands too big for bars and too small for arenas.

**Vogue**
*1516 11th Avenue*
*Seattle*
*(206) 324-5778*

Dance and drink nirvana for black-clad, privacy-phobic "fringe" crowd.

## Movie Theaters

Seattle is a big movie town, and your choices are many, from regional cineplexes, with glitzy lobbies, digital sound, a dozen shoebox-sized theaters, and fake butter, to no-frills discount theaters with squeaky seats and second-run films for two bucks. And then there are the few, proud independent theaters and drive-ins with screens the size of Rhode Island, bravely battling extinction.

MoviePhone in Seattle can be reached at 333-FILM.

**AMC SeaTac 6 North**
*31600 20th Avenue S*
*Federal Way*
*(206) 839-3050*

www.amctheatres.com

**AMC SeaTac 6 South**
*2000 South Seatac Mall*
*Federal Way*
*(206) 839-3050*

www.amctheatres.com

**Cinerama**
*2100 4th Avenue*
*Seattle*
*(206) 441-3653*
www.generalcinema.com

**Pacific Place 11**
*6th and Pine*
*Seattle*
*(206) 652-2404*
www.generalcinema.com

**City Centre Cinemas**
*1420 5th Avenue*
*Seattle*
*(206) 622-6465*
www.enjoytheshow.com

**Factoria Cinemas**
*Factoria*
*(425) 641-9206*
www.enjoytheshow.com

**Grand Cinemas**
*Lynnwood*
*(425) 774-3536*
www.enjoytheshow.com

**Lewis & Clark**
*Seattle*
*(206) 244-2900*
www.enjoytheshow.com

**Meridian 16**
*Seattle*
*(206) 223-9600*
www.enjoytheshow.com

**Northgate Cinemas**
*Northgate*
*(206) 363-5800*
www.enjoytheshow.com

**Redmond Town Center 8**
*Redmond*
*(425) 869-1800*
www.enjoytheshow.com

**Southcenter Cinemas**
*Southcenter*
*(206) 242-6100*
www.enjoytheshow.com

**Regal Cinemas**
www.regalcinemas.com

Seattle businesses were the first to subscribe to Muzak.

**Alderwood 7**
*Lynnwood*
*(425) 776-3535*

**Bella Bottega 11**
*Redmond*
*(425) 562-7230*

**Bellevue Galleria 11**
*Bellevue*
*(425) 451-7161*

**Crossroads 8**
*Bellevue*
*(425) 562-7230*

**Issaquah 9**
*Issaquah*
*(425) 313-5754*

**Mountlake 9 Cinema**
*6009 244th Southwest Mountlake Terrace*
*Mountlake*
*(425) 744-1112*

**Parkway Plaza 12**
*Southcenter*
*(206) 575-1313*

**Seven Gables/Landmark**
www.landmarktheatres.com

**Broadway Market Cinemas**
*425 Broadway E*
*Seattle*
*(206) 323-0231*

**The Crest**
*16505 Fifth Street NE*
*Seattle*
*(206) 363-6338*

**The Egyptian**
*801 East Pine Street*
*Seattle*
*(206) 323-4978*

**Guild 45th**
*2115 North 45th Street*
*Seattle*
*(206) 633-3353*

**Harvard Exit**
*807 East Roy Street*
*Seattle*
*(206) 323-8986*

**The Metro**
*4500 9th Avenue NE*
*Seattle*
*(206) 633-0055*

**Neptune Theatre**
*1303 Northeast 45th Street*
*Seattle*
*(206) 633-5545*

**Seven Gables**
*911 Northeast 50th Street*
*Seattle*
*(206) 632-8820*

**Varsity**
*4329 University Way NE*
*Seattle*
*(206) 632-3131*

## Video Rentals

If you're staying in for the evening and the only things on television are infomercials and tough man competitions, a movie from the local video store might help. Toss a popcorn pouch in the microwave and a "New Release" in the VCR.

Please use these corporate Web site URLs to help locate the store nearest you.

**Blockbuster Video**

www.blockbuster.com

**Hollywood Video**

www.hollywoodvideo.com

**Suncoast Video**

www.suncoast.com

**Tower Records-Video-Books**

www.towerrecords.com

**Video Factory**

www.videofactory.com

**Video Update**

www.videoupdate.com

**Wherehouse Music & Video**

www.wherehouse.com

**MOVING TIP**

If you are intending to transfer to another college, university, or graduate school, you must send your old school written permission to release your sealed transcript to the new registrar.

## Athletics

Because of the stubborn gloom, Seattleites dwell indoors, tinkering with their computers and gazing at the rainswept landscapes, right? Wrong! From casual sculling on morning-serene lakes to "X-treme" mountain biking and snowboarding through the Cascades, we are an active breed. In Seattle, outdoor activities reign . . . even in the rain.

CITY FACT

Each year, over 50,000 fans visit the gravesite of Seattle native Jimi Hendrix. The late guitar impresario is buried at Greenwood Memorial Park in Renton, Washington, a suburb of Seattle.

There are three types of athletes. Pro athletes are the ones who make a gazillion dollars. You'll recognize them. They renegotiate contracts, demand to be traded, and strike. Usually in that order. Recreational athletes are the ones who forget they're not pro athletes. You'll recognize them, too. They limp into the office on Monday mornings. And then there are the child athletes, often the shortest. Child athletes are conspicuous, too. They play for the love of the game.

The Emerald City is one big sandbox for all three. Wanna play?

### PROFESSIONAL SPORTS

Okay, okay. I was a little harsh about pro athletes. Actually, most are conscientious and generous. Or so I'm told. My son, Ashley, was a bat boy and ball boy for the Seattle Mariners last season. He fetched the coveted Louisville Slugger of perennial All-Star Ken Griffey, Jr., and schlepped Gatorades and sunflower seeds for American League Batting Champion Edgar Martinez. Ashley says the Mariners are stand-up guys and I believe him. I'm sure the Sonics and Seahawks are nice fellas, too.

### Baseball

"Take me out to the ball game. Take me out to the crowd . . . ," especially if the crowd is enjoying a ball game at splendiferous Safeco Field. The state-of-the-art, $550-million ballpark is truly amazing. From its nine-acre, 11,000-ton retractable roof to its velvety turf of Kentucky bluegrass and rye, Safeco Field is the most technologically advanced stadium in existence. Best of all, there's not a bad seat in the house. Really.

### Safeco Field

*First Avenue and South Atlantic Street*
*(206) 622-HITS*

www.mariner.org

### Football

In 2002, work will be completed on the Seahawks' brand new, $425-million stadium and exhibition hall. The focal point of the 72,000-seat marvel will be a thirteen-story tower with a digital scoreboard at the top. Will there be other bells and whistles? With Seahawks owner Paul Allen at the helm, you'd better believe it. Allen amassed one of the world's greatest personal fortunes by investing early in Microsoft and diversifying in communications and media. He knows technology and business. And he knows what Seattle wants: the Lombardi Trophy.

### Seahawk Stadium & Exhibition Hall

*201 South King Street*
*(888) NFL-HAWK*

www.seahawks.com

### Basketball

The 17,000-seat Key Arena—which received a $110-million facelift in 1995—is a model of municipal efficiency. Much of the previous structure was re-used or recycled, saving Seattleites $50 million. The rest was financed with city bonds, backed entirely by facility revenues. This strikingly elegant remodel cost taxpayers nothing. But it's the fastbreak, slam-dunk, and three-point shot at the buzzer that keeps cheering fans pouring into Key Arena season after season. One of the NBA's winningest records helps, too.

**Key Arena**
*305 Harrison Street*
*(206) 628-0888*
www.nba.com/sonics

**Hockey**

When Key Arena isn't housing pro hoops, the hardwood gives way to a blanket of ice and the maintenance crew fires up the Zamboni. Temperature at floor-level may drop, but the mercury in the stands rises with each slapshot and power play. From September through March, the arena is also home to the thrilling Seattle Thunderbirds of the Western Hockey League.

**Key Arena**
*305 Harrison Street*
*(206) 448-PUCK*
www.seattlethunderbirds.com

CITY FACT

Microsoft Corporation co-founder and Mercer Island resident Paul Allen is owner of the Seattle Seahawks and the Portland Trailblazers.

**Soccer**

America wasn't too keen on the metric system. We haven't been quick to dip our fries in mayonnaise, either. But one international bandwagon we hopped on is soccer. In Seattle, soccer is the fastest-growing team sport among boys and girls. That's one reason why the Seattle Sounders play fifteen home games in front of a packed house at Renton Memorial Stadium. Soccer: it's a kick! Just don't call it football.

**Renton Memorial Stadium**
*406 North Logan Street*
*(800) 796-KICK*
www.seattlesounders.com

## RECREATIONAL SPORTS

Whatever your sporting pleasure (or pain) is, you'll find valuable information at *www.seattle.citysearch.com.* Or call (206) 684-7092. These, however, are a few of my favorite things.

### Golf

**Ballinger Park Municipal Golf Course**
*23000 Lakeview Drive*
*Mountlake Terrace*
*(425) 775-6467*

**Bellevue Golf Course**
*5500 140th Avenue NE*
*Bellevue*
*(425) 452-7250*

**Carnation Golf Course**
*1810 West Snoqualmie River Road NE*
*Carnation*
*(425) 333-4151*

**Cascade Golf Course**
*14303 436th Avenue SE*
*North Bend*
*(425) 888-0227*

**Mount Si Golf Course**
*9010 Boalch Avenue SE*
*Snoqualmie*
*(425) 888-1541*

**Snoqualmie Falls Golf Course**
*35109 Southeast Fish Hatchery Road*
*Fall City*
*(425) 222-5244*

**Tall Chief Golf Course**
*1313 West Snoqualmie River Road SE*
*Fall City*
*(425) 222-5911*

**Wayne Public Golf Course**
*16721 96th Avenue NE*
*Bothell*
*(425) 486-4714*

**Wellington Hills Golf Course**
*7026 240th Avenue SE*
*Woodinville*
*(425) 485-5589*

**Willows Run Golf Course**
*10402 Willows Road*
*Redmond*
*(425) 883-1200*

### Basketball

The best-kept secret in Seattle's recreational sports is a pick-up game of hoops. It's a Monday night ritual that has been played in the Old Maltby Schoolhouse for nearly thirty years. The game attracts former Sonics and Seahawks, NCAA hopefuls, and just about anyone who plans on bringing their "A" game. Proprietor Ron "Nardo" Nardone and his legendary teammate "Iron" Mike Durbin are pushing sixty, but this unlikely duo of 300-pounders drag players one-third their age up and down the court: frustrating and mystifying their would-be competitors.

**The Old Maltby Schoolhouse Gymnasium**
*Above the famed "Maltby Café"*
*8809 Maltby Road*
*Snohomish*

Local basketball leagues are organized as a service of the Parks & Recreation Department. Cities with the most league activity include:

Seattle: (206) 684-7092

Bellevue: (425) 482-5882

Mountlake Terrace: (425) 775-6477

Kent: (253) 859-3350

You can also locate a friendly game at *www.findhoops.com.*

### Fishing

**Washington State Department of Fish and Wildlife**
*16018 Mill Creek Boulevard*
*Mill Creek*
*(425) 775-1311*

Contact the Department of Fish and Wildlife to obtain a fishing license.

**Creekside Angling Company**
*1660 Northwest Gilman Boulevard #C-5*
*Issaquah*
*(425) 392-3800*
www.creeksideangling.com

**Seattle Public Fishing Spots**

Bitter Lake

Commodore Park

Edmonds Fishing Pier

Golden Gardens Park

Haller Lake

Madison Park

Madrona Park

Magnuson Park

Mount Baker Park

Sayres Memorial Park

Seward Park

Waterfront Park

**Eastside Public Fishing Spots**

Burrow's Landing Pier

Cottage Lake

Enatai Beach Park

Idylwood Park

Juanita Beach

Kiwanis Park

MOVING TIP

Keep a phone book from the city you left. No matter how well you planned your relocation, there will be loose ends to tie up. You'll want to share your relocation adventures with old friends, and the last thing you need is a big bill for directory assistance.

Marina Park

Newcastle Beach Park

Phantom Lake

Pine Lake

Settler's Landing

Waverly Beach

**Cady Lake Manor**
*1471 Northeast Dewatto Road*
*Tahuya*
*(360) 372-2673*
www.cadylake.com

For a weekend getaway, try this Bed and Breakfast nestled on a "fly fishing only" lake.

### Baseball

Most of the following leagues are nationally affiliated. These organizations will help match your skill with an appropriate team:

**American Amateur Baseball Congress**

www.voyager.net/aabc

**United States Amateur Baseball Association**

www.usaba.com

**Pacific Coast Baseball League**

www.pabl.org

**AAU Baseball**

www.aaubaseball.org

**All American Baseball Association**

www.johnstownpa.com/aaaba

**American Women's Baseball League**

www.womenplaying baseball.com

**Men's Senior Baseball League**

www.msbl.com

### Skiing and Snowboarding

For a complete list of ski areas and winter recreation activities, please contact the Washington State Tourism Division at (800) 638-8474.

**Crystal Mountain**

*(360) 663-2265*

A 3,100-foot vertical drop and fifty-two runs for beginners and experts. Nine regular high-speed, and scenic chairlifts. Snowboard-friendly. Located thirty-two miles southeast of Enumclaw on Highway 410.

**Stevens Pass**

*(206) 812-4510*

An 1,800-foot vertical drop covering 1,125 acres, featuring thirty-seven runs, ten chairlifts, and night skiing. Snowboard-friendly. Lodging nearby. Located seventy-eight miles east of Seattle on Highway 2.

**The Summit at Snoqualmie**

*Alpental, Summit West, Summit Central, and Summit East*
*(425) 434-7669*

A 3,300-foot vertical drop with four chairlifts and surface tow. Caters to beginners and intermediates. One pass covers all four ski areas, connected by free shuttle service. 500-foot halfpipe for snowboarders. Night skiing available. Located at Snoqualmie Pass, forty-seven miles east of Seattle on I-90.

**White Pass**

*(509) 672-3101*

Specializing in day and night cross-country skiing. Snowboard school available. Slopeside lodging. Located fifty miles west of Yakima on Highway 12.

### Kayaking and Skulling

**Northwest Outdoor Center**

*2100 Westlake Avenue N*
*Seattle*
*(206) 281-9694*

**Moss Bay Rowing & Kayak Club**

*1001 Fairview Avenue N*
*Seattle*
*(206) 682-2031*

**Washington Park Arboretum & Waterfront Trail**

*2300 Arboretum Drive E*
*Seattle*
*(206) 543-8800*

CITY FACT

Famed crime writer Dashiell Hammett was formerly a Seattle detective.

MOVING TIP

Fill some disposable containers with household cleaners and keep them handy during the move. Your old place will need a once-over, and there's no better time to freshen up the new home than before the furniture arrives.

**Waterfront Activities Center**
*University of Washington*
*Campus at southeast corner of*
*Husky Stadium*
*Seattle*
*(206) 543-9433*

**Smith Cove Marina & Maggie Bluff's Grill**
*2601 West Marina Place*
*Seattle*
*(206) 283-8322*

**Sammamish Rowing Association**
*5022 West Lake Sammamish*
*Parkway NE*
*Redmond*
*(425) 895-1704*

### Hiking

**Bridle Trails State Park**
*(425) 455-7010*

Twenty-eight forested miles of well-maintained multi-use trails. Entrance at 53rd Street NE and 116th Avenue NE (exit #17 off I-405, between Kirkland and Bellevue).

**Burke-Gilman Trail**
*(206) 684-4075*

Fourteen miles of lakeview trails winding gently through Gas Works Park, the University of Washington, and Matthews Beach. In-line skater-friendly. Entrance at 8th Avenue NW in Seattle's Fremont neighborhood.

### Cougar Mountain Regional Wildland Park

*(206) 296-4232*

Fifty miles of trails meander through forests, wetlands, streams, windy bluffs, and wildlife preserves. Canine and equine friendly. Entrance at 18201 Southeast Cougar Mountain Drive, near Issaquah, south of I-90.

### Flaming Geyser State Park

*(253) 931-3930*

Thirty-eight miles of roads and trails, and eighteen miles of Green River banks. Famed "flaming geyser" burns perpetually, with "bubbling geyser" nearby. Raft, kayak, and tube-friendly. Great steelhead fishing. Entrance off Highway 169, 2.5 miles south of Black Diamond.

### North Cascades National Park:

*Take I-5 north to Burlington, go east on Highway 20. Please register at the Visitors Center near Newhalem.*
*(360) 856-5700*

www.nps.gov/noca

Diablo Lake Trail, Sourdough Creek Trail, Thunder Creek Trail, and Happy Creek Forest Walk: a half-million acres of everything from challenging terrain to wheelchair-friendly nature paths. Mountain, lake, and forest scenery also features Colonial campgrounds and tugboat crossings.

### Saltwater State Park

*(253) 661-4956*

Lush, rugged scenery and miles of beach trails. An artificial reef, mooring buoys, and comfortable campsites are popular features. Entrance two miles south of Des Moines on Marine View Drive, off Highway 509.

### Sammamish River Trail

Ten gentle miles of riverside trails have views of Mount Rainier, farms, parks, and the Chateau St. Michelle Winery. Enter from Burke-Gilman Trail at Tracy Owen Station of Marymore Park in Redmond.

### Mountain Biking

For a complete list of mountain biking areas and summer recreation activities, please contact the Washington State Tourism Division at (800) 638-8474.

### Crystal Mountain

*(360) 663-2265*

3,100-foot vertical drop with lifts. Located thirty-two miles southeast of Enumclaw on Highway 410.

### The Summit at Snoqualmie

*(425) 434-7669*

3,300-foot vertical drop with lifts. Located at Snoqualmie Pass, forty-seven miles east of Seattle on I-90.

### Rock Climbing

### Cascade Crags

*2820 Rucker Avenue*
*Everett*
*(425) 258-3431*

Great indoor climbing and professional instruction from elite climbers.

### Climbing Rock

*University of Washington*
*Waterfront Activities Center*
*Seattle*
*(206) 543-9433*

Jocks, physics majors, and non-students take shots at mastering the campus's toughest obstacle.

### Marymoor Park Climbing Wall

*Marymoor Park*
*West Lake Sammamish*
*Parkway SE*
*Redmond*
*(206) 296-2964*

An outdoor, forty-five-foot, man-made pinnacle designed with intermediate and advanced climbers in mind.

**Redmond Athletic Club**

*8709 161st Avenue NE*
*Redmond*
*(425) 883-4449*

One of the top training centers on the Eastside, featuring free-weights, aerobics, personal training, hoops, and several state-of-the-art climbing walls with professional instructors.

**REI Pinnacle**

*222 Yale Avenue N*
*Seattle*
*(206) 223-1944*

Not an urban legend. The titan of recreational equipment retailing has installed a sixty-five-foot pinnacle as the centerpiece of its downtown Seattle flagship. Scale this beast and gaze out the glass atrium as cars zip by on the I-5 freeway.

**Stone Gardens**

*2839 Northwest Market Street*
*Seattle*
*(206) 781-9828*

This Ballard gym preps novice climbers for bouldering and outdoor face climbs.

**Vertical World**

*2123 West Elmore Street*
*Seattle*
*(206) 283-4497*

*15036 B Northeast 95th Street*
*Redmond*
*(425) 881-8826*

Locations in Magnolia and Redmond cater to those who seek levity in a horizontal world.

**MOVING TIP**

Make sure you have arranged to obtain your children's birth certificates and immunization records prior to moving. In most districts, children cannot be registered in school without them.

## HEALTH CLUBS

If you're in shape, you're going to want to stay that way. If you're not, there's no better time to change your life than when you move to a new city. Besides, you'll want to make new friends. Health clubs are a great place to meet people. You can build up your pecs . . . and your Rolodex.

For Free, twenty-four-hour information about fitness, call (206) 442-2880.

- Dial 3400 for advice about designing a weight training program
- Dial 3401 to learn about cardiovascular conditioning
- Dial 3402 for tips about living a more healthy life
- Dial 3403 if you are planning to join a health club

### 24-Hour Fitness

*(800) 204-2400*

www.24hourfitness.com

This place doesn't close its doors. Treadmills, stairclimbers, freeweights, lap pools, hoops, yoga, kickboxing, and convenient locations make excuses difficult. Call for the center nearest you.

### American Woman Fitness

*3080 148th Avenue SE*
*Bellevue*
*(425) 747-8333*

Sorry fellas, this one's just for the ladies. I've never been inside, so I don't know what the center offers. But I bet none of the toilet seats are left up.

### Bally's Total Fitness

*(800) 678-0223*

www.ballyfitness.com

With 350 clubs nationally, this fitness center is great for the relocater and business traveler. Cardiovascular conditioning and circuit training are emphasized, but the aerobics classes draw huge crowds. Call for the center nearest you.

### Columbia Athletic Clubs

*(425) 821-0882*

www.columbiaathletic.com

These places have everything, plus: tennis, golf, and indoor track. Childcare and youth programs are offered, too. Call to arrange a free trial membership.

**The Fitness Edge**
*12033 124th Avenue NE*
*Kirkland*
*(425) 820-SPIN*

www.the-fitness-edge.com

gospinning@the-fitness-edge.com

They say it's the Eastside's premier "Spinning" and fitness studio.

**Fitness Tech Health & Wellness Center**
*10001 Northeast First Street*
*Bellevue*
*(425) 384-1000*

www.fitnesstech.net

Wellness programming and "a new approach to fitness" are emphasized at this Bellevue total health center.

**Gold's Gym**
*10728 Southeast Carr Road*
*Renton*
*(425) 227-9320*

www.goldsgym.com

The original "Muscle Beach" gym in Venice, California, has spawned over 500 franchises worldwide. Hardcore bodybuilders and girly-men alike work out here. Convenient month-to-month memberships are welcomed.

**Pro Sports Club**
*4455 148th Avenue NE*
*Bellevue*
*(425) 885-5566*

www.proclub.com

Nine indoor tennis courts, two pools, 300 machines, two basketball courts, and fifty aerobics classes per week make the "Pro Club" the Northwest's largest athletic club.

CITY FACT

Historic Union Station in Seattle's International District will be headquarters for *Sound Transit:* the new fleet of express buses and high-speed, light-rail commuter trains linking Seattle with Tacoma (south) and Everett (north).

**Pro-Robics Conditioning Clubs**
*3811 Northeast 45th Street*
*Seattle*
*(206) 524-9246*

www.prorobics.com

Aerobics and lots of cardio machines are the focus of these clubs, located in Queen Anne, Laurelhurst, and Inglewood. Tanning and flexible memberships are popular features.

**Redmond Athletic Club**
*8709 161 Avenue NE*
*Redmond*
*(425) 883-4449*

www.racinc.com

One of the newest and largest athletic clubs, this is also the premier fitness place in Redmond. No pushy sales people, just plenty of weights and cardio equipment. Indoor hoops, spinning, rock climbing, and some of the most qualified trainers and massage therapists around make RAC popular with hardbodies and soon-to-be-hardbodies.

**Seattle Athletic Club**
*2020 Western Avenue*
*Seattle*
*(206) 443-1111*

www.sacdt.com

Your Armani hangs in a posh locker room while you burn off the crème brulee from that power lunch. "Events" are big at this downtown Seattle club. Social or athletic, there's something to suit every suit at SAC. Start with an aquatic program, then a little squash. After a few sets with the burnished chrome weights, hit the sauna. Pamper yourself with a massage and you're ready for a smoothie at the café.

**Washington Athletic Club**
*1325 Sixth Avenue*
*Seattle*
*(206) 622-7900*

www.wac.net

Another hotspot for the executive workout. With twenty-one floors of fitness, if this place doesn't have it, it's not good for you. WAC offers restaurants and hotel suites to members and guests. ACSM certified trainers, valet parking, the latest equipment, and locker room stock tips are just a few of the factors that mitigate pricey dues. One session of Swedish or shiatsu massage and you'll apply for life membership. Elite reciprocal clubs worldwide. You may already be a member.

**Yoga Centers**
*2255 140th Avenue NE*
*Bellevue*
*(425) 746-7476*
www.yogacenters.com

The name says it all. This is yoga in a big way. Master relaxation techniques while enhancing circulation and flexibility. Programs are designed to enhance both mind and body.

## YOUTH ATHLETICS

You've seen them. They're whisked from practice to practice in minivans and SUVs. They cover themselves in a lightweight armor of polystyrene padding and scarf down stuff like "power bars" and "engineered drinks." Trophies adorn the bedroom windowsills of these darting creatures. Who are they? Athletica minora, or "child athletes." And if you have one you'll appreciate Seattle's carpool lanes almost as much as ouchless Band-Aids.

**Little League**
www.littleleague.org

Bellevue: (425) 643-8127

Bothell/Kenmore: (425) 485-6421

Eastlake/Redmond: (425) 868-1004

Issaquah: (425) 391-9747

Northshore: (425) 483-8790

Seattle: (206) 937-1928

**PONY League**
www.pony.org

**Babe Ruth League**
www.baberuthbaseball.org

**MOVING TIP**

Pack items in Tupperware containers, suitcases, backpacks, and wastepaper baskets. You'll save packing supplies and time.

### Henderson Ballyard & Northwest Baseball Academy

The two premier training facilities in the Puget Sound area are in the cities of Bellevue and Everett. If your kid has a rifle for an arm and a rocket launcher for a bat, this is where baseball talent is nurtured. Consisting not only of indoor batting cages and pitching lanes, these institutions are lead by some of the most revered instructors in baseball. Under the tutelage of Mark Potoshnik, Dan Spillner, Dave "Hendu" Henderson, and Julio Cruz, many local ballpark rats grow up to be Big Leaguers.

**Dave Henderson's Ballyard**
*13414 Northeast 16th Avenue*
*Bellevue*
*(425) 644-2255*

**Northwest Baseball Academy**
*Mark Potoshnik, owner and director*
*12310 Highway 99 S #122*
*Everett*
*(425) 438-9030*
pitchingnw@aol.com

**Greater Seattle Soccer League**
*9750 Greenwood Avenue N*
*Seattle*
*(206) 782-6831*
www.gssl.org

**Washington State Soccer Association**
*7802 Northeast Bothell Way*
*Kenmore*
*(425) 485-7855*

**Washington State Youth Soccer Association**
*33710 Ninth Avenue S, Suite Eight*
*Federal Way*
*(253) 4-SOCCER*
www.wsysa.com

## Annual or Seasonal Calendar Events

Seattle is a celebration waiting to happen, and the wait is never long. We celebrate at the drop of a hat, as evidenced by the annual "Hat Dropping Festival" sponsored by Chapeau.com. (That was a joke. At the time of this writing there is no such company. By next Wednesday there might be.)

CITY FACT

The Beatles performed for a sellout crowd of 14,300 at the Seattle Center Arena on August 21, 1964.

Sure, we've got all the biggies covered. Christmas is heralded by the "Argosy Christmas Ship Festival," a flotilla of decorated dinghies and mega-yachts joyously traversing Puget Sound and Lakes Washington and Union. The annual festival gives added meaning to Yule "Tide." New Year's Eve is synonymous with "Times Square of the West," a thrilling midnight countdown and block party at the landmark Space Needle. Redmond's Eggstravaganza and Bellevue's Egg Hunt delight and befuddle pastel-clad children who match wits with the Eastside Easter Bunny. Putting the "sound" in Puget Sound is "Ivar's Fourth of July Fireworks Display." This barrage of bursting color draws tens of thousands to the downtown waterfront. Treats, never tricks, are sponsored by merchants and restaurateurs of historic Pike Place Market. Kids from everywhere parade in costume while stuffing their pillow sacks with Halloween goodies. Thanksgiving Day ushers in yet another Northwest tradition: "Northern Lights Holiday Light Park" at Redmond's Marymoor Park. Due to popular demand, this illuminating event has been extended through New Year's Eve.

We also celebrate things you won't find printed on your calendar. Quirky, obscure festivities are what truly define Seattle's uniqueness. If it's tasty, colorful, artsy, or endangered, it's cause celebre. The grape harvest. Strawberry season. Kite flying. Daffodils and cherry blossoms. The salmon run. Shakespeare. Boating Day. The return of the Gray

Whales. International filmmaking. Chocolate—yes, chocolate. We even commemorate June 13th through 19th as "Juneteenth," an African American holiday. Don't try to figure it out. Just enjoy it!

## SUMMER

**AT&T Summer Nights at the Pier Concert Series**
*Pier 62 and Pier 63*
*Seattle*
*(206) 684-4075*

**Ballard Seafoodfest & Bite of Scandinavia**
*Historic Downtown Ballard*
*(206) 684-4093*

**Bite of Seattle**
*Seattle Center*
*(206) 684-7200*

**Bluegrass Festival & Beer Garden**
*Carnation*
*(425) 333-4198*

**Brierfest**
*Brier Park*
*(425) 806-3800*

**Chocolate Festival**
*Downtown Issaquah*
*(425) 392-0661*

**Columbia Winery Summerfest**
*Woodinville*
*(425) 488-2776*

**Down Home Fourth of July**
*Downtown Issaquah*
*(425) 392-0661*

**Evergreen Classic Horse & British Automobile Show**
*Marymoor Park*
*Redmond*
*(425) 885-4014*

**Festival of Northwest Wines**
*North Seattle Community College*
*(206) 527-3600*

**Fourth of July Celebration**
*Bothell Historical Museum*
*(425) 486-1889*

**Fourth of July Fireworks**
*Marymoor Park*
*Redmond*
*(425) 885-4014*

**Fun Run & Briefcase Relay**
*Fremont*
*(206) 684-4075*

**International Kite Festival**
*Long Beach*
*(360) 642-4421*

**Juneteenth Festival**
*Pratt Park*
*Seattle*
*(206) 322-8296*

**Kids' Carnival**
*Robinswood Park*
*Bellevue*
*(425) 452-7156*

**MOVING TIP**

Use towels, T-shirts, and socks as wrapping for delicate items. This cuts down on pricey bubble wrap, and you won't have to pack them separately.

**KOMO KidsFair**
*Seattle Center*
*(206) 684-7200*

**King County Fair**
*King County Fairgrounds*
*Enumclaw*
*(360) 825-7777*

**Kirkland Summerfest**
*Marina Park*
*(425) 822-7161*

**Mural Concert Series**
*Mural Amphitheatre*
*(206) 684-7200*

**Music in the Park Concert Series**
*Mercer Island*
*(206) 236-3545*

**North Bend Alpine Days Festival**
*Snoqualmie*
*(425) 888-4440*

**Northwest Wine Festival**
*The Herbfarm*
*Fall City*
*(425) 222-7103*

**Out to Lunch Concert Series**
*Downtown Seattle*
*(206) 684-4075*

**Outdoor Cinema Season**
*Fremont*
*(206) 684-4075*

**Pacific Northwest Kids Arts & Crafts Fair**
*Bellevue Square and Bellevue Place*
*(425) 454-3322*

**Pacific Northwest Scottish Highland Games**
*Enumclaw*
*(360) 825-3594*

**Redmond Derby Days**
*City Hall Campus*
*(425) 885-4014*

**Rest of Best Fest**
*Downtown Bellevue*
*(206) 363-2048*

**Seafair Hydroplane Races**
*Spirit of Puget Sound*
*(425) 674-3498*

**General Motors Seafair Unlimited Hydroplane Races**
*Lake Washington*
*(206) 728-0123*

**US West Seafair Air Show**
*Lake Washington*
*(206) 728-0123*

**Seafair Milk Carton Derby**
*Green Lake*
*(425) 672-0687*

**Seafair Torchlight Parade**
*Downtown Seattle*
*(206) 728-0123*

CITY FACT

"Wood(inville)stock?" For four days during the summer of 1969, a tiny suburb of Seattle became the epicenter of a festival that rocked the Great Northwest. Sleepy little Woodinville hosted such superstars as The Doors, Chuck Berry, Santana, Guess Who, Led Zeppelin, Ten Years After, Bo Diddley, and Tina Turner.

**Shakespeare in the Park**
*Lynndale Amphitheatre*
*Lynnwood Park*
*(425) 771-4030*

**Shoreline Annual Arts Festival**
*Shoreline*
*(206) 542-1989*

**Sixth Street Fair & Taste of Bellevue**
*Downtown Bellevue*
*(425) 453-1223*

**Solstice Parade**
*Fremont*
*(206) 684-4075*

**Strawberry Festival**
*Burien*
*(206) 244-5662*

**Street Fair**
*Mercer Island*
*(206) 236-3545*

**Summer Concerts on the Green**
*Chateau St. Michelle Winery*
*Woodinville*
*(425) 488-3300*

**Summer Festival**
*International District*
*Seattle*
*(206) 684-4075*

**Wednesday Summer Concert Series**
*Woodland Park Zoo*
*Seattle*
*(206) 684-4800*

## AUTUMN

**Belle Arts Concerts**
*Meydenbauer Center*
*Bellevue*
*(800) 426-8020*

**Bug-A-Boo**
*Woodland Park Zoo*
*(206) 684-4800*

**Fiesta Italiana & Fiestas Patrias**
*Seattle Center*
*(206) 684-7200*

**Floral Fairyland & Poinsettia Festival**
*Molbak's Greenhouse and Nursery*
*Woodinville*
*(425) 483-5000*

**Greek Festival**
*St. Demetrios Greek Orthodox Church*
*Seattle*
*(206) 325-4347*

**Hmong New Year**
*Seattle Center*
*(206) 684-7200*

**Holiday Fest**
*North Bend*
*(425) 888-1211*

**Holiday Markets**
*Fremont*
*(206) 684-4075*

CITY FACT

At the time of its 1999 inaugural season, Seattle's state-of-the-art baseball park, Safeco Field, was the world's most expensive athletic facility. Total construction costs exceeded a half-billion dollars.

**International Auto Show**
*Seattle Exhibition Center*
*(425) 889-9494*

**Kelsey Creek Farm Fair**
*Kelsey Creek Park*
*Bellevue*
*(425) 452-7688*

**Model Railroad Show**
*Science Center*
*(206) 684-7200*

**Newcastle Days**
*Lake Boren Park*
*(425) 649-4444*

**Oktoberfest**
*Fremont*
*(206) 684-4075*

**Safe Halloween, Dahlia Show, & Pumpkin Painting Contest**
*Country Village*
*Bothell*
*(425) 483-2250*

**Salmon Days Festival & Grand Parade**
*Memorial Field and Historic Downtown Issaquah*
*(425) 392-7024*

**Steilacoom Apple Squeeze**
*Steilacoom*
*(253) 581-1900*

**TASTE! Kirkland Festival**
*Peter Kirk Park, Juanita Beach Park, and Marina Park*
*(425) 828-1218*

**Tree Lighting Ceremony**
*Bothell*
*(425) 486-3256*

**Wallingford's Wurst Festival**
*Seattle*
*(206) 684-4075*

**Western Washington State Fair**
*Puyallup Fairgrounds*
*Puyallup*
*(253) 841-5045*

**Woodstack**
*Duvall*
*(425) 788-1185*

**Yulefest**
*Nordic Heritage Museum*
*Ballard*
*(206) 684-4075*

**MOVING TIP**

Locate the garage door openers and make sure you didn't leave spare keys under doormats or rocks. The new tenant will appreciate this.

## WINTER

**Bellevue City Hall Art Show**
*(425) 452-4106*

**Bellevue Home Show**
*(800) 447-1913*

**Chinese New Year**
*International District*
*Seattle*
*(206) 684-4075*

**Christmas Celebration**
*Westlake Center & Downtown Seattle*
*(206) 684-4075*

**Christmas in Seattle**
*Seattle Exhibition Center*
*(425) 889-9494*

CITY FACT

Recreational outfitter Eddie Bauer invented the down parka and established the renowned Eddie Bauer chain of retail clothiers in Seattle.

**Columbia Gorge Food & Wine Extravaganza**
*Columbia Winery*
*Woodinville*
*(425) 488-2776*

**Fat Tuesday & Mardi Gras Celebration**
*Pioneer Square*
*Seattle*
*(206) 622-6235*

**Festival Sundiata**
*Seattle Center*
*(206) 684-7200*

**Garden D-Lights**
*Bellevue Botanical Gardens*
*(425) 451-3755*

**Holiday Show**
*Kirkland Arts Center*
*(425) 822-7161*

**KING 5 Winter Fest**
*Seattle Center*
*(206) 684-7200*

**Northwest Flower & Garden Show**
*Washington State Convention and Trade Center*
*(206) 789-5333*

**The Nutcracker**
*Seattle Center Opera House*
*(206) 441-9411*

**Reindeer Festival**
*Cougar Mountain Zoological Park*
*Issaquah*
*(425) 391-5508*

**Santa Train**
*North Bend to Snoqualmie*
*(425) 888-1211*
*(425) 888-1555*

MOVING TIP

Until you've memorized them, keep your new home or P.O. box address and telephone number in your wallet or purse.

**Seattle International Boat Show**
*Seattle*
*(206) 684-4075*

**Winter Wonderland Performance Series**
*Redmond*
*(425) 556-2900*

**Zoolights**
*Point Defiance Zoo*
*Tacoma*
*(253) 591-5335*

## SPRING

**All Fools Day Celebration & Basset Hound Bash**
*Woodinville*
*(425) 489-2700*

**Cherry Blossom Festival**
*House and Flag Pavillion*
*Seattle Center*
*(206) 684-7200*

**Daffodil Festival**
*Tacoma: (253) 591-5171*
*Puyallup: (253) 841-4321*
*Sumner: (206) 461-5800*
*Orting: (360) 893-2219*

**Gray Whalewatch**
*Seattle Aquarium*
*(206) 386-4320*

**Ikebana International Flower Show**
*Seattle University*
*(206) 296-6000*

**International Wine Fair**
*Union Station*
*Seattle*
*(206) 937-2965*

CITY FACT

Seattle's Woodland Park Zoo earns international awards for its natural "bio-climatic" exhibits, which continue to revolutionize modern zoo design.

**Irish Festival & St. Patrick's Day Celebration**
*Seattle Center House*
*(206) 684-7200*

**Northwest Folklife Festival**
*Seattle Center*
*(206) 684-7200*

**Performing Arts Fest of the Eastside**
*Bellevue*
*(425) 868-5997*

**Pike Place Market Festival**
*Seattle*
*(206) 684-4075*

**Seattle International Children's Festival**
*Seattle Center*
*(206) 684-7200*

**Seattle International Film Festival**
*Seattle*
*(206) 324-9996*

**Seattle Jewish Film Festival**
*King Cat Theatre*
*Belltown*
*(206) 269-7444*

**University District Street Fair**
*University Way*
*Seattle*
*(206) 632-9084*

**Washington Games for the Physically Disabled**
*Seattle*
*(206) 684-4075*

**Whirligig**
*Seattle Center House*
*(206) 684-7200*

**Wild & Wooly Sheep Shearing Festival**
*Kelsey Creek Farm*
*Bellevue*
*(425) 452-7688*

## Public Transportation

### Regional Transit Authority

*821 Second Avenue*
*Seattle, WA 98104*
*(206) 684-6776*

### King County Metro Transit

*821 Second Avenue*
*Seattle, WA 98104*

#### ABOUT METRO TRANSIT

75 million passengers are transported around the Greater Seattle area each year. Buses serving downtown Seattle are bordered by Jackson Street (south), Sixth Avenue (east), Battery Street (north), and the Puget Sound waterfront boardwalk (west). From 6:00 A.M. until 7:00 P.M., bus service is free of charge. Reduced fares are available for senior citizens and disabled persons. All Metro buses are equipped with wheelchair lifts.

Bus Information: (206) 553-3000

Pass Information: (206) 624-PASS

Traffic Update: (206) 684-1420

### Puget Sound Regional Council

*1011 Western Avenue, #500*
*Seattle, WA 98104*
*(206) 464-7090*

### City of Seattle Engineering Department

*600 Fourth Avenue*
*Seattle, WA 98101*
*(206) 684-5349*

**Metro Carpool Ride-Matching**
*(206) 625-4500*

**Metro Vanpools**
*(206) 625-4500*

**Seattle Commuter Services**
*(206) 684-0816*

**Community Transit**
*(206) 778-2185*

**Rideshare**
*(888) 814-1300*

**Pierce Transit**
*(800) 562-8109*

**Seattle Center Monorail**
*(206) 441-6038*

**Park-and-Ride**
*Seattle: (206) 553-3000*
*Eastside: (425) 778-2185*

**Gray Line of Seattle**
*720 South Forest Street*
*Seattle: (206) 624-5077*
*Outside Seattle: (800) 544-0739*

**Greyhound**
*811 Stewart Street*
*(800) 231-2222*

**Washington State Ferries: *"The Nation's Largest Ferry System"***

Seattle: (206) 464-6400

Outside Seattle: (800) 84-FERRY

CHAPTER 7

# What's Out of Town

Being an international focal point has its privileges. By careful design this great city has poised itself as the gateway to Northwest splendor. If you want The Whole: Shebang, Nine Yards, Enchilada, or Kit 'n' Caboodle, you'll find it in Seattle—or at least close by—and getting there promises to be fun. What was an arduous trek for early settlers is now a pleasant drive. A gentle ferry ride. A leisurely afternoon of sailing. Or a stone's skip on a seaplane. If western Washington were a toy box it would be the envy of the neighborhood. Lift up the lid and let your inner child rummage unabashedly through an ocean, a sound, glaciers, volcanoes, gorges, and islands.

To the north is the inviting city of Vancouver, British Columbia. To the east are the renowned Coeur d'Alene resorts. To the south is the awe-inspiring Oregon coastline. And to the west are the timeless San Juan Islands. You may never feel the need to venture beyond the cozy cocoon of Seattle. If you do, though, it's nice to know you won't need a compass to find enjoyment.

## Canada

My children and I love traditions. A summer favorite is spending a few days tooling around British Columbia in a rental RV. Each year I get bolder and the RV gets longer. Last July I navigated a forty-footer through the winding roads of Cultus Lake and broad expanses of Canada's Transcontinental Highway. Once in B.C., we enjoy the same things we do here: camping, miniature golf, horseback riding, paintball, waterparks, boating, etc.. So why put up with the hassles of currency exchange and border inspections? Because in Canada a massive crowd is defined as "four people." A line is when you can faintly see the back of another person's head, and traffic jams occur only when Caribou or Canadian Geese cross the road.

Also, our neighbors to the north tend to be more relaxed. Less paranoid. Horseback riding in the United States requires an act of Congress, posting a surety bond, and signing a twenty-page waiver. All for a half-hour of trotting around a circular track with two guides. Canadians just ask that you bring the horses back before dark. Reigns in hand, you're free to roam through rolling hills of Buttercup and Wild Aster.

**CITY FACT**

Former president Warren G. Harding delivered his last speech in Seattle at the University of Washington Stadium on July 27, 1923. The president died six days later in San Francisco.

If outdoor contests entice you—but getting stung with balls of paint isn't your idea of a vacation—then perhaps fishing is in order. Canada offers some of the best fishing on the continent. Monster lake trout and northern pike are the subjects of lore . . . and record books.

If family outings and fishing aren't quite the action you had in mind, no problem. Vancouver is a glitzy, gleaming metropolis and very singles-friendly. The club scene is as hot as any rival south of the border, maybe hotter. To attract international limelight and potent U.S. dollars, Canada has postured Vancouver as "The Other Gem of the Pacific Rim."

Yet another possibility is Whistler. Located in B.C.'s Blackcomb Mountains, this world-famous ski resort boasts a 7,000-foot crest and thirty-three lifts. *Ski* magazine recently rated Whistler the "Number One Ski Area in North America." After a day on the slopes, the focus shifts to the all-pedestrian Whistler Village, where a dazzling array of eighty restaurants and 150 shops ignite the night. Late-night warmth is found in toasty lodges, bubbling hot tubs, and electric nightclubs. For a three-night stay including lift tickets, plan on $300 per person, double-occupancy.

To get from Seattle to the British Columbia towns of Langley or Alder Grove, then to Cultus Lake:

- take I-5 North to Exit #256, Highway 539
- proceed to the Lynden Border Crossing
- enter Alder Grove on 264th Street/Highway 13
- continue to Freeway #1
- proceed east on the freeway for twenty miles
- follow signs to Cultus Lake attractions

To get from Seattle to the British Columbia city of Vancouver, then to Whistler:

- take I-5 North to Exit #256, Highway 539
- proceed to the Lynden Border Crossing
- enter Alder Grove on 264th Street/Highway 13
- continue to Freeway #1
- proceed west on the freeway to Vancouver/Horseshoe Bay
- connect to Highway 99 North, "Sea to Sky Highway"*
- continue for two hours until reaching Whistler/Blackcomb.

*Rated "The Most Romantic Road in the World" by *Robb Report* magazine.

**Official Whistler Web Site**

www.whistler-resort.com

**Visitor Information**

*(877) 932-0606*

**Ground Transportation**

*(604) 264-8340*

manager@classiclimo.net

**Townhome Rentals**

www.whistler-rental.com

**Weather Updates**

www.whistler-resort.com

**Travel Arrangements**

travel@whistler.net

## Coeur d'Alene, Idaho

Think Idaho. Then think again. Located on I-90, close to the Washington border in the unlikely Idaho panhandle, is a vibrant lakeside city with a funny French name. With Scott Miller–designed golf courses, turn-of-the-century bed and breakfasts, and more than 100 miles of picturesque shoreline, Coeur d'Alene (koor duh lane) is no spud farm. Savvy visitors flock to this resort for its abundant recreation and world-class amenities. You don't have to be a scratch golfer to enjoy the offerings. Nor must you be a duke or duchess to afford a spectacular suite in one of the historic mansion inns.

Coeur d'Alene is about getting away. It's about relaxation. To some that's a morning massage at the spa and an afternoon strolling the galleries. To others it's an afternoon on the courts and an evening at Capone's Sportspub. If dining is how you unwind, try Beverly's or The Wine Cellar. Rustler's Roost at Hayden Lake and Cedars Floating Restaurant are excellent choices, too.

Popular "guest ranches" and bed and breakfast inns can be pricey during peak season. Expect to pay $150 to $300 per couple, per night. The Coeur d'Alene Resort commands between $400 and $550 for luxury accommodations, including greens fees and caddy service. Motor lodges and chain hotels range from $80 to $125 per night. Off-season rates are substantially lower. Public golf courses can be played for under $30.

Commuter flights depart Sea-Tac International Airport for Spokane every half-hour. Shuttle services transport travelers from Spokane Airport thirty-three miles to Coeur d'Alene. To get from Seattle to Spokane, then to Coeur d'Alene:

- take I-5 South to I-90 East
- proceed 285 miles to Spokane
- continue east thirty-three miles, following signs to Coeur d'Alene

**Coeur d'Alene Convention & Visitor's Bureau**

*(800) VISIT-ID*

www.destinationnw.com/idaho/coeurdalene

**Coeur d'Alene Travel Information & Official Web Site**
*(877) 782-9232*

www.coeurdalene.org

info@coeurdalene.org

**The Coeur d'Alene Resort**
*115 Second Street*
*Coeur d'Alene, Idaho 83814*
*(800) 688-5253*

www.cdaresort.com

**Ground Transportation**
*(208) 667-6664*
*(208) 762-7433*

**Free Travel Guide**
*(208) 664-3194*

carrie@coeurdalenechamber.com

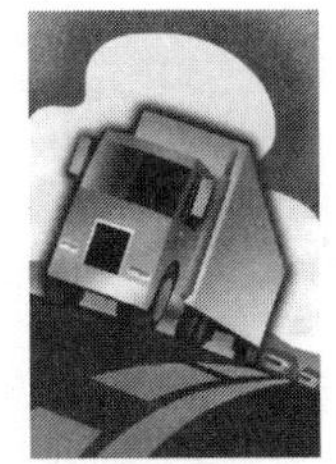

**MOVING TIP**

Don't forget to return the videos and pick up the dry cleaning. Having to take care of this by mail is a hassle.

## Oregon Coast

Oregon 101. It sounds like an introductory course in Oregon State history. Well, in a way, it is. Only your instructor is Mother Nature and your classroom is a 400-mile stretch of breathtaking coastline. Connecting the seafaring village of Astoria and the coastal community of Brookings is the famed Oregon 101/Pacific Coast Highway.

Oregonians treasure—and share—their beautiful coastline. Long ago, the Oregon legislature declared all beaches public domain. That's why you won't find gated oceanfront compounds and sprawling resorts blocking the seascapes. The Oregon coastline is for beachcombers, kite flyers, windsurfers, crabbers and clam diggers, and painters and poets.

Not developers.

The closest thing you'll find to seaside construction is a child building a driftwood fort or a sandcastle at low tide. That's on the ocean side. Inland, you'll find interesting galleries, antique shops, and eateries. Public and private campsites abound. They're always clean and friendly.

After shopping and sightseeing, take a stroll along the tidepools. You'll see little creatures that remind you of the bar scene in Star Wars. They're fascinatingly weird, but resist the temptation to touch them. Left undisturbed they'll return to captivate future generations of beachcombers.

A nice way to top off a day of Oregon 101 is a Dungeness crab and clambake at sunset. The crabmeat is sweet and succulent. And there's nothing like a pot of fresh clams steaming over a crackling fire.

If crab netting and clam digging is wading too close to the wild side, visit The Inn at Otter Crest. It's my favorite place on the coast. The inn straddles a sleepy, lush forest and a dramatic bluff overlooking the Pacific Ocean. From your balcony you can watch whale pods on their seasonal migrations. There are dozens of nature trails and tidepools for the adventurous types. An oceanside pool, spa, and racquet club cater to those in search of traditional resort activities. Convenient dining and magnificent views can be enjoyed at the inn's Flying Dutchman restaurant.

Reservations are suggested during summer months. Campsites range from $5 to $20 per night. Chain hotels and ma and pa motels are common and cost between $65 and $125. Bed and breakfast inns are found along the northern and central coast, and range from $85 to $200. Suites at The Inn at Otter Crest are from $95 to $200, depending upon view and the season.

To get from Seattle to Astoria, Oregon, then down the Oregon 101/Pacific Coast Highway:

- take I-5 South 140 miles to the town of Longview
- proceed southwest onto Highway 4, crossing the Cowlitz River
- turn left onto Highway 411 heading south
- merge with Highway 432 and then Highway 433
- cross Lewis & Clark Bridge to Highway 30
- continue west and follow signs to Astoria and Highway 101
- proceed south on Highway 101 down the Oregon coast

**The Inn at Otter Crest**
*301 Otter Crest Loop*
*Otter Rock, OR 97369*
*(800) 452-2101*

www.ottercrest.com

rooms@ottercrest.com

**Oregon 101**

www.oregon101.com

**Oregon and Washington Coast Guide**

www.nwcoast.com

CITY FACT

Smith Tower, dedicated in 1914, was Seattle's first skyscraper.

**Oregon Coast Alternative Guide**

www.navicom.com/~andrehage/alternacoast.html

**Oregon Coast Campgrounds**

www.ontheoregoncoast.com/campgrnd.html

**Oregon Coast Lodging and Travel Guide**

www.oregoncoastlodging.com

**Oregon Coast Travel and Local Information**

www.pacific101.com/oregon/oregon.html

**Oregon Coast Travel Guide**

www.oregoncoast101.com

**Oregon Coast Vacations**

www.vacationoregon.com

**Oregon Coast Vacation Rentals**

www.deprey.com

### Oregon Coast Virtual Tours

www.oregoncoast.net

www.navicom.com/~andrehage/vtour.html

## The San Juan Islands

I know something about beautiful islands. I grew up in Hawaii. When I tell you that the San Juan Islands are the most heavenly spot in the Pacific Northwest, it's not puffery. It's the truth. Painters have tried to capture the colors, and poets have tried to find the words, but their best efforts fall short. The San Juans are simply indescribable. Even Madison Avenue would have a hard time creating a travel brochure that would do justice to this collection of tiny islands.

Located in North Puget Sound due west of the seaside town of Anacortes, the chain consists mainly of Orcas Island, Lopez Island, and San Juan Island. Together, the islands define straights that attract world-class helmsmen and their yachts. The coastal waters—rich in whale populations—support premier kayaking and scuba diving environments. On land, golf, tennis, and nature activities rule. Some of the world's finest hiking trails can be found on any island, and conscientious campers are welcomed. More traditional lodging is provided by resort hotels and bed and breakfast inns. Vacation rentals are also available. Guests revel in a bounty of boutique restaurants and galleries that are scattered across the isles. Not surprising, the San Juans host weddings and honeymoons year-round.

Aside from private vessels and charters, there are three ways to reach the Islands. To arrive by ferry take I-5 North to Washington State Route 20 West, to Anacortes. Follow the Washington State Ferry signs to the dock. From its Seattle dock, travelers can take the stately Victoria Clipper to Friday Harbor, San Juan Island.

Air travel to Friday Harbor is provided by Harbor Airlines, Kenmore Air, and West Isle Air.

### Marine Activity Director at Roche Harbor Resort

*P.O. Box 2749*
*Friday Harbor, WA 98250*

**Crystal Seas Kayaking**
*(360) 378-7899*

**San Juan Safaris**
*(800) 450-6858*
*(360) 378-1323*

**On-Isle Transportation**
*(360) 378-8887*

**Area Guide for San Juan Islands**
www.sanjuansites.com

**Bed and Breakfast Association of the San Juans**
www.san-juan-island.net

**Ferry Schedules, Lodging, Whale Watching, and Kayaking**
www.friday-harbor.net

**MOVING TIP**

Confirm that your subscriptions, credit/charge card statements, and outstanding bills will be forwarded to your new address. You'll miss your favorite magazines and might inadvertently harm your credit rating if you overlook this detail.

***The Glory***

The premier luxury yacht charter in the Seattle/San Juan Islands Area.

www.mvglory.premier-resorts.com/san_juan_yacht_chart.html

**San Juan Island National Historical Park Visitor's Information**
www.nps.gov/sajh/home.html

CHAPTER 8

# Volunteer and Community Involvement

Seattle is home to some of the wealthiest entrepreneurs and industrialists on the planet. Multitudes of Microsoft millionaires are the subject of lore from Wallingford to Wall Street. One of the most eagerly anticipated business publications is the annual "Forbes 400" list of the wealthiest Americans. These days, the issue reads like a veritable *Who's Who* of Seattle society.

Staggering wealth brings with it certain moral and civic responsibilities. I'm proud to report that the Seattle megarich are among the world's most generous benefactors. But those in the economic stratosphere are not the only ones who give. Average Seattleites can be uncommonly charitable. Those who can't give money often give of their time. Volunteerism, in fact, has become so intricately woven into Northwest culture that organizations have formed with the sole purpose of placing volunteers in other organizations.

As a writer, I'm frequently asked to speak at local schools. It's a request I never decline. Whether addressing wide-eyed high school seniors or waist-high third graders, I always emphasize volunteerism.

Nothing is more important. Money enriches wallets and bank accounts. Volunteering enriches lives.

Me? I like kids. I'm a volunteer Little League coach and elementary school art teacher. My favorite charity is Make-A-Wish Foundation. Community service offers endless opportunities, though. You might gravitate toward environmental concerns. Or animal welfare. Consumer protection. Public health. Perhaps veterans and senior citizens touch your heart. Whatever the cause, please join Seattle's volunteers. You'll never regret it. The Emerald City sparkles brightest when its citizens reach out to one another.

To help find a cause that is most meaningful to you, here are some of the volunteer resources Seattle has to offer.

### Idealist

www.idealist.org

A world of volunteers knowing no boundaries. This site offers access to 20,000 organizations in 140 countries. Tickle the keyboard a little, and you can quickly whittle your search down to the grassroots level. Organizations in Seattle run the gamut from arts to zero population growth. If you can't find a cause here, you better start your own.

### Points of Light Foundation

www.pointsoflight.org

"To engage more people more effectively in volunteer service to help solve serious social problems." There's a lot more than "a thousand points of light" on this site. PLF provides individual and corporate access to volunteer centers, programs, and sponsorship opportunities. It's also a terrific link to United Way of King County. The United Way is a network for community assistance and involvement.

### United Way of King County

*107 Cherry Street, Seventh Floor*
*Seattle, WA 98104*
*(206) 461-3655*

www.uwkc.org

dkuhn@uwkc.wa.org

**Seattle Works—Contact Us**

www.seattleworks.org/contact/index.html

Excellent site for community volunteers. Simply browse the list of updated community projects and pick one you like. The Online Volunteer Response Form is a cinch, or you may call, write, or visit Seattle Works directly.

**Seattle Works**
*510 19th Avenue E*
*Seattle, WA 98112*
*(206) 324-0808*
info@seattleworks.org

**VolunteerMatch Seattle**

www.volunteermatch.org

Part of the Impact Online alliance. This Web site pools of over fifty Seattle area organizations needing volunteers. Visitors can post an opportunity, find an opportunity, or join VolunteerMatch's own "Frontline Fanatics" in outreaching organizations for their data pool.

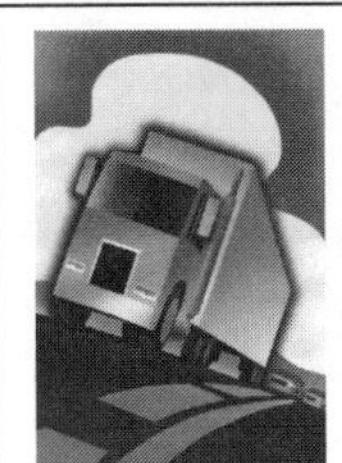

**MOVING TIP**

Aquarium shops and pet stores can advise you about the delicate task of relocating fish. Some even offer transport services.

**Where to Care**

www.thefoundry.org/wheretocare/main.html

A guide for youth volunteers in the Seattle area. An easy-to-navigate Web site, Where to Care conveniently organizes searches by issue, community, skills, and schedule. Detailed descriptions of nonprofit organizations and their missions are included.

## Volunteer Organizations

The following list is just a sample of the many volunteer organizations around Seattle that would be grateful for your support.

**Adopt-A-Park**
*100 Dexter Avenue N*
*Seattle, WA 98109*
*(206) 684-4557*

Truly a "grassroots" effort by neighborhoods to restore and maintain their parks.

CITY FACT

Seattle's Lake Washington and Lake Union are connected to Puget Sound by the Lake Washington Ship Canal. Ships traverse varying water levels—from the lower salt water bay to higher freshwater lakes—by navigating through the Hiram M. Chittenden Locks.

**Allied Arts**
*105 South Main Street, Suite 200*
*Seattle, WA 98104*
*(206) 624-0432*

www.alliedarts-seattle.org

freya_aarts@yahoo.com

Historic preservation, urban design, and arts legislation are among main focuses. It's the oldest arts advocacy in town.

**American Red Cross**
*1900 25th Avenue S*
*Seattle, WA 98144*
*(206) 323-2345*

Helping people to avoid, prepare for, and cope with emergencies.

**Cancer Lifeline**
*6522 Fremont Avenue N*
*Seattle, WA 98103-5358*
*(206) 297-0113*

www.cancerlifeline.org

info@cancerlifeline.org

Information and twenty-four-hour emotional support for cancer patients and their families.

**Chicken Soup Brigade**
*1002 East Seneca Street*
*Seattle, WA 98122*
*(206) 328-8979*

www.csbrigade.org

chicken@sbrigade.org

Provides nourishment and transportation for people with AIDS.

**Crisis Clinic**
*1515 Dexter Avenue N, Suite 300*
*Seattle, WA 98109*
*(206) 461-3210*

Offers intervention for people in crisis. After extensive training, volunteers work the phones.

**Easter Seal Society**
*521 Second Avenue W*
*Seattle, WA 98119*
*(206) 281-5700*

Programs include housing assistance, recreational therapy, and respite care for the disabled.

**Greenpeace**
*4649 Sunnyside Avenue N*
*Seattle, WA 98103*
*(206) 632-4326*

Dedicated to protecting the earth and its inhabitants and promoting environmental issues.

**Make-A-Wish Foundation**
*107 Cherry Street, Suite 305*
*Seattle, WA 98104*
*(206) 623-5300*

www.wish.org

wish@makeawishwa.org

Grants wishes of children with terminal or life-threatening illnesses. Welcomes donations as well as volunteer assistance.

**Peace Action of Washington State**
*5828 Roosevelt Way NE*
*Seattle, WA 98105*
*(206) 527-8050*

Mobilizes citizens through legislative action and community outreach programs.

**Physicians for Social Responsibility**
*4554 12th Avenue NE*
*Seattle, WA 98105*
*(206) 547-2630*

www.wpsr.org

wpsr@wpsr.org

Nonpartisan approach to responsible national defense programs. Promotes education about nuclear arms.

**Seattle Audubon Society**
*8050 35th Avenue NE*
*Seattle, WA 98115*
*(206) 523-4483*

www.seattleadubon.org

Promotes enjoyment and conservation of nature through education.

**Seattle Habitat for Humanity**
*306 Westlake Avenue N, Suite 210*
*Seattle, WA 98109*
*(206) 292-5240*

Ecumenical group that builds and refurbishes homes for sale, at cost, to low-income families.

**Seattle Public Library**
*Fifth Floor Central Library*
*1000 Fourth Avenue*
*Seattle, WA 98104-1193*
*(206) 386-4664*

www.spl.org/volunteer/volunteer.html

volunteer@spl.org

Volunteers act as homework helpers, computer coaches, after-school program assistants, and ESL/literacy advocates.

**Washington Literacy**
*220 Nickerson Street*
*Seattle, WA 98109*
*(206) 284-4399*

www.waliteracy.org

walit@aol.com

Assists adults that read at or below the sixth-grade level.

**Woodland Park Zoo**
*Volunteer Programs*
*5500 Phinney Avenue N*
*Seattle, WA 98103*
*(206) 684-4845*

Volunteers assist with veterinary records, coordinating special events, and providing docent tours.

## Civic Organizations

Here are a few of the most popular civic organizations.

**Boys & Girls Clubs of King County**
*7300 208th Avenue NE*
*Redmond, WA 98052*
*(425) 827-0132*

www.bgckc-kr.org

**Greater Seattle Chamber of Commerce**
*1301 Fifth Avenue, Suite 2400*
*Seattle, WA 98101*
*(206) 389-7200*

www.seattlechamber.com

**Rotary Club of Seattle**
*University District of Seattle, #5030*
*c/o Seattle Yacht Club*
*1807 East Hamlin Street*
*Seattle, WA 98112*
*(206) 325-1000*

www.rotary.org

**Volunteer Firefighters Association**
*163 Village Court*
*Monroe, WA 98272*

www.monroefire.org

george@monroefire.org

MOVING TIP

Open a Seattle checking account and relocate your safe deposit box items a month before you arrive. This will allow you easy access to your assets upon arrival, if necessary.

SECTION FOUR

# Finding the Essentials

CHAPTER 9

# Important Places to Know

Seattle lacks none of the standard amenities of a large city and has a few not found in other cosmopolitan areas of similar size. Relocators can feel pretty confident that the city offers services they need; what complicates matters is that there are so many, not that there are too few, churches, hospitals, pharmacies, markets, and other necessities. Using the following listings, those who are new to the city can find the closest, best, most convenient facility, whatever the service.

## Dry Cleaners and Laundromats

Seattleites are a casual but neat tribe. Because of our mild climate and abundant outdoor activities, many urbanites and suburbanites both favor the "Eddie Bauer" and "REI" look. We love our summer cottons and winter wool blends, but we also favor those synthetic fabrics with funny names like Ebtek, Gortex, and Polartec. Most high-tech, lightweight, and ultradurable sport and leisurewear can be tossed in the washer and dryer. If, that is, you have a washer and dryer. If not, here's a list of Seattle area Laundromats. And just so you don't get "taken to the cleaners," I've tossed in some of the very best dry cleaners in town.

For free twenty-four-hour consumer tips regarding dry cleaning, call (206) 442-2800.

- Press 3230 for information regarding dry cleaning operations and services
- Press 3231 to hear about the latest dry cleaning processes
- Press 3232 to find the right dry cleaner for you
- Press 3233 to receive guidelines for dry cleaning

## DRY CLEANERS

**Ace Cleaners**
*2020 South 320th Street*
*Federal Way*
*(253) 839-1179*

**Aloha Cleaners**
*10575 Northeast 12th Street*
*Bellevue*
*(425) 454-1012*

**Bakker's Fine Dry Cleaning**
*1004 Northeast 50th Street*
*Redmond*
*(206) 526-1909*

**Bella Cleaners**
*8867 161st Avenue NE*
*Seattle*
*(425) 883-9029*

**Betty Brite Dry Cleaners**
*7500-J 196th Avenue SW*
*Lynnwood*
*(425) 774-0222*

**Big W Cleaners & Alterations**
*5025 25th Street NE*
*Seattle*
*(206) 527-6655*

**Campus Cleaners**
*4100 Roosevelt Way NE*
*North Seattle*
*(206) 633-3145*

**City Dry Cleaners**
*8410 Main Street*
*Edmonds*
*(425) 775-4457*

**The Cleaning Center**
*2625 University Village Mall*
*Seattle*
*(206) 522-1033*
www.cleaningcenters.uswest-dex.com

**Corry's Fine Dry Cleaning**
*3800 34th Street W*
*Magnolia*
*(206) 284-8441*

**Corry's Fine Dry Cleaning**
*4640 Union Bay Place NE*
*Laurehurst*
*(206) 634-3238*

**Daniel's Dry Cleaners**
*6923 Coal Creek Parkway SE*
*Newcastle*
*(425) 747-5818*

**Dirk's Fine Dry Cleaning**
*240 Northwest Gilman Boulevard*
*Issaquah*
*(425) 392-3200*

**Emerald City Dry Cleaners**
*850 Rainier Avenue S*
*Seattle*
*(206) 328-0434*

**Forest Park Cleaner**
*17171 Bothell Way NE*
*Forest Park*
*(206) 362-4124*

**Gateway Cleaners**
*1112 N 183rd Street*
*Shoreline*
*(206) 542-4840*

**Helena's Queen Anne Cleaners**
*537 Warren Street N*
*Queen Anne*
*(206) 282-0873*

**Jay's Cleaners**
*2350 24th Street E*
*Mountlake Terrace*
*(206) 328-8158*

**Joinus Cleaners**
*27041 Pacific Highway S*
*Des Moines*
*(253) 839-4864*

CITY FACT

Seattle Center—a major cultural complex of performing arts, science exhibits, retail shops, museums, and an amusement park—is connected to downtown by monorail.

**Kay's Dry Cleaners**
*22941 Highway 99*
*Edmonds*
*(425) 776-3200*

**Kim's Cleaners**
*1018 164th Street SE*
*Mill Creek*
*(425) 743-6867*

**Lake City Sunshine Cleaners**
*12525 Lake City Way NE*
*Lake City*
*(206) 365-0218*

**MOVING TIP**

To prevent breakage, remove lightbulbs from fixtures and pack them separately. Keep the box of lightbulbs in your car, especially if you are arriving after dark.

**Lee's Cleaners**
*17051 Southeast 272nd Street*
*Covington*
*(253) 631-9178*

**Martha Lake Cleaners**
*16420 Sixth Avenue W*
*Lynnwood*
*(425) 743-9009*

**Medina Cleaners**
*1075 Bellevue Way NE*
*Bellevue*
*(425) 451-4433*

**Michael's Fine Dry Cleaning**
*1006 Lake Street S*
*Kirkland*
*(425) 827-2222*

*13200 Old Redmond Road*
*Rose Hill*
*(425) 881-7666*

*10711 Main Street*
*Bellevue*
*(425) 451-1417*

**No-D-Lay Cleaners**
*2117 Queen Anne N*
*Seattle*
*(206) 282-7395*

**Northwest Cleaners of Renton**
*20 Southwest Seventh Street*
*Renton*
*(425) 271-4448*

**Orchard Plaza Cleaners**
*20942 108th Street SE*
*Kent*
*(253) 854-6064*

**Oscar Cleaners**
*2835 78th Street SE*
*Mercer Island*
*(206) 230-9213*

**Personality Cleaners**
*13634 1st Street*
*Burien*
*(206) 243-3200*

**Prestige Cleaners**
*901 Elliott Avenue W*
*Seattle*
*(206) 285-2225*

**Royal Fabric Care Center**
*21445 Pacific Highway S*
*Des Moines*
*(206) 878-11440*

**Seattle's Nicest Dry Cleaners**
*333 Northwest 85th Street*
*Seattle*
*(206) 784-9020*

**Simon & Son**
*16920 Juanita Drive NE*
*Bothell*
*(425) 488-8123*

*15327 Brown Avenue NE*
*Duvall*
*(425) 788-1348*

**Southcenter Cleaners**
*1076 Southcenter Shopping Center*
*Tukwilla*
*(206) 242-8830*

**Sparkle Cleaners**
*2011 Northwest Market Street*
*Seattle*
*(206) 782-7826*

**Stone Dry Cleaners**
*5614 E Lake Sammamish Parkway SE*
*Issaquah*
*(425) 392-8954*

**Strom's Custom Cleaners**
*15223 Sixth Street SW*
*Burien*
*(206) 244-9880*

**Taylor's Fine Dry Cleaning**
*10441 Southeast 240th Street*
*Kent*
*(253) 859-1559*

**Three Brothers Cleaners**
*3210 Beacon Street*
*Seattle*
*(206) 722-0600*

**Villa Dry Cleaner**
*1315 Auburn Way N*
*Auburn*
*(253) 939-5979*

**Wanda's Cleaners**
*2354 Tenth Avenue E*
*Seattle*
*(206) 323-4370*

## LAUNDROMATS

Sit & Spin is a bit of a laundry landmark of downtown Seattle. It's actually quite a hip place to hang out on Friday or Saturday night. Open weekends until 2:00 A.M., this "laundro-theque" offers food, music, and even cocktails to patrons. Rumor has it that half of the clientele already have a washer and dryer at home, but have more fun doing the laundry here.

**Auburn Vibraclean**
*1801 Howard Road*
*Auburn*
*(253) 833-2797*

**Burien Homestyle Laundry**
*14300 First Street*
*Burien*
*(206) 248-3770*

**Clean Laundry Matt**
*6010 Martin Luther King Jr. Way S*
*South Seattle*
*(206) 721-7872*

**Cleveland Street Laundry**
*16421 Cleveland Street*
*Redmond*
*(425) 885-9164*

**Crystal Clean Laundry**
*1718 Bellevue Way*
*Bellevue*
*(206) 323-4969*

**Des Moines Highlander Laundry**
*21837 Marine View Drive S*
*Des Moines*
*(206) 824-7850*

**Edmonds Maytag Laundry**
*184 Sunset Avenue*
*Edmonds*
*(425) 774-1715*

**Hogan's Corner Laudromat**
*5501 25th NE*
*Seattle*
*(206) 526-9754*

**Inglewood Village Laundromat**
*14130 Juanita Drive NE*
*Bothell*
*(425) 823-4304*

**Judy's Laundromat**
*12960 Kent-Kangley Road*
*Kent*
*(253) 631-9501*

**The Laundry Room**
*1313 West Meeker*
*Kent*
*(253) 859-1166*

**Maytag Just Like Home Laundry**
*Northeast 145th and Lake City Way*
*Lake City*
*(206) 362-6278*

**Norge Village Laundromat**
*1905 Southwest Campus Drive*
*Federal Way*
*(253) 874-9603*

**Oliver's Queen Anne Laundry**
*1911 Tenth Street W*
*Seattle*
*(206) 283-1357*

**Otter Wash Laundromat**
*14227 Pacific Highway S*
*Seattle*
*(206) 433-1047*

**Park Lane Laundry Service**
*136 Park Lane*
*Kirkland*
*(425) 822-2550*

**Royal Choice Laundry**
*4012 South 140th Street*
*Tukwilla*
*(206) 431-9174*

**Seattle's Nicest Coin Laundry**
*333 Northwest 85th Street*
*Seattle*
*(206) 784-9020*

**Salmon Creek Coin-Op Laundry**
*11616 Ambaum Boulevard SW*
*Sea Tac*
*(206) 346-0299*

CITY FACT

In the 1980s and early 1990s, Seattle ushered in an era of "grunge," giving rise to such megabands as Pearl Jam, Nirvana, and Soundgarden.

**Sit & Spin**
*2219 Fourth Avenue*
*Seattle*
*(206) 441-9484*

**Splash N Dash**
*18009 Highway 99*
*Lynnwood*
*(425) 672-4965*

MOVING TIP

Keep pets out of the way on Moving Day. This is for the benefit of the animals as well as the movers. Dogs and cats are acutely sensitive to seeing furniture displaced and may exhibit anxiety, including aggression or running away. Remember, too, that some pets may experience confusion, disorientation, and problems with acclimation when relocated. Consult your veterinarian well in advance of Moving Day if you have concerns.

**Super Suds Laundromat**
*3901 Northeast Fourth Street*
*Renton*
*(425) 277-8703*

**12th Avenue Laundry**
*1807 12th Avenue*
*Capitol Hill*
*(206) 328-4610*

**Vince & Mike's Laundromat**
*7903 Rainier Avenue S*
*Seattle*
*(206) 725-5546*

**Wallingford Maytag Laundry**
*2511 North 50th Street*
*Wallingford*
*(206) 548-9252*

**Wilderness Village Laundromat**
*23714 222nd Place SE*
*Maple Valley*
*(425) 432-6351*

## Hospitals and Other Medical Facilities

Our hospitals, university medical center, and research institutes are on the cutting edge of biomedical science. Seattle stands at the forefront of cancer research, immunotherapy, trauma treatment, microsurgery, and neonatal and postnatal care. Several of our private healthcare facilities rank among the nation's most prestigious and richly endowed. In the early 1990s, the Washington State legislature enacted one of the most progressive state healthcare plans in America. Our managed-care programs boast some of the highest enrollee satisfaction ratings, and more and more are modeling their plans after ours.

Notably, too, Seattle's values are beautifully reflected in the continuous support of Children's Hospital, a renowned pediatric facility.

Part of the reason for Seattle's high-quality medical care is that the city benefits greatly as the home of high-tech corporate giants. These companies and their founders, executives, and major shareholders are often generous with their staggering wealth. Some of the finest hospitals and research centers in the world have been recipients of their largesse, and they're right here in Seattle.

## PRIVATE

**Allenmore Hospital**
*1901 South Union*
*Tacoma*
*(253) 572-2323*

**Auburn Regional Medical Center**
*Plaza One, 202 North Division Street*
*Auburn*
*(253) 833-7711*

**Mary Bridge Children's Hospital & Health Center**
*317 S Martin Luther King Jr. Way*
*Tacoma*
*(253) 552-1400*

**Children's Hospital & Regional Medical Center**
*4800 Sand Point Way NE*
*Seattle*
*(206) 526-2000*

**Community Memorial Hospital**
*1450 Battersby Avenue*
*Enumclaw*
*(360) 825-2505*

**Evergreen Hospital Medical Center**
*12040 Northeast 128th Street*
*Kirkland*
*(425) 899-1000*

**Good Samaritan Hospital & Rehabilitation Center**
*407 14th Avenue SE*
*Puyallup*
*(253) 848-6661 (Hospital)*
*(253) 841-5849 (Rehabilitation Center)*

**Group Health Central Hospital**
*201 16th Avenue E*
*Seattle*
*(206) 326-3000*

**Group Health Eastside Hospital**
*2700 152nd Avenue NE*
*Redmond*
*(425) 883-5151*

**Harborview Medical Center**
*325 Ninth Avenue*
*Seattle*
*(206) 731-3000*

**Highline Community Hospital**
*16251 Sylvester Road SW*
*Burien*
*(206) 244-9970*

**Highline Community Hospital Specialty Center**
*12844 Military Road S*
*Tukwilla*
*(206) 244-0180*

**Northwest Hospital**
*1550 North 115th Street*
*Seattle*
*(206) 364-0500*

**Overlake Hospital Medical Center**
*1321 Colby Avenue*
*Everett*
*(425) 261-2000*

**Providence Seattle Medical Center**
*500 17th Avenue*
*Seattle*
*(206) 320-2000*

**Puget Sound Hospital**
*215 South 36th Street*
*Tacoma*
*(253) 474-0561*

**St. Clare Hospital**
*11315 Bridgeport Way SW*
*Lakewood*
*(253) 588-1711*

**St. Francis Hospital**
*34515 Ninth Avenue S*
*Federal Way*
*(253) 838-9700*

**St. Joseph Medical Center**
*1717 South J Street*
*Tacoma*
*(253) 627-4101*

**Stevens Hospital**
*21601 76th Avenue W*
*Edmonds*
*(425) 640-4000*

**Swedish Medical Center**
*747 Broadway*
*Seattle*
*(206) 386-6000*

**Tacoma General Hospital**
*315 South Martin Luther King Jr. Way*
*Tacoma*
*(253) 552-1000*

**THC Seattle**
*10560 Fifth Avenue NE*
*Seattle*
*(206) 364-2050*

**University of Washington Medical Center**
*1959 Northeast Pacific Street*
*Seattle*
*(206) 548-3300*

**Valley General Hospital**
*14701 179th Avenue SE*
*Monroe*
*(360) 794-7497*

**Valley Medical Center**
*400 South 43rd Street*
*Renton*
*(425) 228-3440*

**Vencor Hospital**
*10560 Fifth Avenue NE*
*Seattle*
*(206) 364-2050*

**V.A. Puget Sound Health Center**
*1660 Columbian Way S*
*Seattle*
*(206) 762-1010*

**Virginia Mason Hospital**
*925 Seneca Street*
*Seattle*
*(206) 624-1144*

## PUBLIC

**Columbia Health Center**
*4400 37th Avenue S*
*Seattle*
*(206) 205-6060*

**Downtown Public Health Center**
*2124 Fourth Avenue*
*Seattle*
*(206) 296-4755*

CITY FACT

The theme of the 1962 Seattle World's Fair was "Century Twenty-One."

Keep a tape measure handy at all times throughout the move. Carpenters say, "measure twice, cut once." Movers say, "measure twice, lift once."

**North Public Health Center**
*10501 Meridian Avenue N*
*Seattle*
*(206) 296-4765*

### CANCER RESEARCH

**Fred Hutchinson Cancer Research Centers**
*(206) 667-5000*

**Cancer Information Service**
*(800) 4-CANCER*

### SUBSTANCE ABUSE

**Highline Recovery Service**
*12844 Military Road S*
*Seattle*
*(206) 248-4790*

**Schick Shadel Hospital**
*12101 Ambaum Boulevard SW*
*Seattle*
*(206) 244-8100*

**Seattle Indian Health Board**
*611 12th Avenue S*
*Seattle*
*(206) 324-9360 (Outpatient Clinic)*
*(206) 722-7152 (Inpatient Treatment Center)*

**Swedish Medical Center/Ballard**
*Northwest Market and Barnes Streets*
*Seattle*
*(206) 781-6209*

### HEALTH INSURANCE

**Washington State Insurance Commission**
*(800) 562-6900*

## Grocers and Markets

Like any thriving metropolis, Seattle is peppered with regional chain supermarkets. Albertson's, QFC, and Safeway are the biggies. There's also Top Food & Drug, Thriftway, and Red Apple Markets to keep your pantry well stocked. Larry's is the original yuppie market, and it's a great place to shop if you have Cap'n Crunch and shiitake mushrooms on the same list. They even have a cooking school: (425) 451-2080.

Trader Joe's combines modern notions of bulk distributor pricing and prepared specialty foods with a nostalgic, trading post concept. PriceCostco, the undisputed King of Bulk Discounting, is a local giant with its corporate lair in Issaquah. If you're hosting the Seahawk's offensive line for afternoon tea, make sure you buy a forklift-full of crumpets at PriceCostco.

You aren't officially a Seattlite until you've visited one of the Uwajimaya (ooh-WAH-jih-MY-uh) grocery stores. The stores specialize in Pacific Rim foodstuffs, often venturing into the exotic . . . or even bizarre. Still, I wouldn't buy my lychee juice, gobo, or freshwater eel anywhere else.

Still holding on as a bastion of fresh produce and fish trade is the legendary Pike Place Market, located in the very heart of Seattle. Paintings and greeting cards have depicted images of the mammoth, vintage marquee casting pink reflections on a rain-swept sidewalk for nearly a century. Some people may think of Pike Place as just another tourist site, but it remains a wonderful place for locals to buy their fresh fruits, vegetables, and fish. But be careful, the time-honored practice of relaying huge salmon by way of a bucket brigade is still practiced. Caution: low-flying fish!

Old-fashioned, folksy general stores are alive and well in the countless neighborhood and street corner markets around Seattle. Adding charm, character, and a lively flavor are the ethnic grocers. The Emerald City is a treasure chest of Caribbean, Thai, Indian, East African, Japanese, Latino, Ukrainian, Cambodian, and Hawaiian specialty markets. *Vive la difference!*

**A&M International Grocery**
*14038 Aurora N*
*Seattle*
*(206) 366-8997*

**Aladdin Gyro-Cery**
*4139 University Way NE*
*Seattle*
*(206) 632-5253*

**Alfi's Food & Deli**
*1830 Minor Avenue*
*Seattle*
*(206) 623-8196*

**Auntie Stella's Market**
*1523 Second Avenue*
*Seattle*
*(206) 405-4490*

**Bellevue Oriental Mart**
*900 160th Street NE*
*Bellevue*
*(425) 747-1351*

**Black Diamond Market**
*Highway 169*
*Black Diamond*
*(360) 886-2611*

**The Blue Sun**
*1018 North Central*
*Kent*
*(253) 859-6444*

**Burien Garden**
*13621 Ambaum Boulevard SW*
*Seattle*
*(206) 242-1282*

**Byblos Mini Market**
*22324 Highway 99*
*Edmonds*
*(425) 775-3586*

**Cambodian Market**
*9419 16th Street SW*
*Seattle*
*(206) 767-0531*

**Capitol Hill Market**
*1728 12th Street*
*Seattle*
*(206) 329-4425*

**Central Co-Op's Madison Mkt**
*1600 East Madison Street*
*Seattle*
*(206) 329-1545*

**The Corner Deli**
*656 Northwest 85th Street*
*Seattle*
*(206) 782-3898*

**Crude Awakenings**
*1515 164th Street SW*
*Lynnwood*
*(425) 743-5862*

**DeLaurenti Specialty Food Mkt.**
*1435 First Avenue*
*Seattle*
*(206) 622-0141*

**Dexter Horton Goodie Box**
*710 Second Avenue*
*Seattle*
*(206) 624-5526*

**That Durn Grocery Store**
*4002 Wallingford Avenue N*
*Wallingford*
*(206) 633-0500*

**East African Grocery & Deli**
*2205 East Union Avenue*
*Seattle*
*(206) 860-8211*

**El Mercadito**
*18424 Highway 99, Suite B*
*Lynnwood*
*(425) 744-1546*

**Fishermen's Grocery Store**
*1735 West Thurman Street*
*Seattle*
*(206) 281-7818*

**Golliwog Deli Mart**
*2136 First Avenue*
*Seattle*
*(206) 441-8642*

**Goody Goody Deli Grocery**
*22240 SE 272nd Street*
*Maple Valley*
*(425) 432-3623*

**India Bazaar**
*20936 180th Street SE*
*Kent*
*(253) 850-8906*

**Kilimanjaro Market**
*12519 Lake City Way NE*
*(206) 440-1440*

**La Bodeguita Specialty Foods**
*2528A Beacon Street South*
*(206) 329-9001*

**Little Store West**
*2810 West Lake Sammamish Parkway SE*
*(425) 746-1444*

**Louie's on the Pike**
*1926 Pike Place Public Market*
*(206) 443-1035*

**Madrona Homemade Deli Market**
*3309 East Union Avenue*
*Seattle*
*(206) 324-5771*

**The Market at Crystal Market**
*Crystal Mountain*
*Enumclaw*
*(360) 663-0482*

**Mi Mazatlan**
*16142 Northeast 87th Street*
*Redmond*
*(425) 881-3151*

**Milk Barn Too**
*5610 East Lake Sammamish Parkway SE*
*Issaquah*
*(425) 391-0506*

CITY FACT

The first woman elected mayor of a major American city was Bertha Landes. The year was 1926 and the city was Seattle.

**The Mobile Grocer**
*(206) 363-7447*

**HomeGrocer.com**
*(800) 688-0201*

**99 Cent Store**
*109 Broadway Avenue E*
*Capitol Hill*
*(206) 328-6310*

**NW Halal Mediterranean Grocery**
*15047 Military Road S*
*Sea Tac*
*(206) 431-0941*

**Pakistani & Indian Grocery**
*12325 Roosevelt Way NE*
*Seattle*
*(206) 368-7323*

**PCC Natural Market**
*7504 Aurora Avenue N*
*Greenlake*
*(206) 525-3586*

**Pioneer Organics**
*14001 Lake City Way NE*
*Lake City*
*(206) 440-0996*

**Redmond Country Store**
*7725 159th Place NE*
*Redmond*
*(425) 881-4295*

**Seattle Mediterranean Market**
*22910 Highway 99*
*Edmonds*
*(425) 778-7011*

**Sessions Liquidation Outlet**
*30 West Main Street*
*Auburn*
*(253) 939-1952*

**Shady Park Grocery**
*27848 152nd Street SE*
*Kent*
*(253) 631-5226*

**Smiler Grocery**
*19246 15th Avenue NE*
*Shoreline*
*(206) 364-8215*

**Stock Market Foods**
*6625 132nd Avenue NE*
*Kirkland*
*(425) 881-7602*

**Tiger Mountain Country Store**
*14331 Issaquah-Hobart Road SE*
*Issaquah*
*(425) 392-2265*

**Ukraine International Foods**
*10410 Greenwood Avenue N*
*Seattle*
*(206) 784-8309*
*(425) 747-9012*

**Uwajimaya**
*519 6th Street*
*Seattle*
*(206) 624-6248*

*15555 Northeast 24th Street*
*Bellevue*
*(425) 747-9012*

**Victor's Grocery & Deli**
*11801 Northeast 160th Street*
*Bothell*
*(425) 488-0390*

**Zip Market**
*15253 Bellevue Redmond Road*
*Bellevue*

## Pharmacies

There is such a high concentration of hospitals, general medical centers, and specialized centers around Capitol Hill that residents have dubbed the south Seattle town "Pill Hill." Whether you need a prescription filled or just come down with the sniffles, it's nice to know that a neighborhood pharmacy is close by.

Most chain supermarkets and drug stores have plain old pharmacies. An increasingly common convenience is the twenty-four-hour drive-through pharmacy. "Would you like fries with your Propecia, sir?" Those, too, are part of national or regional chains. They're okay, but I like the Ma and Pa shops, where the pharmacist wears a sweater instead of a lab coat.

Big grocers offering pharmacy service include: Safeway, QFC (Quality Food Centers), Fred Meyer, and Top Food & Drug. Chain pharmacies include: United Drugs, Bartell, Walgreens, Rite-Aid, Longs Drugs, Good Neighbor, Valu-Rite, and Rexall. Even such megastores as Wal-Mart and K Mart will fill your prescription. And then there's PriceCostco, where bodybuilders can buy protein powder in fifty-five-gallon drums and moms can stock up on cough syrup by the vat.

I'd be remiss, though, if I didn't pay homage to a Seattle institution known as Westside Pharmacy, at 5401 California Street SW, (206) 937-5722. Westside Rx offers old-fashioned delivery, but if you prefer to dine-in you can pull up a stool and wash down your Allegra with a yummy latté or refreshing sarsaparilla float from the vintage soda fountain. There's even a deli. Ask your doctor to prescribe the extra-lean Black Forest ham on pumpernickel.

For free twenty-four-hour consumer tips about prescription medications and related topics, call (206) 442-2800.

- Press 3620 for information regarding medications and health insurance
- Press 3621 to hear about the latest pharmacological innovations
- Press 3622 for learning more about children and medication
- Press 3623 to speak with a licensed pharmacist

The following is a list of neighborhood pharmacies.

**CITY FACT**

Washington's number one tourist attraction is Puget Sound.

**AARP Pharmacy Service**
*730 12th Street SE*
*Auburn*
*(253) 833-4570*

**Ballard Plaza Pharmacy**
*1801 Northwest Market Street*
*Ballard*
*(206) 782-7200*

**Bartell Drugs**
*5500 Olympic Drive*
*Gig Harbor*
*(253) 858-7444*

**Bellegrove Pharmacy**
*1605 116th Street NE*
*Bellevue*
*(425) 455-2123*

**Bellevue Apothecary Shop**
*1031 116th Street NE*
*Bellevue*
*(425) 454-3358*

**Bridgeport Professional Pharmacy**
*3021 Griffin Street*
*Enumclaw*
*(360) 802-2441*

**Briggs Pharmacy**
*2201 North 56th Street*
*Seattle*
*(206) 632-7613*

**Cabrini Medical Tower Pharmacy**
*901 Boren Avenue, Suite 100*
*Seattle*
*(206) 682-1011*

**Cascade Pharmacy**
*3915 Talbot Road S*
*Renton*
*(425) 271-7025*

**Clark's Pharmacy**
*15615 Bellevue-Redmond Road*
*Bellevue*
*(425) 881-0222*

**Cornell's Valley Pharmacy**
*4300 Talbot Road S*
*Renton*
*(425) 228-2210*

**Cornerstone Pharmacy Services**
*2502 Fifth Avenue*
*Seattle*
*(206) 448-0932*

**Covington Pharmacy**
*17239 Southeast 272nd Street*
*Covington*
*(253) 631-1200*

**Dick's Pharmacy**
*1811 156th Street NE*
*Bellevue*
*(425) 747-2301*

**Don Plumlee's Pharmacy**
*4130 East Madison*
*Seattle*
*(206) 324-1188*

**Dong Nai Pharmacy**
*620 South Jackson Street*
*Seattle*
*(206) 624-4238*

**Douglass Drug Store**
*8301 161st Street NE, Suite 101*
*Redmond*
*(425) 885-1831*

**Duvall Family Drugs**
*15325 Brown Avenue NW*
*Duvall*
*(425) 788-2644*

**Eastern's Pharmacy**
*515 Minor Avenue*
*Seattle*
*(206) 622-6094*

**Evergreen Pharmacy**
*12911 120th Avenue NE*
*Kirkland*
*(425) 821-8888*

**Five Corners Pharmacy**
*8403 Main Street*
*Edmonds*
*(425) 776-0168*

**Gateway Pharmacy**
*18320 Midvale Avenue N*
*Shoreline*
*(206) 542-3110*

**Hadfield's Pharmacy**
*21701 76th Avenue W*
*Edmonds*
*(425) 744-1799*

**Georgetown Pharmacy**
*6111 13th Street S*
*Seattle*
*(206) 763-0288*

**Healthtek Pharmacy**
*1221 Madison Avenue*
*Seattle*
*(206) 292-6254*

**Issaquah Medical Center Pharmacy**
*450 Northwest Gilman Boulevard*
*Issaquah*
*(425) 392-8650*

**Jim's Pharmacy**
*2987 Griffin Street*
*Enumclaw*
*(360) 825-6523*

**Juanita Bay Pharmacy**
*13520 100th Avenue NE*
*Kirkland*
*(425) 821-4009*

**Lakeshore Pharmacy**
*325 Parkplace Center*
*Kirkland*
*(425) 822-4123*

**Lakeside Drug**
*Redmond Center*
*Redmond*
*(425) 885-2323*

**Lakeside Mercer Drugs**
*8441 Southeast 68th Street*
*Mercer Island*
*(206) 232-3000*

**Look's Issaquah Pharmacy**
*1520 Northwest Gilman Boulevard*
*Issaquah*
*(425) 392-5151*

**Look's Mercer Island Pharmacy**
*2775 78th Street SE*
*Mercer Island*
*(206) 232-2222*

**Manhattan Pharmacy**
*17833 First Street S*
*Normandy Park*
*(206) 243-7500*

**Madrix Pharmacy**
*13210 Southeast 240th Street*
*Kent*
*(253) 630-3833*

**Medicine Man Pharmacy**
*323 North 85th Street*
*Greenwood*
*(206) 789-0800*

**Medicine Shoppe**
*22505 Marine View Drive S*
*Des Moines*
*(206) 824-4127*

**Mill Creek Pharmacy**
*15808 Mill Creek Boulelvard*
*Mill Creek*
*(425) 481-7575*

**Newport Hills Drug**
*5620 119th Street SE*
*Bellvue*
*(425) 746-8161*

**Ostrom's Drugs**
*44 Northeast 181st Street*
*Kenmore*
*(425) 486-7711*

**Padgett Pharmacy**
*18322 Bothell Way NE*
*Bothell*
*(425) 486-5811*

**Peckenpaugh Drug**
*1123 East Main Street*
*Auburn*
*(253) 833-8020*

**Providence Community Pharmacy**
*1600 East Jefferson Street, Suite B-1*
*Seattle*
*(206) 320-2699*

**Riverton Family Pharmacy**
*15045 Pacific Highway S*
*Tukwila*
*(206) 242-8221*

**Sand Point Clinic Pharmacy**
*4575 Sand Point Way NE*
*Seattle*
*(206) 523-5700*

**Seoul Pharmacy**
*31260 Pacific Highway S*
*Federal Way*
*(253) 946-3968*

**Specialized Prescription Services**
*1319 Dexter Avenue N*
*Seattle*
*(206) 217-0993*

**Sunscript Pharmacy**
*15405 53rd Street S*
*Tukwila*
*(206) 241-7828*

**Three Tree Professional Pharmacy**
*16259 Sylvester Road S*
*Burien*
*(206) 244-4100*

**Tokuda Drugs (Delivery and Mail)**
*609 South Main Street*
*Seattle*
*(206) 624-7098*

**UPC Health Network**
*34012 9th Avenue S, Suite 6*
*Federal Way*
*(253) 661-2474*

**Vashon Pharmacy**
*17617 Vashon Highway SW*
*Vashon Island*
*(206) 463-9118*

**Village Drug**
*22117 Southeast 237th Street*
*Maple Valley*
*(425) 432-1234*

**White Center Pharmacy**
*9601 16th Street SW*
*White Center*
*(206) 763-2500*

**Woodinville Medical Center Pharmacy**
*17000 140th Avenue NE*
*Woodinville*
*(425) 485-2900*

## Places of Worship

One measure of Seattle's cultural diversity are the many places of worship in and around the greater metropolitan area. From great cathedrals and temples to neighborhood churches and country chapels, Seattle's places of worship represent every world religion, all of which are part of the woven cloth that is our community.

### ASSEMBLY OF GOD

**Angle Lake Neighborhood Church**
*18617 42nd Avenue S*
*Sea Tac*
*(206) 244-7600*

### BAPTIST

**Crossroads Baptist Church**
*14434 Northeast Eighth Street*
*Bellevue*
*(425) 747-6750*

**Grace Baptist Church**
*17123 13th Avenue W*
*Lynnwood*
*(425) 743-9520*

**Queen Anne Baptist Church**
*2011 First Street N*
*Queen Anne*
*(206) 282-7744*
www.qabc.org\

**MOVING TIP**

Disconnect and drain all appliance hoses. Stow them and related materials, including exhaust ducts, filters, and assembly manuals or directions, inside its appliance. Depending upon the model, replacement parts might be hard to locate, and you'll want to use your appliances shortly after arriving.

**Seattle First Baptist Church**
*Seneca and Harvard*
*Seattle*
*(206) 325-6051*

## BUDDHIST

**Dharmadhatu Buddhist Meditation Center**
*919 East Pike Street*
*Seattle*
*(206) 860-4060*
www.shambhall.org/center/seattle

**White River Buddhist Temple**
*3625 Auburn Way N*
*Auburn*
*(253) 833-1442*

**Seattle Buddhist Temple**
*1427 South Main Street*
*Seattle*
*(206) 329-0800*

## CATHOLIC

**Corpus Christi Chapel**
*204 Sixth Avenue N*
*Edmonds*
*(425) 771-9208*

**Holy Family Church**
*15216 21st Street SW*
*Burien*
*(206) 246-1230*

**Our Lady of the Lake Church**
*8900 35th Avenue NE*
*Seattle*
*(206) 523-6776*

**St. Francis of Assisi Church**
*9622 20th Street SW*
*Seattle*
*(206) 767-6220*
www.brigadoon.com

## EPISCOPAL

**All Saints' Episcopal Church**
*5150 South Cloverdale*
*Cloverdale*
*(206) 721-0285*

**St. Alban's Episcopal Church**
*21405 82nd Place W*
*Edmonds*
*(425) 778-0371*

**St. Mark's Episcopal Cathedral**
*1245 Tenth Avenue E*
*Seattle*
*(206) 323-0300*

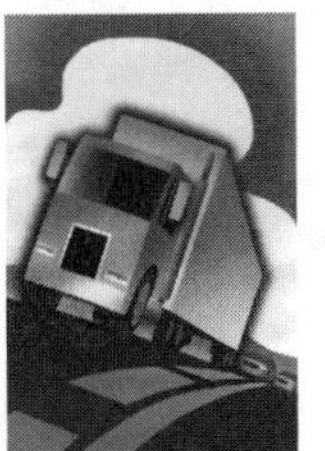

**MOVING TIP**

Arrange to have trash disposed of at both residences: the one you are vacating as well as the one to which you are relocating. You'll be surprised how much trash is generated on both ends of a move.

## HINDU

**Vedanta Society of Western Washington (Ramakrishna Mission)**
*2716 Broadway E*
*Seattle*
*(206) 323-1228*

**International Society for Krishna Consciousness**
*1420 228th Street SE*
*Issaquah*
*(425) 391-3293*

## ISLAMIC

**Evergreen Islamic Institute**
*6210 188th Avenue SW*
*Lynnwood*
*(425) 774-8852*

**Islamic Center of the Eastside**
*14700 Main Street*
*Bellevue*
*(425) 746-0398*

**Islamic Idriss Mosque**
*1420 Northgate Way*
*Seattle*
*(206) 363-3013*

## JEWISH

**Beth Ha Shofar-Messianic**
*13001 37th Street S*
*Tukwilla*
*(206) 246-5345*

**Bet Chaverim Community Synagogue of South King County**
*25701 14th Place S*
*Des Moines*
*(253) 946-4406*

**Congregation Tikvah Chadashah Gay & Lesbian**
*1122 East Pike Street, #734*
*Seattle*
*(206) 329-2590*

**Herzl-Ner Tamid Conservative Congregation**
*3700 East Mercer Way*
*Mercer Island*
*(206) 232-8555*

**Temple B'nai Torah**
*15727 Northeast Fourth Street*
*Bellevue*
*(425) 603-9677*

## LUTHERAN

**Our Redeemer Lutheran Church**
*11611 Northeast 140th Street*
*Kirkland*
*(425) 821-2424*

**Trinity Lutheran Church**
*1200 Tenth Street E*
*Seattle*
*(206) 324-1066*

## METHODIST

**First United Methodist Church**
*811 Fifth Avenue*
*Seattle*
*(206) 622-7278*

**Lake Washington United Methodist**
*7525 132nd Avenue NE*
*Kirkland*
*(425) 885-3311*

**Calvary Temple of Seattle**
*6810 Eighth Street NE*
*Seattle*
*(206) 525-7473*
www.ctseattle.com

**MOVING TIP**

When transporting firearms, be sure to comply with all state and federal interstate regulations. Remove rounds, secure all safety locks, and pack ammunition separately. Most important, *keep firearms and ammunition beyond the reach of children at all times.*

## MORMON

**Church of Jesus Christ of Latter-Day Saints**
*9500 Myers Way S*
*Seattle*
*(206) 764-0848*

**Church of Jesus Christ of Latter-Day Saints**
*15205 Southeast 28th Street*
*Bellevue*
*(425) 746-3440*

**Church of Jesus Christ of Latter-Day Saints**
*11852 140th Street SE*
*Renton*
*(425) 226-8686*

## NONDENOMINATIONAL AND INTERDENOMINATIONAL CHRISTIAN

**The City Church**
*9051 132nd Avenue NE*
*Kirkland*
*(425) 803-3233*
www.thecity.org

CITY FACT

The top employer in the Greater Puget Sound area is The Boeing Company. As the world's largest aircraft manufacturer, Boeing's 110,000 employees earned a 1998 payroll of nearly $6 billion.

**Eastside Christian Church**
*4242 Jones Avenue NE*
*Renton*
*(425) 226-1874*

**Eastside Foursquare Church**
*14520 100th Avenue NE*
*Bothell*
*(425) 488-2500*
www.eastsidechurch.org

**Edmonds Church of Christ**
*8703 216th Street SW*
*Edmonds*
*(425) 778-9612*

**Federal Way Mission Church**
*405 South 312th Street*
*Federal Way*
*(253) 529-3935*

**First Christian of Seattle**
*1632 Broadway*
*Seattle*
*(206) 322-0487*

**Greenwood Christian Church**
*8018 Fremont Avenue N*
*Seattle*
*(206) 783-5510*

**Highline Christian Church**
*14859 First Avenue S*
*Burien*
*(206) 243-4333*

**Hope of Seattle Church**
*6195 92nd Avenue SE*
*Mercer Island*
*(206) 275-1042*

**Issaquah Christian Church**
*10305 238th Way SE*
*Issaquah*
*(425) 392-5848*

**Joint Youth Ministry of Mercer Island**
*8501 Southeast 40th Street*
*Mercer Island*
*(206) 230-8109*

**Lakeside Community Church**
*10522 Lake City Way NE*
*(206) 417-1436*
www.lakesidecommunity.org

**Light of the City Ministries**
*708 SW 13th Street*
*Renton*
*(425) 277-3861*

**Mountlake Terrace Christian**
*5304 232nd Street SW*
*Mountlake Terrace*
*(425) 778-3931*

**New Beginnings Church**
*21705 58th Avenue W*
*Mountlake Terrace*
*(425) 771-8343*

**New Hope Christian Church**
*22804 44th Avenue W*
*Mountlake Terrace*
*(425) 771-4673*

**Overlake Christian Church**
*9900 Willows Road NE*
*Redmond*
*(425) 702-0303*

**Park Ridge Chapel**
*3805 Maltby Road*
*Bothell*
*(425) 481-8801*

**River of Life Fellowship**
*10410 Southeast 216th Street*
*Kent*
*(253) 859-0832*

**Seattle Christian Assembly**
*19931 Forest Park Drive NE*
*Seattle*
*(206) 362-7384*

MOVING TIP

Flattened boxes, carpet remnants, old towels, welcome mats, and automobile floor mats are great for moving heavy items and protecting hardwood or tiled floors.

**Summit View Community Church**
*1810 116th Avenue NE*
*Bellevue*
*(425) 646-0661*

**West Seattle Christian Church**
*4400 42nd Street SW*
*West Seattle*
*(206) 932-2098*

## United States Postal Service

**Consumer Affairs**
*(800) 275-8777*

**Military Mail**
*(206) 553-2326*

**Sea-Tac Airmail Center**
*16601 Air Cargo Road*
*Sea-Tac*
*Administrative Support:*
*(800) 275-8777*

### POST OFFICES

The following are Seattle area branches and stations of the United States Post Office. All telephone inquiries are directed to a single toll-free number: (800) 275-8777.

**Ballard Station**
*5706 17th Street NW*
*Seattle*

**Bellevue Branch**
*1171 Bellevue Way NE*
*Bellevue*

**Bitter Lake Station**
*929 North 145th Street*
*Seattle*

**Broadway Station**
*101 Station E*
*Seattle*

**Burien Branch**
*609 Southwest 150th Street*
*Burien*

**Columbia Center Station**
*701 Fifth Avenue*
*Seattle*

**Columbia Station**
*3727 S Alaska Street*
*Seattle*

**Des Moines Branch**
*22203 Seventh Street*
*Des Moines*

**East Union Station**
*1110 23rd Street*
*Seattle*

**Georgetown Station**
*620 South Orcas Street*
*Seattle*

**Greenwood Station**
*8306 Greenwood Street N*
*Seattle*

**Interbay Annex**
*2010 15th Street W*
*Seattle*

**International Station**
*4141 Sixth Avenue S*
*Seattle*

**Kenmore Station**
*6413 Northeast 181st Street*
*Kenmore*

**Kirkland Branch**
*721 4th Street*
*Kirkland*

**Lake City Station**
*3019 Northeast 127th Street*
*Seattle*

**Magnolia Station**
*3211 West McGraw Street*
*Seattle*

**Mercer Island Post Office**
*304 78th Street SE*
*Mercer Island*

**North City Branch**
*17233 15th Avenue NE*
*Shoreline*

**Northgate Station**
*11036 8th Avenue NE*
*Seattle*

**Old Federal Station**
*909 First Avenue*
*Seattle*

**Pioneer Square Station**
*91 South Jackson Street*
*Seattle*

**Redmond Branch**
*16135 Northeast 85th Street*
*Redmond*

**Riverton Heights Branch**
*15250 32nd Street S*
*Sea Tac*

**Seafirst Finance**
*1001 Fourth Avenue*
*Seattle*

**MOVING TIP**

Pack items that you seldom use first and load them on the truck first.

**Seahurst Post Office**
*2116 Southwest 152nd Street*
*Burien*

**Skyway Branch**
*7633 South 126th Street*
*Seattle*

**Tukwila Branch**
*225 Andover Park W*
*Tukwila*

**University Station**
*4244 University Way NE*
*Seattle*

**Wallingford Seattle Station**
*1329 North 47th Street*
*Seattle*

**Wedgewood Station**
*7724 35th Avenue NE*
*Seattle*

**West Seattle Station**
*4412 California Avenue SW*
*Seattle*

**Westwood Village Station**
*2721 Southwest Trenton Street*
*Seattle*

**Woodinville Station**
*17000 610 Wood-Snoho Road NE*
*Woodinville*

CHAPTER 10

# Local Schools and Colleges

The Greater Puget Sound area provides fertile ground for cultivating educated and enlightened minds of all ages. Time and again, public opinion surveys confirm that Seattleites rank education as Priority One. Voters' behavior reflects this belief; they routinely and overwhelmingly pass public school bonds and initiatives. The Seattle public school district underwent a dramatic overhaul in the 1990s, producing one of the nation's most progressive reform programs. Today, nearly 90 percent of Seattle's young adults hold high school diplomas, and 40 percent have earned bachelors or higher degrees, ranking above San Francisco, Washington, D.C., Chicago, and New York City.

The offerings are rich. Seattle has a full spectrum of educational opportunities for everyone. Complementing the public school districts are some of the finest private, parochial, and alternative schools in the United States.

The city is also a cornerstone of higher education in the Pacific Northwest, and the University of Washington is at the core of public, graduate, and advanced research. But it isn't alone. College-bound students can choose from among many institutions, plus large community colleges, small religious universities, and vocational/technical institutes.

From preschool to grad school, here's a look at education around Seattle.

## Preschool and Day Care

For free twenty-four-hour consumer tips about child care, call (206) 442-2800.

- Press 3220 to know what to observe and what questions to ask
- Press 3222 to better ensure a quality child care experience
- Press 3223 to learn appropriate activities and programs

Nearly 3,000 licensed day-care providers operate in the Greater Puget Sound area. Of these, 80 percent are home-based, authorized to care for six or fewer children. Most other providers are minicenters, which are allowed up to twelve children. Infant care costs about $175 per week. Weekly care for toddlers runs about $150. Expect to pay upwards of $120 each week for preschool enrichment. To help locate weekday care for your child, contact these helpful agencies:

**Child Care Resources**
*2915 East Madison Street, Suite 305*
*Seattle*
*(206) 461-3708*
www.4ccare.com

**Child Care Resources**
*15015 Main Street*
*Bellevue*
*(425) 865-9350*

**Camp Fire's Phone Friend**
*8511 15th Avenue NE*
*Seattle*
*(800) 543-8255*

**Family Child Care Association**
*1225 Fourth Avenue S, Suite A*
*Seattle*
*(206) 467-1552*

**Kidcare**
*(800) 756-KIDS*

**Kids Haven**
*9715 Firdale Avenue*
*Edmonds*
*(206) 546-9594*

**Neighborhood House**
*905 Spruce Street*
*Seattle*
*(206) 461-8430*

Here are a few of the most recognizable and established child-care and preschool centers serving Seattle area families:

**Children's World Learning Centers**
*22137 68th Avenue S*
*Kent*
*(253) 872-2447*

www.childrensworld.com

- Preschool and school-age learning programs, limited infant centers
- Learning stimulated through fun and exploration
- Individual creativity and positive self-concept fostered
- Transportation available
- Parents welcome

**Childtime Children's Centers**

www.childtime.com

- Before and after school program
- Programs vary by location
- Parents welcome

*9329 244th Street SW*
*Edmonds*
*(206) 542-0789*

*135 South 312th Street*
*Federal Way*
*(253) 946-1137*

*23211 61st Avenue S*
*Kent*
*(253) 854-9939*

MOVING TIP

Don't forget to clean out your car's trunk before moving. Every bit of space counts. Save a little room for things you may purchase along the way (nonperishable groceries, clothing, souvenirs, etc.).

*4306 156th Street NE*
*Redmond*
*(425) 869-3949*

*4311 Northeast Fifth Street, Building A*
*Renton*
*(425) 277-1696*

*1000 Second Avenue, Suite 204*
*Seattle*
*(206) 382-9869*

**Kid's Country Learning Centers**

- Infants to twelve years
- Age-appropriate curriculum
- Nurtures individual interests and development
- Member USDA Food Program
- Closed-circuit monitors
- Large, well-equipped outdoor play areas

*101 10th Street*
*Auburn*
*(253) 931-1993*

*21135 Highway 410*
*Bonnie Lake*
*(253) 862-2840*

*22703 Bothell-Everett Highway*
*Bothell*
*(425) 486-0260*

*14400 Ambaum Boulevard SW*
*Burien*
*(206) 242-5437*

*12625 4th Avenue W*
*Everett*
*(425) 353-4488*

*24221 Southeast Kent-Kangley Road*
*Maple Valley*
*(425) 413-1173*

*19935 State Road 2*
*Monroe*
*(360) 794-0161*

**Kid's Haven**

www.uswestdex.com/kidshaven

- Ages one to twelve
- Owned and directed by registered nurse
- Staff medical doctor
- Christian learning

*9715 Firdale Avenue*
*Edmonds*
*(206) 546-9594*

**KinderCare**

www.kindercare.com

- Age-appropriate learning programs emphasizing social, emotional, physical, and intellectual development
- Ages six to twelve years
- Furnishes meals and snacks
- Transportation available
- Parents welcome

*2916 Auburn Way N*
*Auburn*
*(253) 939-1833*

*12415 Southeast 41st Place*
*Bellevue*
*(425) 747-4267*

*20613 Bothel-Everett Highway*
*Bothell*
*(425) 485-5253*

*18020 Des Moines Memorial Drive*
*Burien*
*(206) 244-3069*

*205 East Casino Road*
*Everett*
*(425) 348-5444*

*33504 13th Place S*
*Federal Way*
*(253) 874-2822*

*4341 West Lake Sammamish Parkway SE*
*Issaquah*
*(425) 643-2917*

**CITY FACT**

Seattle is nestled on the shores of two large lakes and a sound, flanked by two major mountain ranges. Nearby are dozens of islands, the Straits of Juan de Fucha, and the Pacific Ocean.

*25400 Pacific Highway S*
*Kent*
*(253) 941-8698*

*11404 Slater Avenue NE*
*Kirkland*
*(425) 828-3583*

*7330 196th Street SW*
*Lynnwood*
*(425) 778-7961*

*22040 Southeast Wax Road*
*Maple Valley*
*(425) 432-2855*

*15711 Mill Creek Boulevard*
*Mill Creek*
*(425) 745-4484*

*15202 Redmond Way*
*Redmond*
*(425) 885-2377*

*1225 Anacortes Avenue NE*
*Renton*
*(425) 271-0733*

**La Petite Academy**

www.lapetite.com

- Enriching preschool and school-age programs
- Sibling and extended hours care
- Summer programs
- Ages six weeks to twelve years

*13231 Bothell-Everett Highway*
*Bothell*
*(425) 338-1651*

*508 South 348th Street*
*Federal Way*
*(253) 838-0061*

*11440 Northeast 116th Street*
*Kirkland*
*(425) 821-0907*

*24037 132nd Avenue SE*
*Kent*
*(253) 630-1541*

*12918 Mukilteo Speedway*
*Lynnwood*
*(425) 347-4267*

*2800 Milton Way*
*Milton*
*(253) 952-6607*

*1006 39th Avenue SE*
*Puyallup*
*(253) 840-1093*

*410 228th Avenue NE*
*Redmond*
*(425) 868-5895*

*4735 East Marginal Way S*
*Seattle*
*(206) 764-3492*

*2771 Northwest Myhre*
*Silverdale*
*(360) 692-7187*

**Merrylarks**

- Ages one month to twelve years
- Total growth through cultural, social, and academic programs
- Natural outdoor environment
- Degreed teachers

*16121 3rd Avenue NE*
*Shoreline*
*(206) 363-3236*

**Quality Child Care**

- Low student/teacher ratio
- Ages one month to five years
- Developmentally appropriate programs, emphasizing individual care
- Field trips, gymnastics, drama, art, music, computers
- Summer program includes swimming
- Large playground
- Diapers and nutritious meals included

*1118 12th Avenue*
*Seattle*
*(206) 324-KIDS*

**Temporary Child Care Services**

www.seattlenanny.com

- National Nanny Training Institute nannies
- Temporary sitters: four-hour minimum
- Overnight care
- Nanny tax and payroll service available
- CPR certified

*417 Denny Way, Suite 302*
*Seattle*
*(888) 439-KIDS*

**Toyland Childcare Nights & Weekends**

- Ages one month through kindergarten
- "The First Unique Children's Bed & Breakfast"
- FBI-checked caregivers
- Nutritious meals
- CPR and first aid certified
- Educational activities including computers
- Co-op options; most subsidies accepted

**MOVING TIP**

Secure large mirrors and framed glass between mattresses, and be sure helpers at both ends of the move know that you've done so.

*16564 Southeast 19th Street*
*Bellevue*
*(425) 649-9029*

**Whizz Kids Academy**

- Ages one to six
- Full-service preschool
- "A Great Place To Be A Kid"

*18512 Ballinger Way NE*
*Lake Forest Park*
*(206) 362-6519*

*2450 33rd Avenue W*
*Magnolia*
*(206) 284-2253*

*11715 15th Avenue NE*
*Northgate*
*(206) 364-0650*

**MOVING TIP**

Whenever possible, use a dolly or hand truck. They'll save time, help prevent scratches, and spare you additional back pain.

**YMCA**

- Safe, supervised before and after school child care
- "A Good Place For Your Child To Grow"

*14230 Bellevue-Redmond Road*
*Bellevue*
*(425) 746-9900*

*9260 California Avenue SW*
*Fauntleroy*
*(206) 937-1000*

*17874 Des Moines Memorial Drive*
*Highline*
*(206) 244-5880*

*909 Fourth Avenue*
*Seattle*
*(206) 382-5340*

*1220 Northeast 175th Street*
*Shoreline*
*(206) 364-1700*

*4515 36th Street SW*
*West Seattle*
*(206) 935-6000*

## Public Elementary and Secondary School Districts and Private Schools

Combined enrollment in Seattle Area Public School Districts is just under 50,000. Another 16,000 students are enrolled in 350 private, parochial, and alternative schools in and around Seattle.

### SEATTLE AREA SCHOOL DISTRICTS (ELEMENTARY, MIDDLE, AND HIGH SCHOOL)

**Auburn**
*915 Fourth Street NE*
*Auburn, WA 98002*
*(253) 931-4900*

**Bellevue**
*12111 Northeast First Street*
*Bellevue, WA 98005*
*(425) 456-4000*

**Edmonds**
*20420 68th Avenue W*
*Lynnwood, WA 98036*
*(425) 670-7000*

**Enumclaw**
*2929 McDougall Avenue*
*Enumclaw, WA 98022*
*(360) 825-2588*

**Federal Way**
*31405 18th Avenue S*
*Federal Way, WA 98003*
*(253) 945-2000*

**Highline**
*15675 Ambaum Boulevard SW*
*Burien, WA 98166*
*(206) 433-0111*

**Issaquah**
*565 Northwest Holly Street*
*Issaquah, WA 98027-2899*
*(425) 837-7000*

**Kent**
*12033 Southeast 256th Street*
*Kent, WA 98031-6643*
*(253) 813-7000*

**Lake Washington**
*16250 Northeast 74th Street*
*Redmond, WA 98052*

**Mercer Island**
*4160 86th Avenue SE*
*Mercer Island, WA 98040*
*(206) 236-3330*

**Northshore**
*18315 Bothell Way NE*
*Bothell, WA 98011-1983*
*(425) 489-6000*

**Renton**
*300 Southwest Seventh Street*
*Renton, WA 98055*
*(425) 204-2300*

**Riverview**
*32240 Northeast 50th Street*
*Carnation, WA 98014*
*(425) 333-4115*

**Seattle**
*815 Fourth Avenue N*
*Seattle, WA 98109*
*(206) 298-7000*

**Shoreline**
*18560 First Avenue S*
*Shoreline, WA 98155*
*(206) 267-6111*

**Tacoma**
*25720 Maple V./Black D. Road SE*
*Maple Valley, WA 98038*
*(425) 432-4481*

**Tukwila**
*4640 South 144th Street*
*Tukwila, WA 98168*
*(206) 901-8000*

**Vashon Island**
*20414 Vashon Highway SW*
*(206) 463-2121*

**White River**
*240 North "A" Street*
*Buckley, WA 98321*
*(360) 829-0600*

## SEATTLE AREA PRIVATE SCHOOLS (ELEMENTARY, MIDDLE, AND HIGH SCHOOL)

**Bertschi School**
*2227 10th Avenue E*
*Seattle, WA 98102*
*(206) 324-5476*

Emphasizes individual styles in a group environment.

**Blanchet High School**
*8200 Wallingford Avenue N*
*Wallingford, WA 98103*
*(206) 527-7711*

Stresses preparation for college.

**Bush School**
*405 36th Avenue E*
*Seattle, WA 98112*
*(206) 322-7978*

Advocates experiential learning.

**Epiphany School**
*3710 East Howell Street*
*Seattle, WA 98122*
*(206) 323-9011*

Tempers traditional curriculum with fine arts and performing arts. Stresses problem solving and critical thinking.

**Evergreen School**
*15201 Meridian Avenue N*
*Shoreline, WA 98133*
*(206) 364-0801*

Encourages self-motivation and individual curriculum. Emphasizes foreign language and global studies.

**Holy Names Academy**
*728 21st Avenue E*
*Seattle, WA 98112*
*(206) 323-4272*

College preparation and advanced placement steer curriculum. Leadership and honors programs strongly encouraged.

**King's Elementary School**
*19531 Dayton Avenue N*
*Seattle, WA 98133*
*(206) 546-7258*

General studies curriculum with focus on Bible and chapel.

**MOVING TIP**

Shorter moves usually require multiple trips and can often equal the mileage of longer moves. In either case, treat your car to some preventive maintenance three weeks before the move. If the mechanic detects a problem, you have adequate time for repairs. Have the oil, oil filter, and air filter changed and top off all fluids. Look carefully for signs of worn hoses and regularly monitor tire pressure and wear patterns. Double-check your spare tire.

**King's High School**
*19303 Fremont Avenue N*
*Seattle, WA 98133*
*(206) 546-7241*

Emphasizes college preparation and Christian faith.

**Lakeside Schools**
*14050 First Avenue NE*
*Seattle, WA 98125*
*(206) 368-3600*

Liberal arts curriculum. Community service stressed. Considered among the region's finest. Large percentage of students go on to Ivy League schools.

**Morningside Academy**
*1633 12th Avenue*
*Seattle, WA 98122*
*(206) 329-9412*

Specialized attention for learning and attention deficits. Outdoor programs and field trips promote experiential learning.

**Northwest School**
*1415 Summit Avenue*
*Seattle, WA 98122*
*(206) 682-7309*

College preparation emphasized through integrated humanities and global studies.

**O'Dea High School**
*802 Terry Avenue*
*Seattle, WA 98104*
*(206) 622-6596*

College preparation emphasized. Exceptional computer and math facilities.

**Perkins Elementary School**
*4649 Sunnyside Avenue*
*North Seattle, WA 98112*
*(206) 329-3260*

Emphasizes Catholic development. Arts and computer skills stressed.

**St. Joseph's School**
*700 18th Avenue E*
*Seattle, WA 98112*
*(206) 329-3260*

Emphasizes Catholic development. Strong music and science programs.

**Seattle Academy of Arts & Sciences**
*1432 15th Avenue*
*Seattle, WA 98112*
*(206) 323-6600*

College preparation through demanding science and communications curriculum.

**Seattle Country Day School**
*2619 Fourth Avenue N*
*Seattle, WA 98109*
*(206) 284-6220*

Curriculum aimed at highly capable and creative children.

**Seattle Hebrew Academy**
*1617 Interlaken Drive E*
*Seattle, WA 98112*
*(206) 323-5750*

Both secular and Judaic curricula.

**Seattle Preparatory School**
*2400 11th Avenue E*
*Seattle, WA 98102*
*(206) 324-0400*

College preparation stressed.

**Spruce Street School**
*411 Yale Avenue N*
*Seattle, WA 98109*
*(206) 621-9211*

Integrated learning program emphasizes humanities and arts.

**University Prep**
*8000 25th Avenue NE*
*Seattle, WA 98115*
*(206) 523-6407*

Liberal arts, stressing language and literature. Outstanding science labs.

**Villa Academy**
*5001 Northeast 50th Street*
*Seattle, WA 98105*
*(206) 524-8885*

General elementary curriculum. Seventy-five percent go on to attend Seattle Prep.

MOVING TIP

Before Moving Day, master the art of tying a secure, standard, and easily released knot. Take a moment to teach this skill to one another, and stick with it throughout the move. This is especially important if you will be staying at motels along the way. Obscure knots aren't safe, and they take a long time to untie.

**West Seattle Christian School**
*4401 42nd Avenue SW*
*Seattle, WA 98116*
*(206) 938-1414*

Christian elementary curriculum. Emphasizes traditional studies and values.

**Westside Place**
*1310 North 45th Street*
*Seattle, WA 98103*
*(206) 634-0782*

Well-rounded curriculum for promising children with histories of difficulties in traditional schools.

**Zion Academy**
*4730 32nd Avenue S*
*Seattle, WA 98118*
*(206) 723-0580*

"Open Court" practiced. Parental involvement a must. Phonics and Marva Collins methodology.

## EASTSIDE PRIVATE SCHOOLS (ELEMENTARY, MIDDLE, AND HIGH SCHOOL)

**Bellevue Children's Academy**
*2120 South Jackson Street*
*Seattle, WA 98144*

*1402 140th Avenue NE*
*Bellevue, WA 98007*
*(425) 649-0791*

Emphasizes social, emotional, and academic growth.

**Bellevue Christian School**
*1601 98th Avenue NE*
*Bellevue, WA 98004*
*(425) 454-4402*

Preschool through high school. Christ-centered education. Extensive bus service.

**Christa McAuliffe Academy**
*(509) 575-4989*

www.cmacademy.org

Pioneering Internet access to education and distance learning. Kindergarten through twelfth grade.

**Chrysalis School of Independent Studies**
*14241 Northeast Woodinville-Duvall Road*
*Woodinville, WA 98072*
*(425) 481-2228*

Focuses on individually tailored learning programs.

**Cougar Mountain Academy**
*5410 194th Street SE*
*Issaquah, WA 98027*
*(425) 641-2800*

Traditional academic approach to general studies curriculum. Nonsecular, nondenominational. "Living classroom" concept and after-school electives offered.

### Hillside Student Community

*5027 159th Place SE*
*Bellevue, WA 98006*
*(425) 747-6448*

Preparatory middle school emphasizing academic achievement without elitism. Wooded campus designed to inspire arts and sciences.

### Solomon School

*7620 242nd SW*
*Edmonds, WA*
*(425) 774-2929*

solomons@seanet.com

Curriculum designed to inspire "mind, body, and spirit." Low student/teacher ratio. Supervised after-hours study program.

### Hamlin Robinson School

*(206) 763-1167*

www.aa.net/~meyerfm/hrs

### The Overlake School

*20301 Northeast 108th Street*
*Redmond, WA 98053*
*(425) 868-1000*

Stresses college preparation. Strong in sciences but broad spectrum of studies offered. Outdoor education emphasized.

### Soundview Private School

*6515 196th Avenue SW*
*Lynnwood, WA 98036*
*(425) 778-8572*

General studies with art appreciation emphasized. Physical fitness without organized competition. Low student/teacher ratio.

### Springhurst

*10737 124th Avenue NE*
*Kirkland, WA 98033*
*(425) 827-7617*

Elementary school for gifted and talented students.

The home of Microsoft Corporation co-founder and chairman, Bill Gates, was constructed at a cost of $65 million. Property taxes are estimated at $575,000 annually.

**Thomas Academy**
*8207 South 280th Street*
*Kent, WA*
*(253) 852-4437*

Preschool through middle school. Interaction, negotiating, and diplomacy encouraged. Process, not product oriented. Fifteen to sixteen students per class.

**North Creek School**
*1510 196th Street S*
*Bothell, WA*
*(425) 481-4141*

Preschool through eighth grade. Mixed ages and mixed grades, with individual contract studies and group learning. "Environmental trails." Parent involvement.

## Colleges, Universities, and Art & Technical Institutes

**Bellevue Community College**
*3000 Landerholm Circle SE*
*Bellevue, WA 98007*
*(425) 641-0111*

www.bcc.ctc.edu

Premier community college. Nationally known. The 20,000 students study everything from accounting to zoology. Many transfer to the University of Washington.

**Edmonds Community College**
*68th Avenue W*
*Lynnwood, WA*
*(425) 640-1500*

www.edcc.com

The 10,000 students come from sixty countries. Strong technical arts programs for professional credentials and continuing education. General education credits transfer well.

**Shoreline Community College**
*16101 Greenwood Avenue N*
*Shoreline, WA 98133*

www.shoreline.ctc.edu/~welcome

Offers fifty degree and certification programs; 12,000 students. Liberal arts for students planning to transfer; vocational and technical programs for others.

**Highline Community College**
*2400 South 240th Street*
*Des Moines, WA 98198*
*(206) 878-3710*

www.highline.ctc.edu

Focuses on continuing education and occupational programs for associate of arts degrees and other credentials. Good general education program for transfer to four-year college or university.

**Seattle Community College District**
*1500 Harvard Avenue*
*Seattle, WA 98122*
*(206) 587-4100*

www.sccd.ctc.edu

Accredited curriculum offers associate of arts degrees and professional credentials. Focuses on professional development through continuing education programs. Distance learning encouraged.

**North Seattle Community College**
*9600 College Way N*
*Seattle, WA 98103*
*(206) 527-3600*

Satellites offer convenient campuses.

**Seattle Central Community College**
*1701 Broadway*
*Seattle, WA 98122*
*(206) 587-3800*

**South Seattle Community College**
*6000 16th Avenue SW*
*Seattle, WA 98106*
*(206) 764-5300*

**Lesley College**
*1806 East Lynn Street*
*Seattle, WA 98112*
*(206) 860-0065*

www.lesley.edu

Accredited college offering programs for working professionals.

On long trips, don't try to take perishable foods, especially heat-sensitive or opened dairy-based products. Nothing derails a move like food poisoning and a trip to the hospital.

Weekend format available. Graduate programs in the arts, human services, education, and management.

**City University**
*335 116th Avenue SE*
*Bellevue, WA 98004*
*(800) 426-5596*

www.cityu.edu

Private, nonprofit institution mainly serving working adults. Fifty accredited programs at undergraduate and graduate level. Most faculty have worked in the field they teach. The twenty locations offer day, evening, and weekend classes and distance learning.

CITY FACT

Biotech is one of the fastest growing industries in Seattle, currently accounting for 140 companies, 13,000 jobs, and $2 billion in revenue. By 2005, this will more than double.

**Renton**
*919 Southwest Grady Way*
*(425) 637-1010*

**Northgate**
*2150 North 107th Avenue*

**Bellevue**
*335 116th Avenue SE*
*(425) 637-1010*

**Everett**
*1000 Southeast Everett Mall Way*
*(425) 353-0727*

**Tacoma**
*2111 South 90th Avenue*
*(253) 539-8499*

**Silverdale**
*3100 Bucklin Hill Road*
*(360) 692-1800*

**Puget Sound Christian College**
*410 4th Avenue N*
*Edmonds, WA 98020*

Accredited college with emphasis on Christian studies.

**Henry Cogswell College**
*2802 Wetmore Avenue*
*Everett, WA 98201*
*(425) 258-3351*

www.bhenrycogswell.edu

Private, nonprofit four-year college offering trimester (year-round) bachelor's degree programs. Focus is on business, computer sciences, and engineering.

**Antioch University**
*2326 Sixth Avenue*
*Seattle, WA 98121*
*(206) 441-5352*

www.seattleantioch.com

Bachelor of arts in liberal studies. Graduate programs in psychology, education, and management. Focus is on tailoring adult studies around personal and professional goals.

**Bastyr University**
*14500 Northeast Juanita Drive*
*Kenmore, WA 98028*
*(425) 823-1300*

www.bastyr.edu

Professional credential, undergraduate, and graduate programs in psychology, behavioral science, and alternative medicine.

**Western Washington University**
*Old Main 230*
*Bellingham, WA 98225*

www.wce.wwu.edu

Liberal arts studies on remote, scenic campus. Business and fine arts popular. Strong international studies program. Woodring College of Education and Huxley College of Environmental Studies renown.

**Seattle University**
*900 Broadway*
*Seattle, WA 98122*
*(206) 296-6000*

www.seattleu.edu

One of twenty-eight Jesuit colleges in the United States. More than 6,000 students enrolled in forty-five undergraduate, and thirty-one graduate programs. Doctoral degrees in law and education offered.

**Seattle Pacific University**
*3307 Third Avenue W*
*Seattle, WA 98119*
*(206) 281-2051*

www.spu.edu

Accredited Christian university of arts, sciences, and professional studies. Nearly 4,000 undergraduate and graduate students. Course offerings in forty-three major fields; master's degree available in ten disciplines, doctorate in two.

# City Fact

Seventy-two bolts fasten the Space Needle to its foundation. Each bolt is thirty feet long, enabling the 605-foot structure to withstand winds of up to 200 miles per hour.

**University of Puget Sound**
*1500 North Warner*
*Tacoma, WA 98416*
*(253) 756-3100*

www.ups.edu

Strong undergraduate liberal arts program. Excellent international courses, including Asian studies.

**Cornish College of the Arts**
*710 East Roy Street*
*Seattle, WA 98102*
*(206) 323-1400*

Respected performing arts program. Accredited degrees in art, dance, design, music, and theater production.

**Northwest College of Art**
*16464 State Highway 305 NE*
*Poulsbo, WA 98370*
*(360) 779-9993*

www.nca.edu

Bachelor of fine arts degrees in visual communications, with majors in fine arts and design. Accredited. Good financial aid programs for qualified applicants.

**The Art Institute of Seattle**
*2323 Elliott Avenue*
*Seattle, WA 98121*
*(206) 448-6600*

www.ais.edu

Accredited technical program with 3,000 students. Focus is on practical, business applications of creative arts. Career-oriented studies include industrial design, visual merchandising, music and video, and commercial photography. Strong computer arts program.

**Lake Washington Technical College**
*11605 132nd Avenue NE*
*Kirkland, WA 98034*
*(425) 739-8100*

www.lwtc.ctc.edu

Considered one of the finest public two-year technical colleges in the state. 20,000 full- and part-time students. Strong in business, health care, technology, and transportation. Associate of applied science degree offered in forty programs.

**Seattle Vocational Institute**

*(206) 587-4950*

www.sccd.ctc.edu

See Seattle Community College District.

**University of Washington**

*4014 University Way NE*
*Seattle, WA 98105*
*(206) 543-9198*

www.washington.edu

Major public research university with sixteen schools on main campus. Seattle campus and branch campuses in Bothell and Tacoma. Offers 5,000 courses in 100 academic fields. 26,000 undergraduate students and 9,000 graduate students. World-class medical centers and clinics. Research and graduate programs internationally known. Total value of federal grants ranks in top five nationally. Considered finest institute of higher education in the Northwest.

SECTION FIVE

# Finding a Job

CHAPTER 11

# Working in the City

For the history buff in a hurry, here's a three-word chronology of Seattle's spectacular economic evolution: agriculture, industry, technology. Agricultural opportunities for today's Seattleites are limited. Most homes offer enough space to pamper a PVG (Personal Vegetable Garden). Apartments and condominiums can usually be fitted with a window box large enough to yield all the parsley you'll need. And with fluorescent lighting, you just might be able to nurture a Chia Pet at the office.

The good news is that industrial opportunities around Seattle are abundant, and technological prospects are, in a word, boundless.

The Emerald City started out as a humble mill town. Outfitting the Klondike gold miners set in motion an economic chain reaction. To this day, apparel and specialty retailing remain integral components of Seattle commerce. Homegrown companies like Nordstrom, Eddie Bauer, REI, Costco, Loew's/Eagle, and Starbucks have combined annual revenues of more than $30 billion. Wholesale and retail trades provide employment for 385,000 people of Greater Seattle, or one fourth of the total workforce.

Catering to the miners also gave rise to Seattle's booming hospitality industry long before the city became a favorite destination for tourists and a prestigious hub for international travel. Tourism is now Washington's fourth-largest industry, and Seattle gets the lion's share. Each year, eight million camera-toting tourists and conventioneers cheerfully pump $3 billion into King County coffers, keeping 56,000 hospitality workers whistling.

Perhaps more than any other industry, it was aircraft and aerospace engineering that launched Seattle into international prominence. Boeing's growth—charted over the last eighty-five years—ascends as proudly as one of the corporate giant's mighty 777s. At present, a healthy 16 percent of the workforce in the Greater Seattle area is dedicated to durable goods manufacturing. Of these 260,000 employees, nearly 120,000 work for the world's largest aircraft manufacturer. But unlike the 1970s, when a national recession nearly crippled Boeing, Seattle is no longer overly dependent upon its largest employer to sustain economic stability and growth.

Enter Microsoft Corporation, its countless corporate offspring, and Seattle's "Platinum Era of Technology."

Although dwarfed by Boeing's staggering 1999 revenues of $51 billion, Microsoft's hefty yield of $18 billion—coupled with average annual growth of 40 percent—is a lightning rod for Wall Street analysts and investors. The coveted stock of the world's largest software manufacturer remains the bedrock of the most revered mutual funds. Today, more than 2,000 software companies operate in the Puget Sound area alone. In 1998, Seattle's 23,500 software engineers shared compensation of $6.77 billion, including stock options. That's a jaw-dropping average of $287,700 apiece!

**CITY FACT**

Microsoft Corporation is one of 2,000 software development companies in the Greater Puget Sound area.

It doesn't end here. Seattle-based technologies have spawned such industries as bioinformatics, genomics, telemedicine, and environmental engineering. Although still in the fledgling stage, these cutting-edge sciences offer unlimited promise. Seattle's 140 biomed companies have already added 13,000 jobs and $2 billion to the pot. By 2005, this contribution will double.

Such opportunities have defined a vital economic corridor dubbed the Cascadia Region. The Emerald City is the centerpiece of this 400-mile stretch from Eugene, Oregon, to Vancouver, British Columbia. The Cascadia Region hosts eight million residents and accounts for a quarter trillion dollars in annual economic output. The region is so robust that if it were an independent nation it would boast the world's tenth-largest economy.

Oh, and if you're worried that you may have missed the boat, relax. Employment projections for 2010 add a rosy hue to the Emerald City. The City of Seattle Office of Governmental Relations forecasts that local employment will increase by a substantial 21 percent, in contrast to a national average increase of 15 percent. Historical performance of municipal bond issues and Seattle's current Moody's rating (Aaa) are very impressive. Consumer confidence is further demonstrated by a healthy appetite for new construction.

In short, whether you're a people person, a worker bee, or a technoid, Seattle's a great place to hitch your wagon to a star.

## Income Versus Cost of Living

### Median Family Income, Metropolitan Seattle

| | |
|---|---|
| *1993:* | *$48,000* |
| *1994:* | *$49,800* |
| *1995:* | *$51,500* |
| *1996:* | *$53,900* |
| *1997:* | *$55,100* |
| *1998:* | *$60,200* |
| *1999:* | *$62,600* |
| *2000:* | *$65,500 (projected)* |

### Average Individual Income, Metropolitan Seattle

**Wages for Unskilled Labor**

| | |
|---|---|
| *Hourly range:* | *$5.82–$15.48* |
| *Annual range:* | *$12,106–$32,199* |
| *Average annual income:* | *$22,153* |

### Wages for Skilled Labor

| | |
|---|---|
| *Hourly range:* | *$8.14–$29.32* |
| *Annual range:* | *$16,932–$60,986* |
| *Average annual income:* | *$38,959* |

### Wages for Entry Level Management

| | |
|---|---|
| *Hourly range:* | *$12.63–$19.11* |
| *Annual range:* | *$26,271–$39,749* |
| *Average annual income:* | *$33,010* |

### Wages for Middle Management

| | |
|---|---|
| *Hourly range:* | *$16.18–$31.97* |
| *Annual range:* | *$33,655–$66,498* |
| *Average annual income:* | *$50,077* |

### Wages for Upper Management

| | |
|---|---|
| *Hourly range:* | *$25.47–$48.92* |
| *Annual range:* | *$52,978–$101,754* |
| *Average annual income:* | *$77,366* |

### Total Compensation Packages for Senior Executives

| | |
|---|---|
| *Average salary:* | *$114,000* |
| *Average bonus/stock options:* | *$81,000* |
| *Average total compensation:* | *$195,000* |

### Cost-of-Living Index

| | |
|---|---|
| *Seattle:* | *115* |
| *National:* | *100* |

### Unemployment Rate

| | |
|---|---|
| *Seattle:* | *3.10 percent* |
| *National:* | *4.04 percent* |

### Employment Demand

| | |
|---|---|
| *Demand for labor:* | *very high* |
| *Demand for non-labor:* | *high* |

### Key Areas of Economic Expansion

*software engineering*
*medical technology*
*biotechnology*
*genetic engineering*
*telecommunications*
*wood products*
*aerospace*
*apparel design/retail*
*fish processing*
*finance and insurance*
*electronics*
*commercial construction*
*wholesale food*
*kindred products*

MOVING TIP

Mark boxes on the sides and top. Use "FRAGILE" and arrows designating the top when necessary.

## Finding Your Job in Seattle

Seattle has been labeled a hotbed of successful business start-ups. Contributing factors include: a skilled and educated workforce, capacity for local manufacturing, access to international markets, government support, and availability of research and development facilities. Washington ranks first in the U.S. for per capita exports. Growing at an annual rate of 5 percent, international export is the most dynamic sector of Seattle's economy. One out of three jobs is linked to import/export industries. So if you think the best way to get to the top is to start at the top, Seattle provides fertile ground for entrepreneurs.

These aren't secrets that I'm telling you. Word's out: Seattle's markets are hotter than a firecracker on the Fourth of July. Perhaps you're one of the lucky thousands to receive a company transfer to Seattle. If so, congratulations, your job awaits you! Still luckier are the retirees who will migrate to the Northwest instead of following the

Florida-bound flock. They will soon be spending their days restaurant hopping, flyfishing, boating, and using GPS uplinks to pinpoint the next RV campsite.

But unless self-employment, a company transfer, or retirement is your reason for relocating to Seattle, you'll need a job. Be selective. Right now, and in the foreseeable future, it's an employee's market. There are more than enough jobs to go around, literally. Landing the right one will allow you opportunities to enjoy the Pacific Northwest to its fullest.

You already have at least two things going for you: record low unemployment; and the Internet. 3.1 percent unemployment means you won't be facing a lot of competition. Access to the World Wide Web means you can research companies, seek career counseling, locate recruiters, and post your résumé. All this at the touch of a key and at the speed of light. If you're not online, get online. The King County Library System offers free Internet access during library hours.

When it comes to pursuing a career, let your conscience be your guide. Let the Internet be your co-pilot.

This chapter will provide you with some resources that can help you find the right job.

## Executive Search Firms and Personnel Agencies

Finding yourself in a new town without local contacts and references can be a disadvantage. Personnel agencies can help. They are often instrumental in securing employment with a reputable company. Agencies run the gamut from specializing in temporary labor and clerical representation to presenting senior management candidates to corporations and executive search firms, also known as headhunters. Endorsement by a personnel agency could be viewed by prospective employers as a sign of credibility. Beware. There is a price to pay for the services of private agencies and search firms. The questions are "who will pay?" and "how much?"

For free twenty-four-hour consumer tips regarding personnel agencies, call (206) 442-2880.

- Press 3990 for advice about writing an effective résumé
- Press 3993 to help refine networking skills

- Press 3992 to learn how personnel agencies operate
- Press 3991 to help prepare for interviewing
- Press 3338 for information about seeking temporary employment

The following is an index of executive search firms, personnel agencies, and technical agencies.

**Accountants Executive Search**
*600 108th Avenue NE*
*Bellevue*
*(425) 635-0700*

www.aocnet.com

Specializes in bookkeeping and accounting jobs for clients without degrees and executive placement for CPAs, controllers, and CFOs.

**Aerotek**
*1407 116th Avenue NE*
*Bellevue*
*(425) 462-9350*

www.aerotek.com

Provider of highly trained technical support for engineering, biochemistry, and business.

**Aquent Partners**
*1525 Fourth Avenue*
*Seattle*
*(206) 623-3800*

www.aquentpartners.com

Provides placement for computer arts professionals, emphasizing Web graphics.

CITY FACT

Seattle is home to the world's first revolving restaurant, the Space Needle.

**Art Source, Inc.**
*188 106th Avenue NE*
*Bellevue*
*(425) 688-0094*

www.artsource.com

Focuses on digital media careers for creative computer types.

**Berkana International**
*18907 Forest Park Drive NE*
*Seattle*
*(206) 361-1633*

www.headhunters.com

Specialize in executive search for I/T senior management.

Software engineers, telecom, and aerospace recruits for start-ups as well as large corporations.

**Business Careers**
*15 South Grady Way*
*Renton*
*(206) 447-7433*

www.businesscareers.com

One of the largest and most established agencies with focus on entry/mid-level management, accounting, and sales professionals.

CITY FACT

Seattle was *Fortune* magazine's pick as "Best City for Work and Family."

**Career Clinic**
*6920 220 Street SW, Suite 107*
*Mountlake Terrace*
*(425) 673-1994*

www.careerclinic.com

Clients start and jump-start careers in diverse fields, including high technology, insurance, construction, and administration.

**Career Improvement Group**
*4010 Stone Way N*
*(206) 545-1155*

www.cignw.com

Gatekeepers to "unpublished" job market. Offer full-service career planning, interview coaching, salary negotiating, and a free workshop.

**Career Solutions, Inc.**
*16400 Southcenter Parkway*
*Tukwilla*
*(206) 575-6266*

www.adamscareersolutions.com

General placement agency covering a broad spectrum of disciplines, industries, and career assistance.

**Center for Career Alternatives**
*2401 Hewitt Avenue*
*Everett*
*(425) 252-6400*

www.snownet.org/cca

Nonprofit agency providing educational programs, vocational training, and summer youth employment.

**Computer Personnel, Inc.**
*8224 15th Avenue NE*
*Seattle*
*(206) 985-0282*

www.cpi-seattle.com

Well-established I/T specialists staffing temporary and full-time opportunities.

**Conmarke USA, Inc.**
*18717 76th Avenue W*
*Lynnwood*
*(425) 712-1948*

www.conmarke.com

Unique marine engineering niche, providing leads for nautical designers and drafters.

**Creative Assets Digital Talent**
*101 Yesler Way*
*Seattle*
*(206) 682-6005*

www.creativeassets.com

Matches clients with digital arts companies needing Web designers, html pros, and art directors.

**Data Partners**
*11100 Northeast Eighth Street*
*Bellevue*
*(425) 451-1030*

www.datapartners.com

Source for mid/senior level managers and I/T consultants to link with Fortune 500 firms. Boasts premier client base.

**Diverse Employment Opportunities**
*1932 First Avenue*
*Seattle*
*(206) 441-6838*

www.diverseemployment.com

An "organic" approach to partnering with companies. Understands diverse corporate cultures and philosophies. Boasts high first-match success rate.

**Goto & Company**
*10907 177 Court NE*
*Redmond*
*(425) 869-8092*

hiroshigoto@msn.com

Specializes in Japanese companies and Asian markets. Serves needs of import/export, international banking and finance, and semi-conductor trades.

**Guidance Service, Inc.**
*1010 South 336th Street*
*Federal Way*
*(253) 925-8605*

www.guidance-services.com

Provides employment services for healthcare administrators, RNs, and LVNs.

**Guidance Service, Inc.**
*1010 South 336th Street*
*Federal Way*

www.guidancestaffing.com

Provides employment services for office managers, accountants, and office administrators.

**Houser Martin Morris & Associates**
*110 110th Avenue NE*
*Bellevue*
*(425) 453-2700*

www.houser.com

Large, established agency offers executive search and recruiting I/S, I/T, finance, legal, mechanical, sales, marketing, and accounting, to name a few.

**Human Resources, Inc.**
*9725 Southeast 36th Street*
*Mercer Island*
*(206) 889-9070*

hrmercer@accessone.com

Results-oriented agency places temporary and permanent office staffers in positions from file clerk to human resources.

**Sakson & Taylor**
*4300 Aurora Avenue N*
*Seattle*
*(206) 548-2240*

www.sakson.com

Forte is matching communications technology companies with highly skilled professionals.

**Interim Technology, Inc.**
*18000 Pacific Highway S*
*Seattle*
*(206) 431-9500*

www.interim.com

Agency staffs impressive client base of multinational I/T firms with help desk, data center, and networking technicians. Offers temporary and permanent jobs.

**Lab Support, Inc.**
*900 Fourth Avenue*
*Seattle*
*(206) 622-6323*

www.labsupport.com

Provides full spectrum of lab opportunities for technicians from bottlewashers to microbiologists.

**Law Dawgs, Inc.**
*1201 Third Avenue*
*Seattle*
*(206) 224-8244*

www.lawdawgs.com

Specializes in executive search for attorneys, as well as placing paralegals, legal secretaries, and law clerks. No affiliation with University of Washington.

**Legal Ease**
*615 Market Street*
*Kirkland*
*(425) 822-1157*

www.legalease.com

Matches attorneys with law firms. Agency even finds partners and associate partners.

**Management Solutions**
*320 108th Avenue NE*
*Bellevue*
*(425) 646-6300*

www.mgmtsolutions.com

Executive search and recruiting efforts focus on senior managers in finance and accounting.

**NestBuilders**
*16149 Redmond Way, Suite 412*
*Redmond*
*(425) 869-4276*

www.thenestbuilder.com

Residential real estate brokerage offering careers in sales and consultation.

**Opus Corporation**
*777 108th Avenue NE*
*Bellevue*
*(425) 688-1904*

www.opusco.com

Source for strategic placement of I/T pros: programmers, analysts, and Java Web developers.

**MOVING TIP**

Talk to your veterinarian about your pet's special needs well in advance of Moving Day. Most moving companies will not assume responsibility for pets or plants. Your pet may require a portable kennel or even sedatives.

**Oxford & Associates**
*1220 116th Avenue NE*
*Bellevue*
*(425) 451-4772*

www.oxfordcorp.com

Focus on providing software and mechanical firms with experienced engineers.

**Professional Resource Group**
*10655 Northeast Fourth Street*
*Bellevue*
*(425) 451-0060*

www.prg-performers.com

Specializes in mortgage lending.

**Renee Feldman & Associates**
*8533 Second Avenue NE*
*Seattle*
*(206) 527-0980*

feldexec@aol.com

Well-established agency offering industrial-oriented sales and sales management placement. Also electromechanical, chemical, and plastics industries.

**Rod Asher & Associates**
*411 108th Avenue NE*
*Bellevue*
*(425) 646-1030*

www.asher.com

General search and recruiting for a broad range of disciplines and industries.

**Susan Schoos & Associates**
*140 Lakeside Avenue*
*Seattle*
*(206) 324-4942*

susan@susanschoos.com

Veteran "boutique" recruiting firm. Small but effective. Fields of expertise include publishing, manufacturing, engineering, and construction.

**Transitions, Inc.**
*514 12th Avenue*
*Seattle*
*(206) 325-4353*

www.transition-inc.com

An up-and-coming firm with focus on management, clerical, and light industrial careers for clients.

**Volt Services Group**
*22232 17th Avenue SE*
*Bothell*
*(425) 806-1900*

Industry leader for permanent, temporary, contract, or temp-to-hire. Management, engineering, and software, among many other offerings.

**What's New, Inc.**
*1424 Fourth Avenue*
*Seattle*
*(206) 467-4972*

www.whatsnew.com

Modeling and talent agency.

**Windermere Real Estate**
*9327 Fourth Street NE*
*Everett*
*(425) 335-4666*

www.windermere.com

Industry leader offering careers in real estate brokerage and sales.

**Woods & Associates**
*1221 2nd Avenue, Suite 330*
*Seattle*
*(206) 623-1216*

Veteran job finder supplying temporary and recruit-for-hire opportunities. Focus is on legal and litigation support, healthcare, advertising, and public relations.

**TheWriteStuff**
*4534 University Way NE*
*Seattle*
*(206) 548-1111*

www.writestuff.com

Niche agency serving Web site text writers, copywriters, and translators. Good start for technical communications pros.

## Temporary Jobs

The following is an index of nationally recognized agencies specializing in temporary labor and administrative support.

**Accountemps**
*601 Union Street, Suite 4300*
*Seattle*
*(206) 749-9161*

www.accountemps.com

Financial staffers. Focus on accounting, bookkeeping, payroll, credit, and collections.

**Accounting Partners**
*500 108th Avenue NE*
*Bellevue*
*(425) 450-1990*

www.apartner.com

**MOVING TIP**

Resist the temptation to rest a large rental truck's retractable ramp on a curb or step. Slight movements of the truck can create unstable footing, and people or furniture might be damaged.

**Affinity Staffing Group**
*401 Parkplace Center, Suite 301*
*Kirkland*
*(425) 822-0300*

www.affinitystaff.com

Temp and temp-to-hire, but offers lots of TLC with office skills training and career support.

**Available Personnel Services**
*801 Southwest 150th Street, Suite 212*
*(425) 454-4204*

www.availablepersonnel.com

Office openings and more. Temp and temp-for hire for food service, Burien assembly, warehouse, and general.

**Business Temps, Inc.**
*1200 112th Avenue NE, Suite P-100*
*Bellevue*
*(425) 454-4300*

bustemps@televar.com

From mailroom clerks to executive assistants. Focus is on speedy placement of temporary office staffers.

**Contractor's Labor Pool**
*030 Tacoma Mall Boulevard, Suite A*
*Tacoma*
*(253) 472-6408*

www.clp.com

Largest private labor resource for construction trades and general labor.

**ConsultNet**
*1800 112th Avenue NE, Suite 310*
*Bellevue*
*(425) 637-9700*

www.consult-net.com

Specializes in temporary jobs for computer professionals. Client server, e-commerce, mainframe, Web, network architecture, and more.

**Comforce Technical Services**
*4002 148th Avenue NE*
*Redmond*
*(425) 883-2233*

www.comforce.com

redjobs@rhotech.com

Microsoft-certified solutions provider. Brings temporary technical support to I/S and I/T environments. Programmers, developers, NT administrators, and PC techs placed.

**Hospitality Services, Inc.**
*10564 Fifth Avenue NE*
*Seattle*
*(206) 368-9039*

www.hsinw.com

Quick placement in hotel and restaurant industries.

**Kelly Services**
*999 Third Avenue*
*Seattle*
*(425) 454-7230*

www.kellyservices.com

The original industry leader matching qualified applicants with local businesses. Now staffing tech temps, too.

**Labor Ready**
*(888) 24-LABOR*

24/7 jobs. Same-day pay. Industrial, hospitality, assembly, construction, and warehouse work. Credit lines offered.

**ManPower**
*12720 Gateway Drive S, Suite 103*
*Tukwila*
*(206) 241-9005*

www.manpower.com

Offers immediate placement and basic computer skill training to ready workers. Mostly office and light industrial, but staff technical openings with qualified people.

**MedTemps, Inc.**
*1200 112th Avenue NE, Suite C-110*
*Bellevue*

ringham@staffing.nu

Specialize in trained medical office personnel. Mostly temp and temp-for-hire, but some direct hire, too.

**NuWest Group, Inc.**
*1200 112th Avenue*
*Bellevue*
*(425) 637-9500*

www.staffing.nu

Accounting and general office staffing. Good start for customer service reps and receptionists.

CITY FACT

*Money* magazine picked Seattle as "Best City in the West."

**PAC Personnel, Inc.**
*17965 Northeast 65th Street*
*Redmond*

www.pacpersonnel.com

Mainly staffs light labor jobs, as well as general office and clerical positions.

**MOVING TIP**

Don't pack belongings in grocery store produce boxes, which are often host to spider eggs. You won't want to infest your new home when they hatch. Use boxes that contain canned, bottled, or dry goods. Liquor stores are a good source for boxes.

**Randstad**
*15 South Grady Way*
*Renton*
*(425) 204-9466*
www.randstadna.com

Staffs mainly office support, but also legal, accounting, and light industrial.

**Remedy Intelligent Staffing**
*19203 36th Avenue W*
*Lynnwood*
*(425) 771-5431*
www.remedystaff.com

Fast-growing agency staffs office jobs, as well as light industrial and technical positions.

**Temporarily Yours**
*1000 Second Avenue, Suite 3550*
*Seattle*
*(206) 386-5400*
www.tempyoursseattle.com

Well-established agency staffs temporary openings in diverse industries, including legal and travel.

## Job Banks

It used to be called job "hunting," and for good reason. You'd get up at the crack of dawn, dress to blend with the environment, arm yourself with a high-powered résumé, and set off to prowl the urban jungle. Today, things are a little more civilized. Finding a job is still an adventure, but much of the search exists in the ethereal wilds of the Internet. It's here—where the beast of bandwidth reigns supreme—that you'll cross paths with an awesome creature.

It's called a job bank, and it's big. Really big. It can absorb millions of hits a day. But job banks are your friends. Stalked carefully, they can lead you out of Cyberspace and into Seattle's lushest territory: the Land of Employment.

Job banks host massive online databases with jillions of job listings. Because job banks make their money by advertising employers, you can use them for free. You can search by geography, company, or industry. Most job banks also offer advice about résumés, cover letters, interviewing, and negotiating a salary. Often, you are even allowed to post your résumé. Some can be tricky to navigate, so here's a list of popular, user-friendly job banks.

### America's Job Bank

www.ajb.dni.us

Huge. Over a million listings. Overwhelming at first, you'll appreciate some nice features. Specific sub-searches are designed to save time. You can register with the site, allowing you to save and print searches.

### Best Jobs USA

www.bestjobsusa.com

This site is particularly useful to the relocator, since it features profiles of major U.S. cities, including Seattle. In addition to résumé posting, you can research companies and view articles from Employment Review.

### CareerCast

www.careercast.com

A tasty cyberstew of newsgroups and links to employer's own Web sites.

### Career.com

www.career.com

Another biggie. Whether you're a highly specialized pro or wading into corporate waters for the first time, this site provides a broad spectrum of domestic and international jobs. The site is designed well, offering alternative search techniques. There are countless company profiles and even an online résumé workshop.

### CareerExchange

www.careerexchange.com

Focuses on high-technology offerings. A particularly welcomed feature are the professional chat rooms, which provide excellent networking opportunities.

### CareerMosaic

www.careermosaic.com

An up-and-comer. This job bank contains the standard company profiles, résumé postings, and career tips, as well as an excellent database of travel jobs and multinational corporations.

### CareerPath.com

www.careerpath.com

If you can't seem to give up newspaper classifieds but hate inky fingers, this site's for you. Over ninety major U.S. newspapers contribute to an impressive database. All the traditional trimmings, plus a great source for job fairs.

### CareerScape

www.careerscape.com

Tailor-cut for tech-types needing computer jobs. Industry trends, employment news, and lots of direct links to technology companies.

### Employers Online

www.employersonline.com

Straightforward job searching. This site is particularly useful for trained professionals looking for continuation or advancement within their specialized industry. CPAs, engineers, healthcare administrators, and I/T professionals will love EO.

**Headhunter.net**

www.headhunter.net

A hot one for executives and top-level salespersons. A detailed search form helps match clientele with corporate profiles. Caveat emptor: enhanced searches and personalized services can add "upgrade fees."

**JobOptions**

www.joboptions.com

Plenty of garden-variety search and post features, but this bank has something really slick. JobOptions will e-mail you new job postings that match your needs. Just take a minute to answer their questionnaire. Also, you can compare your present salary with similar jobs or industry averages.

**Jobs.Internet.com**

www.jobs.internet.com

A great source for Internet opportunities and more. Personal Service Agents help you find your match.

**JobTrak**

www.jobtrak.com

A great one for college students and recent grads. This site features jobs from 1,000 university career centers. Password required, so pick one up at your campus.

CITY FACT

The only father and son to hit back-to-back homeruns were Seattle Mariners Ken Griffey Sr. and Ken Griffey Jr.

**JobWarehouse**

www.jobwarehouse.com

Jobs from A to Z. A rich source for high-tech jobs posted by employers and recruiters. The site hosts lots of links to company Web sites, where you can cut and paste your résumé.

### Monster.Com

www.monster.com

Don't let the name scare you. It's really one of the easiest sites to use. You can even search by a single keyword to find one of 300,000 jobs. Freelancers and contract workers will love "Monster Talent Market."

### The Origin Group

www.origingroup.com

If actuarial, employee benefits, or human resources is your thing, this job bank's for you. Compare your qualifications and salary to similar openings, or post inquiries to prospective employers.

### Preferred Jobs

www.preferredjobs.com

A+ for clever innovations. Take a tour of this virtual job fair and visit employer booths. You'll find job descriptions as well as career and industry advice. Bookmark links to your dream companies.

**MOVING TIP**

Professional quality two-inch transparent tape is worth the extra money.

### Recruiting-Links.com

www.recruitinglinks.com

A truly unique design. You'll enjoy browsing a thoughtful collection of links, pitting the power of your résumé against the needs of select employers.

### TechJobBank

www.techjobbank.com

Cut to the chase with this site. You can link not just to company Web sites, but to their specific job pages, too. Nice features include "confidential" and "private" résumé posting, career resource assistance, and employment newsgroups.

### TopEchelon

www.topechelon.com

Recruiting and outplacement services. If you're searching for contract, temporary, or permanent placement, this could be a good one.

### TopJobs USA

www.topjobsusa.com

Meat and potatoes. Narrow your search by state, city, industry, and job title. This site's not big on frills, but it does feature career advice and helpful hints for no-nonsense job seekers.

### Vault Reports Job Board

www.vaultreports.com/jobboardhtml

A good one for metropolitan searches. VRJB provides job notification by e-mail, and a feature called "Company Snapshots." This is free, but more detailed reports are on a fee-for-service basis.

## Job Fairs and Career Drives

Quick description: Job fairs are like a convention of job seekers. They are sponsored by trade associations and private promoters. The purpose is to get employers and prospective employees together. Face to face. Some job fairs are huge and host hundreds of companies from a variety of industries. Others are smaller and feature a select group of companies from a specific industry. Career drives are usually sponsored by industry leaders. Their representatives spend a few days at colleges and universities speaking with students and graduates. However, many career drives take place at temporary recruiting centers which are open to the public. Large corporations often maintain their own recruiting centers year-round.

Job fairs and career drives are—and aren't—what they used to be. Many convention centers and university campuses still host seasonal career expos, complete with bright lights, booths, barkers, and brochures. However, the Internet now brings its virtual version of these events to you, in your home, where you can sport a tee shirt and jeans. No traffic. No parking. No dry cleaning.

What you sacrifice in promotional pens and complimentary mints is exchanged for more comprehensive, leisurely searching. You can leave a virtual résumé at most virtual booths, saving untold dollars in pricey cotton stock, printing, and postage fees.

Why, then, do conventional job fairs and career drives remain so popular? Because of the human factor. There is no substitute for a smile, a handshake, and the all-important first impression. Looking at annual reports, many companies appear similar. But visit a Microsoft booth, then an IBM booth, and you'll see just how polarized two corporate cultures can be. Most of us are fortunate to possess all five senses. When it comes to searching for career opportunities, use everything you've got.

Here are some resources for learning more about job fairs and career drives—both real and virtual.

## THE REAL DOMAIN

### Big Bend Community College

*DeVries Activities Center*
*7662 Chanute Street*
*Moses Lake*
*(509) 762-5351*

marys@bbcc.ctc.edu

An annual event attended by 100 companies. More than just job recruitment and employer information, the fair features work search workshops, too.

### Diversity Recruitment Committee Job Fair

*Spokane Community College Lair*
*Spokane*
*(509) 323-1252*

jecash@careerpathservices.org

Full-spectrum internship, graduate recruitment, and general public employment opportunities. The fair brings companies from both private and public sectors.

**Fort Lewis ACAP**
*ACAP Job Fair Team*
*(253) 967-3250*

acapjobs@lewis.army.mil

Hosts ongoing series of "Mini-Fairs" and "Special Employment Fairs." Usually held twice monthly, events focus upon the specialized recruiting efforts of ten to twenty employers per industry.

**Northwest Career, Job, and Education Expo**
*Seattle Center Exhibition Hall*
*305 Harrison Street*
*Seattle*
*(253) 884-3407*

kaffercom@foxcomm.net

10,000 job seekers and hundreds of companies. Administration, healthcare, high technology, retail management, and sales are among the many industries represented.

CITY FACT

Fourteen million passengers rode Seattle ferries in 1998. Destinations included: Bainbridge Island, Vashon Island, and the Kitsap Peninsula towns of Bremerton, Kingston, and Southworth.

**The Northwest Employment Expo**
*Best Western Lakeway Inn*
*714 Lakeway Drive*
*Bellingham*
*(360) 671-1011*

www.employmentexpo2000.com/objective.html

"Barrier-free networking environment," says *Business Pulse Magazine.* This fair has a little bit of everything, including community business forums and workshops.

**"Pathways to Your Future" Job Fair**

*Westfield Shoppingtown*
*Vancouver*
*(360) 992-2155*

www.clark.edu

Career and job information clearinghouse for more than 100 Seattle-area businesses. The annual fair provides more than just networking. There's free résumé critiques, job search workshops, and a "Dress for Success" fashion show. "Pathways" is sponsored by colleges, private industry, and the Washington State Employment Security Department.

**The Peninsula College Job Fair**

*Peninsula College*
*1502 East Lauridsen Boulevard*
*Port Angeles*
*(360) 417-6548*

leslie@pcadmin.ctc.edu

Fifty local and regional employers focusing on entry-level recruitment. Information about technical training and job search workshops are offered.

MOVING TIP

Save money by "piggybacking a rig." That is, share the storage capacity and cost of a moving van with a party who is also relocating to Seattle.

**Pierce College Career Fair**

*Pierce College*
*Lakewood Campus*
*9401 Farwest Drive*
*Lakewood*
*(253) 964-6705*

wmazikow@pierce.ctc.edu

Open to students, graduates, and the general public. Seventy-five Puget Sound–area companies are represented. The fair also features workshops on how to secure state and city employment.

### Snohomish County Job Fair

*Everett Community College*
*2000 Tower Street*
*Everett*
*(425) 338-9278*

www.evcc.ctc.edu/depts/admin/pr/events/jobfair.html

A megafair. Education, finance, banking, government, aerospace, and wireless communications are just a fraction of the industries represented.

### Snohomish County Workfirst Job Fair

*Holiday Inn Hotel & Convention Center*
*101 128th Street SW*
*Everett*
*(425) 673-3204*

No-frills, no-nonsense. Bring a quiver of résumés and plan to interview on the spot. This fair is stocked with employers chomping at the bit to hire. Industries represented include finance, transportation, healthcare, retail, and light manufacturing.

### Walla Walla Community College State Career & College Exposition

*Walla Walla Community College Conference Center*
*500 Tausick Way*
*Walla Walla*
*(877) 992-9922*

jimwillis@po.ww.cc.wa.us

Big name, big opportunities. Educational requirements for careers are the focus of workshops and symposiums. If you have what it takes, your job awaits. If not, counselors and industry experts can help you identify necessary credentials. Associate of Arts to Ph.D. welcome.

### THE VIRTUAL DOMAIN

**American Preferred Jobs**
www.preferredjobs.com

**Career City**
www.careercity.com

**Career Fairs**
www.careerfairs.com

**Career Service Center**
careers@admsec.wwu.edu

**EmploymentSpot**
www.employmentspot.com

**Hospital Jobs Online**
www.hospitaljobsonline.com

**Seattle Preferred Jobs**
www.seattlejobs.net

**TechUniverse**
www.techuniverse.com

**Virtual Job Fair**
www.vjf.com

**WorkSource Washington**
www.worksource.wa.gov

CITY FACT

The Boeing Company owns the world's largest building, their *Final Assembly Facility* in Everett.

## Internet Career and Job Resources

No matter how many job fairs and workshops you plan on attending, you'll never match the awesome exposure of the Internet. Besides, we're talking about Seattle—"Silicon Forest." Everything is done online in this town. So boot up and grab your mouse.

### About.com

www.about.com

A simple search of the Seattle/Tacoma area will reveal: job directories, callboards, referral services, Chamber of Commerce data, and newspaper classifieds.

### Access Washington

www.access.wa.gov

A prime site for local employment information and services. The handy Work Source Washington link can help you hit paydirt. Offerings include Résumé Center, Job and Career Guide, Career Events and Counseling, and Local Connections.

### Careers.org

www.careers.org

Career Resource Center has it all. From students to retirees reentering the job market, there's something for everyone. Use the "Job Sleuth" to investigate companies, or network with Seattle professional and trade association members.

### City of Seattle Employment Opportunities and Information

www.ci.seattle.wa.us/jobs/html

Postings of municipal jobs and more. Links to government agencies are neatly packaged with internships, apprenticeships, and career development tips.

### Digital City—Seattle

www.home.digitalcity.com/seattle/visitorsguide/html

Explore Seattle opportunities from top to bottom. The nifty Jobs & Careers department is rich with employee assistance programs. Also, the site lets you test your market value and earning potential.

**IncPad**

www.jobcenter.com

Everything in an electronic nutshell. 1,200 companies, links to HR associations, salary statistics, and help with personal presentation.

MOVING TIP

If you store boxed items in your new garage, be careful. Very few garages are fully insulated, and temperature-sensitive items (e.g., photographs, paintings, videocassettes, and food) may be permanently damaged.

**Seattle.CitySearch.com**

www.seattle.citysearch.com

Career Center serves up interesting fare with City, Company, and Industry Research. Use your Personal Search Agent to navigate through oodles of fresh listings.

**Seattle Insider.com**

www.seattleinsider.com

Edge out the competition with this one. Site prides itself on maintaining inside track on local job market and employment trends.

**Seattle.net**

www.seattle.net

Local links and job resources with a view toward homespun technologies.

**Suite 101.com**

www.suite101.com

Career Development section outfits the urban job hunter. Feature articles and suggested readings add to the mix. A major list of links and productive discussion groups combine to round out a complete site.

### Washington Employment Web Pages

www.members.aol.com

1,500 links are just the beginning. Information resources and referrals are designed with the relocator in mind.

### Welcome to Seattle

www.oz.net

Conveniently bundles employment and housing. The site offers easy access to the most solid employers in the northwest, as well as joblines and classifieds.

### Worksource Seattle—King County

www.skcpic.org

Programs are a specialty. The user can choose between group and individual consultation on an open, no-fee basis. Maps are particularly helpful to the relocator, as are Partner Links.

## University Career Resources and Employment Opportunities

Educational institutions can help you find a job. All of the campuses have career centers. Helping people get jobs is good for a university in several ways. First, it reflects well on the quality of the institution when a company hires a graduate. Second, that new hire may soon find herself in a position to recruit other graduates, helping to foster corporate relations with the university. Last, an alumnus will likely feel indebted to the university for career assistance, and gratitude is often expressed in annual donations to endowments. However, unless you're an enrolled student or an alumnus, job placement services can be limited.

Before you register for Computer Programming 101, know this: Advanced technology lures students and researchers to Seattle like bears to honey. As campus enrollment grows, so does the university's need for administrators, faculty, and staff. So even if you're not relocating to Seattle as a freshman or transfer student, you may still be able to find your niche in one of the hundreds of university jobs available.

These Puget Sound–area universities offer student and alumni career resources, as well as university employment opportunities.

**MOVING TIP**

Telephone service should be disconnected by Moving Day, so make sure your cellular phone is fully charged or that you have sufficient prepaid calling cards in your wallet or purse. Purchase a "cigarette lighter" adapter if necessary, but avoid needing change for pay phones. Arrange for your new service to begin the day you arrive at your new house and give the new phone number to anyone who might need to reach you.

**Pacific Lutheran University**
*Tacoma, WA 98447*
*(253) 531-6900*
www.plu.edu

**Seattle Pacific University**
*3307 Third Avenue W*
*Seattle, WA 98119-1997*
*(206) 281-2000*
www.spu.edu

**University of Puget Sound**
*1500 North Warner Street*
*Tacoma, WA 98416*
*(253) 879-3100*
www.ups.edu

**University of Washington**
*Employment Office*
*P.O. Box 354550*
*Seattle, WA 98195-4550*
*(206) 543-9198*
www.washington.edu

**Western Washington University**
*516 High Street*
*Bellingham, WA 98225-9009*
*(360) 650-3440*
www.wwu.edu

# INDEX

## D

## N

# About

Because moving affects almost *every aspect* of a person's life, Monstermoving.com is committed to improving the way people move. Focusing on an individual's needs, timing, and dreams, the site provides everything for the entire lifestyle transition and every stage of the move. Free service provider content, interactive products, and resources give consumers more control, saving them time and money, and reducing stress. Site features include cost-of-living comparisons, home and apartment searches, mortgage calculators and services, an interactive move-planning application, an address change service, relocation tax advice, and virtual city tours. Monstermoving.com is committed to remaining the most effective, comprehensive, and lifestyle-centric point of service for everyone involved in moving.

Monstermoving.com is part of the Interactive Division of TMP Worldwide (NASDAQ: "TMPW;" ASX: "TMP"). For information, visit *www.monstermoving.com* or call (800) 567-7952.

## Use the Internet to Find the Perfect Job for You

This fast-track guide gives you the tools and resources you need to achieve the job search results you want simply and easily all in one weekend. Inside you'll find:

- **An overview of the electronic job market**
- **Suggestions for researching your job target**
- **An overview of career Web sites**
- **And much more!**

This easy-to-read book simplifies the process of launching your job search online and helps you do so in a matter of a few days.

ISBN 0-7615-2452-5
Paperback / 336 pages
U.S. $24.99 / Can. $36.50

**To order, call (800) 632-8676 ext. 4444 or visit us online at www.primatech.com**